SUPPLEMENTARY VOLUME LXXXI
2007

THE
ARISTOTELIAN
SOCIETY

THE SYMPOSIA READ AT THE JOINT SESSION
OF THE ARISTOTELIAN SOCIETY AND THE
MIND ASSOCIATION, HOSTED BY THE
UNIVERSITY OF BRISTOL AT THE UNIVERSITY
OF THE WEST OF ENGLAND, JULY 2007

PUBLISHED BY
The Aristotelian Society
2007

First published 2007 by
The Aristotelian Society

© The Aristotelian Society 2007

ISBN 0 907111 56 4
ISSN 0309-7013

Printed in Great Britain by 4 Word Page and Print Production, Bristol.

ACTIVITIES AND PUBLICATIONS
The Society, founded in 1880, meets fortnightly in London to hear
and discuss philosophical papers. The Society's website is at
www.aristoteliansociety.org.uk. The *Proceedings* are published as a
journal in one annual printed edition, with three online journals ap-
pearing via Blackwell Synergy in March, June and September. The
Supplementary Volume, published annually in June, contains the
papers to be read at the Joint Session of the Aristotelian Society and
the Mind Association in July. Information about subscription rates,
back copies and other Aristotelian Society publications is available
at the end of this volume.

CONTENTS

PROGRAMME

JOINT SESSION OF THE ARISTOTELIAN SOCIETY AND
THE MIND ASSOCIATION, UNIVERSITY OF BRISTOL,
6–8 JULY 2007

Friday 6 July	5.00 pm	Christopher Hookway Inaugural Address: *Fallibilism and the Aim of Enquiry* Chair: Thomas Baldwin
Saturday 7 July	9.00 am	James Ladyman and Bas C. van Fraassen *Scientific Structuralism* Chair: Richard Bradley
	11.00 am	James Lenman and Michael Ridge *Expressivism and Epistemology* Chair: Ralph Wedgwood
	2.00 pm	*Graduate Papers*
	4.30 pm	*Submitted Papers — Open Sessions*
	8.00 pm	Ursula Coope and Christopher Shields *Aristotle on Action* Chair: David Charles
Sunday 8 July	9.00 am	Peter Millican and Helen Beebee *Humes Old and New* Chair: Harold Noonan
	11.00 am	Theodore Sider and Katherine Hawley *Neo-Fregeanism and Quantifier Variance* Chair: Bob Hale
	2.00 pm	*Submitted Papers — Open Sessions*
	4.30 pm	*Submitted Papers — Open Sessions*
	8.00 pm	Scott Soames and Keith Hossack *Actuality* Chair: Dorothy Edgington

THE INAUGURAL ADDRESS

CHRISTOPHER HOOKWAY

FALLIBILISM AND THE AIM OF INQUIRY

Philosophers such as Richard Rorty and Donald Davidson have argued
that it is a consequence of accepting fallibilism that truth cannot be our
aim in inquiry. The paper examines these arguments, compares them with
some apparently similar arguments employed by philosophers in the
pragmatist tradition, and uses some pragmatist ideas to show how the arguments can be defused.

I

Is Truth the Aim of Inquiry? Common sense would suggest that the
answer to the question 'Is truth the aim of inquiry?' is an emphatic
'Yes'. When we carry out an investigation, we would never know-
ingly rest content with a conclusion that we believe to be false, or
that we do not take to be true. However it can be questioned in a
number of different ways. Section two surveys some strategies for
questioning whether truth can be our aim, and section three explores an argument due to Richard Rorty and Donald Davidson
which is designed to show that if fallibilism is correct, then truth
cannot be our aim. Section four begins the criticism of this argument by comparing some ways of understanding fallibilism, and
then, in section five we explore how at least one form of pragmatist
epistemology begins by, apparently, endorsing something close to
Rorty's argument, but avoids the conclusion that truth cannot function as an aim of inquiry. Section six draws some conclusions.[1] First,
we begin to clarify what is at issue.

Inquiry is a goal-directed activity that aims to find something out.
I can inquire into an unlimited range of matters: whether the tank of

---

[1] This paper addresses just one issue about truth and pragmatism that is raised by Rorty's
work—see for example the papers in Rorty (1998). There are others, some concerned more
directly with his rejection of the correspondence theory of truth, some concerned with for
example, how far a norm of truth determines which systems of predicates (which 'vocabu-
laries') we should use. Bilgrami (2000) address a wider range of such topics than are considered here.

©2007 THE ARISTOTELIAN SOCIETY
Proceedings of the Aristotelian Society Supplementary Volume LXXXI

my car is full of petrol; how much petrol the tank contains; how to fill the tank; why I ran out of petrol; whether truth is the aim of inquiry; and so on. If truth were the aim of inquiry, this would have implications for what would count as success in any of these inquiries. It would also have a role in explaining what normative standards should be followed in carrying out inquiries; we should regulate inquiries in ways that that will contribute to their successfully uncovering truths. Talking of truth as *the* aim of inquiry cannot be right. We seek answers to our questions which are relevant, illuminating and useful, so truth is, at most, one among a set of standards that we use in evaluating inquiries. The issue concerns whether it belongs in that set at all. Thus Donald Davidson, who denies that truth can be an aim of inquiry, also denies that truth is a value (2005, p. 6), or that it is a 'norm, something for which we strive' (2005, p. 7). The question whether truth should be our aim in inquiry is intimately connected with the question whether, in regulating and evaluating our inquiries, we have to use standards that employ the concept of *truth* or that depend upon properties that are intimately linked to truth.

Although the issues may be related, the question whether truth is the aim of inquiry is not the same as the question whether truth is the aim of belief, which has been discussed recently (see, for example, Velleman, 2000; Owens, 2003). No one could dispute that when we inquire, we engage in a goal-directed activity; inquiry is a kind of action. Believing is not an action, and many beliefs have never been matters for investigation or inquiry. I am concerned with the norms that govern *activities*, not the norms that govern our engagement with cognitive *states* such as beliefs.

II

Strategies for Denying that Truth is Our Aim. In this section, we survey some different strategies that could be employed in order to challenge the apparent platitude that, when we inquire, our aim is to arrive at the truth. One possibility is to accept the platitude for what it is, but to deny that it has the philosophical importance it is commonly supposed to have. If, for example, we accept a minimalist account of truth, holding that there is no more to truth than is captured by the familiar Tarskian biconditionals, or if we think that a disquotational schema reveals all there is to truth, then we may be able to question whether the concept of truth is sufficiently *substantive* to be used to identify a goal or be used to ground norms for inquiry. A similar conclusion may be drawn if we accept a caricature of William James's claim about truth: if a proposition's being true is explained in terms of it being right to believe it, then talk of truth must depend upon an *independent* account of the norms that govern inquiries and the regulation of belief.

A second possibility is that what we seek is something *other* than truth. We require a good solution to a problem, an effective cognitive instrument, a satisfying all encompassing understanding of some subject matter, and so on. On some views, these desiderata are not best evaluated in terms of *truth*, nor need their assessment depend upon the use of truth related norms. Even if we record our agreement with such a conclusion using the word 'true', the norms that we follow in carrying out our inquiry are not to be explained by reference to demands encapsulated in that property, Rather, the norms derive directly from the need to understand, or to solve our problem, or to obtain an instrument that will serve our purposes. We may call our results 'true' because they are things it is right to endorse; but we need not explain their being rightly endorsed in terms of their truth.

The third strategy takes truth more seriously, yet, in identifying goals for inquiry, settles for something *less*. Such arguments may be based on sceptical concerns or on fallibilism about our beliefs. Some forms of Pyrrhonian scepticism denied that we could ever be confident that we had reached the truth and proposed instead that we should be content to stop our inquiries as soon as we had something that fitted our experience. Van Fraassen's empiricist approach to science could be seen as embracing a modest goal for theoretical inquiries on the grounds that we cannot see how it is possible for us to be warranted in thinking that theoretical beliefs are genuinely true (van Fraassen, 1980).

A weaker challenge of the same kind takes seriously the fact that when we try to control our inquiries we need rules that tell us when we can stop. It is always possible to ask more reflective questions about how the inquiry has gone. We can ask about whether our evidence is reliable enough, whether it is sufficient, about whether we should inquire further about whether our evidence is sufficient, and so on. In many cases, we are content with a conclusion that has a good chance of truth, or that represents what it is reasonable to assert at the current stage of our inquiries. Even if we can be confident that we shall reach the truth in the end, our grounds for confidence that we have reached the truth now may be limited. And it may not matter greatly to us that this is so. In that case, should we deny that truth is our aim?

In the next section I shall consider an argument employed by both Rorty and Davidson for the strong conclusion that truth *cannot* be our aim in inquiry. Both conclude that our goal should be justified belief, and neither seems to accept the view that our standards of justification can be grounded in our grasp of truth. The argument rests upon a fundamental principle that Rorty describes as 'pragmatist'. One might suppose that Rorty's reasons for rejecting the idea that truth should be our goal would depend upon his acceptance of an account of our use of 'true' which emphasizes its disquotational properties and supplements this by mentioning some expressive functions that it is used to perform. We use the word to endorse propositions and also cautiously to express the idea that what seems right to us now may, in future, be rejected (Rorty, 1991, ch. 8). This would be a strategy of the first kind. However, the reasons Rorty gives for denying that truth could be our aim suggest the third strategy that I described. This is clear when we see that when Davidson refined, developed and endorsed Rorty's argument, he employed the premiss that truth is *objective*. His argument sought to establish that if truth is objective and fallibilism is true, then truth cannot be our aim in inquiry (Davidson, 2005, ch. 1).

Section three examines the argument used by Rorty and Davidson. Since the doctrine of fallibilism is involved in Davidson's argument and in Peirce's theory of inquiry, section four considers how fallibilism should be understood and how it might affect the attitudes we should take towards the results of our inquiries. Then, in section five, we consider a related argument employed by another pragmatist, Charles Sanders Peirce. In the course of this discussion, we identify some different ways in which the concept of truth could be involved in the regulation of inquiries. The final section tries to answer the question posed in the title by considering the role of *reasons* in the ways in which we regulate inquiries.

III

'Pragmatist' Arguments (1). Richard Rorty's (1995, ch. 1; 2000) argument for the conclusion that our aim in inquiry cannot be, or should not be, truth exploits a general principle that he describes as 'pragmatist' because it implies that a goal can only be taken seriously if its achievement would make a difference in practice. We cannot aim for something if it makes no practical difference whether we achieve our aim or not. Unless we can tell whether we have achieved our aim or not, then it would make no difference that could affect our practice. This is expressed by a pragmatist slogan:

> [Y]ou can only work for what you could recognize. (Rorty, 2000, p. 4)

Suppose I leave my house with the goal of walking to my office in the University. The aim will guide my conduct by causing me to carry out actions that are means to the achievement of that aim. I shall turn left out of the door; I continue past the shops and down the hill; and I then turn into the University entrance before taking the lift to the twelfth floor. It also guides my action by telling me when to stop: once I have arrived at the philosophy department and entered the room with my name on the door, I have finished. And in order for my aim to serve this second role, I need to be able to recognize that I have arrived at my office: in this case, my name on the door, the familiar furniture and piles of papers all provide reasons for thinking that I am now in my office. The activity of inquiry works in the same way: my aim of finding out the time of the next train to London guides me in adopting suitable means for acquiring that information; and it also determines when I can stop my inquiry. Once I have discovered the time of the train, I can stop inquiring. In order to know when to stop, I need to be able to recognize when I have succeeded in my aim. If my aim is to reach the truth, then I must be able to recognize when I have done so.

As noted above, both Rorty's argument and Davidson's more careful presentation of a related argument rely upon the fallibilist claim that, no matter how careful we are in our investigations, we can go wrong. It is this possibility that somehow rules out the possibility that truth is our goal. We shall discuss more fully how fallibilism is to be understood below. For the present, we should identify three different levels of fallibility, using the example of my consult-

ing the train company's web site as a method for finding out about
train times. First, however good this method is, I can go wrong because I execute it poorly: I may misread what it says on the screen,
or I may mistype when I enter my request for information. Second,
the method may be reliable only under certain circumstances: trains
run late and are cancelled; schedules are changed. So, even if the
method is generally reliable, there will be occasions when it will let
me down, through no fault of my own. Third, I may be wrong in my
belief that this method is a good one: perhaps the company failed to
update the website when the schedules were changed. It appears to
be Rorty's view that, since any of these possibilities could have the
result that my well-conducted inquiry did not arrive at a true belief,
it is not possible that finding a true belief is (part of) my goal. How
does that argument work? It is probably best to look at the Davidsonian version.

In his paper 'Truth Rehabilitated', Donald Davidson has offered a
more carefully worked out version of Rorty's argument.[2] Davidson's
version argues for a conditional conclusion: if truth is objective,
then it cannot be our aim in inquiry. To obtain from this the conclusion that truth is not our aim, we require the premiss that truth is
objective, one that Davidson endorses. Like Rorty's argument, Davidson's depends upon a doctrine commonly linked to an acceptance
of the objectivity of truth: fallibilism. So the conclusion is:

> If truth is objective and fallibilism holds, then truth is not the
> aim of inquiry.

Davidson's characterization of what is involved in truth being objective is:

> [T]he truth of a belief or sentence is independent of whether it is justi-
> fied by all our evidence, believed by our neighbors, or is good to steer
> by. (Davidson, 2005, p. 7)

Evidence, the dispositions of our fellows, and the effects of acting
on a belief are all phenomena that are detectable. So the objectivity
of truth ensures that however well a proposition fits the evidence,

---

[2] Although I shall not discuss it here, I should emphasize that Davidson (2005, p. 7, n. 5)
takes his argument to be different from Rorty's. The latter rejects the objectivity of truth,
denying that there is a practical difference between truth and justification.

however well our friends support it, and however useful it is, the belief could still be false. And Davidson's three characterizations of
fallibilism take off from this characterization of objectivity:

(i) Truths do not come with a mark like the date in the corner
     of a photograph that distinguishes them from falsehoods.

(ii) However long and well we inquire, we shall be left with fal-
     lible beliefs.

(iii) We will never *know for certain* which of our beliefs are
     true.

From these claims, Davidson concludes that truth is neither 'visible
as a target' nor 'recognizable when achieved'. The final conclusion
is, then, that 'there is no point calling [truth] a goal'. Moreover, we
must also reject the idea that it is a *norm*: 'something for which to
strive'. And since truth is not a value, 'the pursuit of truth' is an
empty enterprise. Even then, we may want to *talk* about the pursuit
of truth if by this we mean only that 'it is often worthwhile to increase our confidence in our beliefs by collecting further evidence or
checking our calculations' (Davidson, 2005, pp. 6–7). But using the
word 'true' in this way is not sufficient for treating *truth* as a norm.

Rather than exploiting conceptual links between belief and 'taking to be true', he relies on a very strong version of Rorty's 'pragmatic' slogan. Unless there are times at which we can conclusively
ascertain that some belief is true, truth can't be an aim or a norm. It
would follow from this that 'settled belief' cannot be our aim either:
there is no guarantee that inquiry will reach a stage at which we can
establish conclusively that belief is (permanently) settled. The challenge to be met in understanding Davidson's argument is to see why
he accepts such a strong constraint on possible goals. Once again,
fallibility has a substantial role.

If truth is objective, according to Davidson, then whether a proposition is true is *not* determined by the sorts of considerations we
rely on in determining what we should believe. In practice, we accept something as true because of its evidential support, or because
belief in it contributes to the success of our activities. In such cases,
we shall say that our belief that p is grounded in considerations C.

In most cases, such considerations will provide us with reason for
accepting some propositions that answers the question that is the
target of our inquiry. It seems to follow from Davidson's characterization of *objective truth* that, if truth is objective, then:

> If C obtains, then it is true that *p*

is neither necessarily true nor a priori knowable: such connections
are contingent and rarely exceptionless; and our knowledge of them
is not grounded in our mastery of the concept of truth. If our acceptance of a proposition is always grounded in such considerations, then the considerations that we take as signs of success in our
inquiry do not guarantee that we have been successful.

This is the crucial piece of background to the issue raised by
Rorty and Davidson. Their arguments suggest that we can distinguish two ways of describing such cases:

(1) Our goal is to arrive at a true answer to our question, and
we adopt fallible means of achieving this goal.

(2) Our goal is to arrive at answer to our question that reasonable people would judge to be a reasonable choice of answer.

There are two components to (2). One of these is social: if people
we judge to be reasonable or competent do not share our views
about which arguments or beliefs are reasonable, and we have no
special reason for thinking that their judgement lacks value on this
occasion, then, other things being equal, it is rational for us to reflect on whether our views should be revised. We rely upon the
judgements of our competent fellows in trying to minimize the effects of our fallibility. The other is that it is not necessary to say that
our goal is truth: we do not make use of the concept of truth in the
reflective regulation of our inquiries and opinions. Position (1), by
contrast, retains the view that, in spite of our fallibility, there is
point in the claim that our aim is *truth*. We need to ask what
grounds there are for preferring (1).

The arguments we have been examining depend upon two basic
theses. The first is Rorty's 'pragmatist' principle: we can only aim
for what we can recognize. As it stands, this is not very clear, partic-

ularly concerning what is required for being able to recognize *whether* some outcome has been obtained. One interpretation would be that it must be decidable for us whether the outcome has been secured. Only slightly less demanding would be the requirement that we can, in some favourable circumstances, 'know for certain' that we have achieved what we set out to achieve. A much weaker interpretation would hold that it is enough that, in some circumstances, we can arrive at assessments of our degree of success that are reasonably reliable, albeit defeasible. If we adopt the stronger kind of reading of the principle, it seems very implausible: there are many kinds of goals that can be reasonably adopted which do not conform to it. For example, someone can aim to make a lasting contribution to philosophy, even if their ability to recognize whether they have done so is both limited and fallible. At best, we might suppose, they can achieve something that they can reasonably *hope* will satisfy their long-term goal. Similar patterns are found when people aim to prepare their children for the challenges their lives will present. A natural response to this is to say that although we may be fallible in determining whether we have achieved our goal, we need a clear grasp of what achieving it would consist in, what it would mean for a book to make a lasting contribution or for a child to be well brought up. But, once again, it seems that there can be indeterminacy and fallibility in our grasp of this. At the very least, Rorty's principle is not evidently true when taken as a general claim about goals of actions.

The second thesis is that fallibilism threatens the satisfaction of the first if our goal is truth. Since Davidson expresses fallibilism as claiming that we can't be absolutely certain of anything, there is reason to think that the argument rests on a 'demanding' version of 'what we can recognize'. At this stage, it is unclear whether the demanding version of *being able to recognize* is supposed to be invoked for any kind of goal (as seems most likely) or whether it is required particularly for the case of inquiry. It is a strong requirement, and does not seem very plausible that, if our aim is to be the discovery of object truth, we require the capacity to be 'absolutely certain' of our success. The relation between fallibilism and certainty is an important issue here that we must now address.

IV

Two Ways to Characterize Fallibilism. Fallibilism is difficult to define. We can start from the observation that we have many beliefs
that we actively regard as fallible, we can understood how these beliefs are acquired in ways that are compatible with their being false.
We rely on someone's testimony and they turn out to be insincere or
mistaken; we base our beliefs upon evidence while aware that more
evidence may show that we were mistaken; we know we often form
beliefs upon the basis of reasons while unaware of potential defeaters. So one way to characterize fallibilism could take this as a starting point: a defender of *global fallibilism* holds that, for any
proposition at all, either we can see how we might be mistaken in
believing this proposition or, if we were properly rational in our reflections, we would be able to recognize the possibility of error.

   In such cases, we can follow C. Delaney in describing fallibilism as
a distinctive 'attitude of mind' (Delaney, 1993, p. 110): we recognize
that a well-supported belief may yet turn out to be false; we cannot
insulate ourselves from all possibility of error. Such observations
suggest that we often take ourselves to be right to believe propositions when we recognize that there is a real, albeit slight, possibility
of error. This sort of understanding of fallibilism can encourage the
idea that our acceptance of propositions should always have a de-
tached or tentative character: the possibility of error must be real.
Thus readers of the final sections of Quine's 'Two Dogmas of Empiricism' sometimes seem to take him to be committed to the idea that
we can be aware of the real possibility that we may turn out to be
wrong to accept, for example, elementary truths of arithmetic or logical laws. And it is then natural to respond that, for many such propositions, the possibility of error cannot be seriously entertained.

   There is another way of understanding even global fallibilism that
does not have this consequence. Perhaps lack of 'absolute certainty'
is compatible with the sort of ordinary certainty that arises when
the possibility of error cannot really be entertained or taken seriously. This may be suggested by Hilary Putnam's characterization of
fallibilism: 'There is never a metaphysical guarantee to be had that
such-and-such a belief will never need revision.'[3] The talk of '*abso-*

---

[3] For discussion of this, see Putnam (1995, pp. 151–81).

lute certainty' and '*metaphysical* guarantee' is supposed to extend our sense of fallibility beyond these familiar cases to cover all of our beliefs, including examples where we feel wholly certain of propositions and cannot readily imagine any circumstances in which we might come to abandon our acceptance of them. One way in which we might do this is to begin by defining *infallibility*, and then characterize fallibilism as the view that there are no propositions that are 'infallible' so understood. Here is one way in which this might work.

When we describe a judgement or belief as 'infallible', we identify it as belonging to an epistemic kind of which, of necessity, all members are true. If direct reports of sense-data are infallible, then, necessarily, all direct reports of sense-data are true; if reports of one's sensations are infallible, then all such reports are true; if intuitions of the rational structure of reality are infallible, then all such intuitions are correct. This assignment to a kind identifies a metaphysical feature of the judgement or belief that guarantees its truth. (This must be a non-trivial matter: we do not show that a judgement is infallible by assigning it to the class of 'veridical judgements', for example.) If this is how we understand infallibility, then we can show that a judgement is *fallible* by demonstrating that there is no such kind to which it belongs. And this suffices to show that it is not infallible even if we feel totally certain of it and we cannot conceive of what might lead us to revise our judgement. The fallibility of a proposition consists in the absence of a distinctive metaphysical explanation of its infallibility. And it is compatible with this that, as things stand, we cannot imagine or conceive how we might be mistaken. I suggest that Putnam's talk of 'metaphysical guarantees' and Peirce's appeal to 'absolute certainty' should be understood in terms of this understanding of fallibility: nothing is absolutely certain because no judgement belongs to an epistemic kind which rules out the possibility of error.[4]

This characterization of infallibility may face problems: there may be judgements of which we do not feel confident, yet which, for all that, belong to epistemic kinds that guarantee their truth. Suppose that we adopt a disjunctivist account of perception: perceptual

---

[4] This way of understanding fallibilism is useful for understanding the later sections of Quine's 'Two Dogmas of Empiricism'.

judgements are factive, so all perceptual judgements, of necessity, are true. Yet we may be unconfident of our judgement because we are unsure whether it is a judgement of perception or, perhaps, a member of a different epistemic kind, a report of illusion or hallucination, for example. There are two ways to deal with such examples. We might revise the characterization of infallibility to require that the belief *detectably* belongs to a kind which guarantees its truth. Alternatively, we might accept that fallibilism does not extend to all our judgements, recognizing the infallibility of perceptual ones, while also insisting that our beliefs *about* whether a given judgement is a perceptual judgement are fallible. I shall not discuss this further here.

Support for this way of understanding Peirce's position can be found in his explanation of why his fallibilism extends to the claim that twice two is four (Peirce, 1910/1958, par. 108). He acknowledges that he feels 'not the slightest real doubt of it' (1910/1958, par. 109); and, indeed, 'that it would be difficult to imagine a greater folly than to attach any serious importance' to the rather strained reasons for doubting it that he manages to dredge up (1910/1958, par. 108). He begins by noting that even 'computers' occasionally make errors in simple multiplications, which he takes to establish that doing a calculation just once does not provide an absolute guarantee that no error has been made: that a belief is the result of simple multiplication does not guarantee its truth. Perhaps repetition of the calculation, possibly by different people, enables us to progress from a conclusion that we feel very certain of, one that we cannot imagine we could be in error about, into one that is '*absolutely certain*'. Since it would be absurd to see just one calculation as enabling us to cross this metaphysical boundary, the safest recourse is to acknowledge that we are often extremely certain of the results of calculations but conclude that 'man is incapable of absolute certainty' (1910/1958, par. 108). This rests on the assumption that if there is a real distinction between fallible and 'absolutely infallible' beliefs, it needs to be a sharp one: there cannot be borderline cases between the fallible and the *absolutely* infallible; and Peirce agrees with Quine that philosophy cannot provide a sharp boundary of this kind. He denies that we can be 'absolutely certain' that twice two is four, and this is grounded on the demonstration that we cannot identify a significant epistemic kind to which this judgement belongs and which guarantees its truth. I suspect that something similar is going on in the closing sections of 'Two Dogmas of Empiricism': once the analytic–synthetic distinction and a reductionist verificationism are abandoned, we have to recognize that, even if we can't conceive of how we could be brought to question them (or to see them as anything other than certain), we have no way of proving that (no metaphysical guarantee that) they are absolutely infallible. And it can support this that we know that (very rarely) what has seemed to be wholly certain has been abandoned.

If this is correct, then a commitment to fallibilism is compatible with great confidence and certainty in the adequacy of most of our opinions and methods. It does not occur to us to question their reliability, although we can offer no philosophical reason for absolutely ruling out the possibility that we may, one day, decide that this certainty and confidence was misplaced. The lack of such reason, of course, does not provide the slightest reason for concern about whether our certainty should be questioned. We can also notice some connections between the characterization of fallibilism and some well-known features of pragmatist epistemology. Again I can register this point only schematically. When do we need reasons or justifications for our beliefs? We need reasons and justifications when we change our mind. When we form an opinion about something that we have previously been agnostic about, or when we come to doubt what we had previously, we need to be able to defend what we do. When faced with reasons to doubt something, then, if we are to continue in the belief, we may need reasons for ignoring those reasons for doubt. If I am certain of something, and I am not faced with reasons for doubting it, then my inability to give concrete reasons for believing this proposition will normally have no rational impact upon my certainty. Once again, confident, non-tentative certainty is compatible with the lack of explicit reasons for thinking that this confidence is absolutely secure.

V

Pragmatist Arguments (2). Rorty was not the first to argue against identifying the aim of inquiry as *truth*, and not even the first pragmatist to do so. In his paper 'The Fixation of Belief', Charles Peirce

(1877/1992, ch. 7) presents an argument for the conclusion that, when doing epistemology, we should identify the aim of inquiry as 'settled belief' and not as 'true belief'.[5]

> We may fancy that [settled belief] is not enough for us, and that we seek, not merely an opinion, but a true opinion. But put this fancy to the test, and it proves groundless; for as soon as a firm belief is reached, we are entirely satisfied, whether the belief be true or false. The most that can be maintained is that we seek a belief that we shall *think* to be true. But we think each one of our beliefs is true, and, indeed, it is mere tautology to say so. (Peirce, 1877/1992, p. 115)[6]

These remarks occur as part of an extended thought experiment designed to identify the most fundamental norms that govern our beliefs and inquiries, and we must be careful not to be misled by taking them out of context. However, we should begin by taking in them at face value, in which case they derive the denial that our aim in inquiry is true belief from the observation that we cannot believe a proposition unless we also believe that the proposition in question is true.[7]

Consider two reflective questions I might ask about my belief that *p*:

(1) Is my belief that *p* true?
(2) Am I right to believe that *p*?

Peirce's argument seems to take it for granted that if it is correct to say that my aim in inquiry is *true belief*, then the most illuminating way in which I can reflect upon my belief is to begin by asking (1). But if I genuinely believe that *p*, then I am already committed to an-

---

[5] For further discussion of the issues addressed in this section, see for example, Hookway (2004), Misak (2004b).

[6] David Wiggins (2004, pp. 97–9) suggests that this is just a mistake. Peirce appears to say that there is no practical difference between seeking the truth and seeking something that we will think is true, and Wiggins remarks that this is analogous to identifying the directive to 'do your duty' and the directive to 'do what you think is your duty'. Whether this is a mistake may depend upon the role it occupies in Peirce's complex thought experiment. As Wiggins himself emphasizes, by the time the thought experiment is finished, we can draw such distinctions and rely upon them in our reflections. I am unclear whether it follows from this that Peirce cannot make the point he does at the beginning of the exercise.

[7] Although the arguments used by Rorty and Peirce are superficially similar, there are differences: Rorty's argument exploits the gap between truth and justification; while Peirce's argument exploits the lack of a gap between belief and taking something to be true.

swering *that* question in the affirmative. Reflection on my opinion requires me to ask (2), in the expectation that our mastery of epistemic norms will guide us in taking that inquiry further.

To simplify what is already a rather schematically presented thought experiment, Peirce explores our certainties about what sorts of things will destabilize our beliefs: what sorts of things are we committed to treating as reasons to suspend judgement in what we already believe? He does this by identifying some methods of belief formation that cannot be self-consciously employed. Once we recognize that our belief is formed in one of these ways, the belief (ceteris paribus) will be unsettled. These flawed methods involve allowing the question of what propositions we should belief to be determined by, for example:

(a) My own subjective exercise of will in choosing which belief I shall adopt.

(b) My deference to some authority who will determine what should be believed by an act of will determining what everyone should believe.

(c) My subjective tastes or preferences, accepting the propositions whose acceptance we find 'agreeable'.

By the end of the paper, he has concluded that we could not take seriously the question what norms of *belief* we should adopt unless we believed:

> There are real things, whose characters are entirely independent of our opinions about them; those realities affect our senses according to regular laws, and, though our sensations are as different as our relations to the objects, yet, by taking account of the laws of perception, we can ascertain by reasoning how things really are, and any man, if he have enough experience and reason enough about it, will be led to the one true conclusion. (Peirce, 1877/1992, p. 120)

What should be believed is not determined by the will of any individual or by anything subjective. Our acceptance of this set of views (or, most likely, a more complex and sophisticated set of views along these general lines) guides us in which questions we should ask when we answer question (2) above. It will be evident that we do not always interact causally with the objects of our knowledge in the way suggested here. Wiggins (2004, p. 105) has proposed that what Peirce wanted to say is better expressed by using a form of words that Peirce himself employs elsewhere: we seek a belief which is 'determined by circumstances not extraneous to the fact [in question]'.

These formulations raise a host of questions about, for example, how they can be applied to a priori knowledge or moral knowledge (but see Wiggins, 2004, pp. 107–8, for suggestions about how this could work), how we should qualify the claim that anyone who has sufficient experience, and thinks about the matter long enough and well enough, will share our opinion. It is clear that it offers a broadly realist view of the objects of inquiry and our ability to learn about them. Does the endpoint of the thought experiment, then, lead Peirce to retract (or qualify beyond recognition) his earlier insistence that truth is not the aim of inquiry? And how far does this differ from the sort of position that, as we have seen, is defended by Rorty?

In the sequel to 'The Fixation of Belief', Peirce clarified the concept of truth, although, as always, he does not discuss the concept of truth in much detail. Moreover, what he provides is a 'pragmatic clarification' rather than the familiar kind of analysis that involves identifying the necessary and sufficient conditions for some representation to have the property of truth.[8] In nearly all cases, his clarifications of truth are devices for getting a handle on the concept of reality. Having offered a verbal definition of the real by remarking, 'That whose characters are independent of how you or I think is an external reality', he recognizes that he needs to explain what this kind of mind-independence comes down to in practice. He does this, first by clarifying truth: 'The opinion which is fated to be ultimately agreed to by all who investigate is what we mean by the true, and the object represented in this opinion is the real.' It follows from this that if I take some proposition to be true, then I anticipate that anyone who inquires into it long enough and well enough would end up

---

[8] There is a widespreaed consensus that pragmatist theories of truth are not in direct competition with attempts to provide traditional analyses of that concept. Recent publications that emphasize this point include Misak (2004a), Hookway (2000, ch. 2; 2004) and Wiggins (2004).

endorsing that proposition. Of course, it is compatible with this that, for many truths, it is, in practice, not possible for anyone to complete the investigations that would be required in order to accept what they are 'fated' or 'destined' to accept. Moreover, since most propositions are vague, lacking in fully determinate content, there is no reason to suppose that all inquirers are fated to resolve such indeterminacies in the same way. If a proposition is fully determinate, then consensus will be forthcoming unless we are unable to acquire sufficient representative evidence or we do not inquire carefully and attentively enough. But that will rarely be our position.

This is a very schematic description of a complex position. But we can make some observations about the resulting pragmatist account of truth that provide a useful foil for considering the Rorty-Davidson argument. First, the position is compatible with fallibilism: if we inquire well enough and long enough, we are 'fated' to reach the truth; but it may be consistent with this that we never have *conclusive* reason to think that we have inquired long enough or well enough. Indeed, in a letter written late in his life, Peirce wrote:

> I do not say that it is infallibly true that there is any belief to which a person will come if he were to carry his inquiries far enough. I only say that that alone is what I call truth. I cannot infallibly know that there is any truth.[9]

So these views about truth are fallible claims about what we commit ourselves to when we take something to be true, or when we inquire into the truth of something. Presumably Peirce sees no reason to doubt these claims, indeed they reflect certainties which he sees no reason to doubt. If we treat these claims (and many others) as fallible certainties about truth, as contributing to our understanding of how what is true is independent of what anyone actually thinks about the matter, then it is hard to see why truth cannot be part of our goal, however fallible our means of identifying it may be.

In describing his own views about truth, William James happily endorsed the claim that true propositions 'agree with reality'. Like Peirce he endorses the platitude. And both saw the role of a pragmatist clarification as a guide to how we are able to apply the concept in practice, or how we are able to evaluate propositions in order to

---

[9] This passage is cited in Delaney (1993, p. 46).

find out which of them are true. In doing this, they do not seek a set of analytic necessary and sufficient conditions. And they do not require that the clarification be something that is known *a priori*: it is fallible but certain. And he information it provides concerns *truth*, it is not about justification or knowledge or something else.

If that is right, then truth can be our goal, once elaborated more fully in pragmatist terms. And it is then easy to see how the concept can have a role in our evaluations. One aspect of this comes from the 'social' dimension of what Peirce has to say. Leaving aside issues about vagueness, then reflection on truth shows us that if two people disagree, at least one of them must either lack relevant evidence or have gone wrong in processing the evidence that they possess. It cannot be the case that both have inquired long enough and well enough yet their conclusions are different. So if I treat a proposition as truth-apt, then the disagreement of those that I respect gives me a reason to reconsider my position. (As Huw Price (2003) has pointed out, this is the pragmatist account of how propositions evaluable as true or false are differentiated from, for example, expression of taste. The norm of truth 'gives disagreement its immediate normative character'.) When I commit myself to a proposition's being *true*, then I commit myself to the fact that any further evidence that leads me to revise my opinion will, if I continue to investigate the matter appropriately, turn out to be misleading. The formulation also enables me to address issues of when to stop my inquiries. I rely on information about the circumstance in which further well-conducted inquiry is unlikely to disrupt a current opinion. I may be able to tell that any subsequent inquirer will be less well placed than me to have a relevant opinion. And so on.

So exploring another example of pragmatist thinking on this matters illustrates how truth can have a normative role, and can have a role in setting our goals, even if both our grasp of the concept of truth is fallible, the ways in which we derive normative standards from our concept are fallible, and the methods we use in attempting to conform to these goals are fallible, and the beliefs we employ in applying these norms are fallible.

However, questions may still be raised about how far the sort of position just described undermines the claims made by Davidson, in particular. I shall mention just two of these questions here. First, it may be disputed whether the sort of position just described is compatible with the claim that truth is *objective*. (Since Rorty's argument does not depend upon this assumption anyway, this may not be of fundamental importance.) The clarification of the concept of truth that we find in Peirce's writings relates truth to what would be believed if inquiry continued for long and enough and was conducted well enough. This is compatible with denying that a true proposition must be justified by 'all our evidence'. That we are all certain that what survives effective inquiry is true says nothing about whether we could ever complete such an inquiry, and, as we have seen, Peirce allows that the link between truth and convergence is fallible. We need not treat these claims about truth as analytic or as embodying necessary truths or a priori knowable propositions. All that is claimed is that these are certainties that we all share, and which we can confidently rely upon in planning our inquiries and judging on the truth-values of propositions. It is one way of understanding how truth is independent of what anyone actually thinks, or will think, on the matter that does not condemn us to scepticism. We have no reason to doubt these claims about truth, and (perhaps) we cannot imagine encountering reason to deny them. But this does not require them to be grounded in semantic rules or to be anything other than deeply embedded contingent propositions.

VI

Reasons and Truth. I have asserted that we can pursue goals without having a capacity to identify with 'absolute certainty' whether we have achieved them. We may believe that we have reliable indicators of success, but these may be fallible or inconclusive. Often we *hope* that things will see us right, but we have no guarantee of this. Unless we have a strongly internalist conception of practical rationality, one which holds to the implausible view that *everything* which is relevant to assessing the success of our actions is available to us, there is no reason to treat fallible indicators as unsatisfactory.

There is a natural response to this. If we are fallibilists, then we have to be confident that standards are available that enable us to correct our beliefs in the face of future evidence. They guide us in identifying reasons for doubting our beliefs and reasons for revising or qualifying them. If truth is objective, then facts about such reasons are neither necessary truths nor knowable a priori: they too are fallible. We revise our opinions in the light of our background beliefs and our general conception of how things are. But there is no necessary or a priori connection between these beliefs and conceptions and the truth: we do not rely upon them because they *are* true or because they are guaranteed to enable us to discover the truth. The appeal to truth appears to provide grounding for our standards but does not in fact do so.

One way in which we criticize our standards of justification, and our standards for identifying reasons, is that we discover cases in which relying upon them leads us to acquire false beliefs. We find reasons to believe that these standards and methods are unreliable; or we find reason to doubt that they are reliable. But, of course, the judgements we make when we identify these reasons are themselves fallible. And there is no guarantee that such reflection makes it more likely that our beliefs will be true. We may feel certain of the standards we follow, but in order for the concept of *truth* to have a normative role in these reflections, there must be a necessary or a priori connection between our standards and the search for truth. And it is not clear that there is one.

I have tried to suggest that such concerns are misplaced. Confidence requires certainty, we may suppose, but it does not require 'absolute certainty'. We have many confident beliefs about indicators of truth and about the reliability of methods of inquiry, etc. Perhaps we cannot provide conclusive justification of such claims, but such justification is needed only when we are changing our views or responding to reasons for doubting what we take to be certain. Fallibilism, I have argued, challenges the idea that we have certain sorts of conclusive justifications available, but it need not challenge the many certainties that we have no reason to doubt. If many of these certainties concern truth, then there is no reason to deny that the concept of truth has a normative role in our inquiries. And since this claims do not establish a priori connections between truth and the fate of inquiry, perhaps we can hold on to the idea that truth is 'objective'.

It may seem surprising that Davidson could take *so* seriously an objective conception of truth yet deny that it has a role in setting the aims for our inquiries. But there is quite a deep issue involved here. When we try to make sense of a concept, for example *truth*, we often

explore connections between that concept and others: the concept
we wish to understand forms part of a family of concepts which are
used together in our cognitive practices. When we think about truth,
there are several families of concepts to which we might appeal.
Most commonly—and this is true of pragmatists like Peirce and
James—the concept of truth is explored through its relations to concepts like *belief, doubt, inquiry, assertion, knowledge* and so on (see,
for example, Misak, 2004a). We focus on the role of the concept in
the arena of *epistemic* reflection. If that is the right way to think of
the concept, then it is likely that it will have a role as one of the components of our goal in inquiry. And in that case, our understanding
of the concept will emphasis connections with *evidence, agreement
with other people*, and so on: the sorts of things to which we appeal
in settling our beliefs. A second related family of concepts concerns
how we think about our actions and projects: if our beliefs are true,
then this contributes to the success of our actions. True beliefs are
ones that it is good to 'steer by'. Both of these families of concepts introduced ideas, in thinking about truth, which Davidson would ex-
clude from a truly 'objective' account of truth.

   Davidson's own work studies truth in connection with a different
family of concepts: truth is understood by exploring its connections
with belief (as in the other cases) but also in connection with *meaning, interpretation, translation*, and so on. We understand the concept through exploring its role in semantics, not through its role in
epistemology. And somehow he ends up with a position that holds
that we can be confident that, on the whole, our beliefs are true
(and anti-sceptical position), but that we do not achieve this by actively pursuing truths and employing standards that are defended by
showing that they stand in intimate relations to truth. We have
many beliefs about what reality is like, and we are confident that,
on the whole, they are true. But any of them *might* turn out to be
mistaken. Our reasons can be defended by reference to what we
take ourselves to know about our surroundings. We defend them by
reference to things that we take to be true, but, for Davidson, in doing this we are not guided by reflection on the constitutive role of
the concept of truth.[10]

---

[10] Earlier versions of this material were delivered to a workshop on epistemic normativity at
the University of Cork, and to the University of Palermo. I am very grateful for comments
received on both of those occasions.

REFERENCES

Bilgrami, A. 2000: 'Is Truth a Goal of Inquiry? Rorty and Davidson on Truth', in Brandom (2000, pp. 242–61).

Brandom, R. (ed.) 2000: *Rorty and his Critics* (Oxford: Blackwell).

Davidson, D. 2005: *Truth, Language and History* (Oxford: Clarendon Press).

Delaney, C. F. 1993: *Science, Knowledge, and Mind* (Notre Dame, IN: University of Notre Dame Press).

Hookway, C. 2000: *Truth, Rationality, and Pragmatism* (Oxford: Clarendon Press).

——2004: 'Truth, Reality and Convergence', in Misak (2004b, pp. 127–50).

Misak, C. J. 2004a: *Truth and the End of Inquiry*, expanded paperback edition (Oxford: Clarendon Press).

——(ed.) 2004b: *The Cambridge Companion to Peirce* (Cambridge: Cambridge University Press).

Owens, D. J. 2003: 'Does Belief Have an Aim?', *Philosophical Studies*, 115, pp. 283–305.

Peirce, C. S. 1877/1992: 'The Fixation of Belief', in *The Essential Peirce*, vol. 1, ed. Nathan Houser and Christian Kloesel (Bloomington and Indianapolis, IN: Indiana University Press).

——1910/1958: 'Kinds of Reasoning', in *Collected Papers of Charles Sanders Peirce*, vol. 7, ed. A. Burks (Cambridge, MA: Harvard University Press).

Price, H. 2003: 'Truth as Convenient Friction', *Journal of Philosophy*, 100, pp. 167–90.

Putnam, H. 1995: *Words and Life* (Cambridge, MA: Harvard University Press).

Rorty, R. 1998: *Truth and Progress* (Cambridge: Cambridge University Press).

——1991: *Objectivity, Relativism and Truth* (Cambridge: Cambridge University Press).

——2000: 'Universality and Truth', in Brandom (2000, pp. 1–30).

van Fraassen, B. 1980: *The Scientific Image* (Oxford: Oxford University Press).

Velleman, D. 2000: *The Possibility of Practical Reason* (Oxford: Clarendon Press).

Wiggins, D. 2004: 'Reflections on Inquiry and Truth Arising from Peirce's Method for the Fixation of Belief', in Misak (2004b, pp. 87–126).

Scientific Structuralism
James Ladyman and Bas C. van Fraassen

I—James Ladyman

On the Identity and Diversity of Objects in a Structure

The identity and diversity of individual objects may be grounded or un-grounded, and intrinsic or contextual. Intrinsic individuation can be grounded in haecceities, or absolute discernibility. Contextual individuation can be grounded in relations, but this is compatible with absolute, relative or weak discernibility. Contextual individuation is compatible with the denial of haecceitism, and this is more harmonious with science. Structuralism implies contextual individuation. In mathematics contextual individuation is in general primitive. In physics contextual individuation may be grounded in relations via weak discernibility.

I

Introduction. According to Jonathan Lowe, 'two different individuals cannot both individuate, or help to individuate, each other. This is because individuation in the metaphysical sense is a determination relation ... As such, individuation is an *explanatory* relation' in the metaphysical sense of 'explanatory' (2003, p. 93, his emphasis). He goes on: 'Certainly, it seems that any satisfactory ontology will have to include self-individuating elements, the only question being which entities have this status—space-time points, bare particulars, tropes, and individual substances all being among the possible candidates'. Presumably Lowe's implicit argument is as follows: to say in virtue of what a thing is the thing it is and not any other—to give its principle of individuation—is thereby to explain the facts about the identity and diversity of it and other related things; explanations must appeal to what is already given, therefore relations between individuals cannot individuate those same individuals. This conclusion is widely accepted and is often expressed thus: 'Relations presuppose numerical diversity and so cannot account for it.'[1]

---

[1] I first heard this pithy formulation from Jeremy Butterfield in conversation, though he may not endorse it. The issue was famously discussed by Russell (1911), and also by Allaire (1963; 1965), Chappell (1964), and Meiland (1966); see MacBride (2006).

©2007 The Aristotelian Society
Proceedings of the Aristotelian Society Supplementary Volume LXXXI

Philosophers of a more empiricist bent disagree with Lowe about the need for self-individuating elements and look instead to the properties of objects to ground their individuality. Most have thought that the properties in question must be restricted to intrinsic properties and spatiotemporal relations, and have assumed that facts about the identity and diversity of individual objects must be ontologically and conceptually prior to their relations to other individuals in a structure. Hence, they agree with Lowe that individual objects cannot individuate or help individuate each other but must have what John Stachel (2005) calls 'intrinsic individuality'.[2]

The *ante rem* structuralism about mathematics defended by Stewart Shapiro among others, and the ontic structural realism about physics defended by Steven French and myself among others, are both metaphysical positions.[3] They have in common the idea that relational structure is ontologically more fundamental than individual objects. There are of course important differences between them, the most essential of which is that ontic structural realism is a form of realism about the modal (causal or nomological) structure of the world, whereas *ante rem* structuralism is only concerned with mathematical reality. Nonetheless, similar metaphysical controversies about the identity and diversity of individuals within a structure have arisen within the debates about each doctrine. It is therefore of

---

[2] Stachel criticizes Putnam for assuming that individuality must be intrinsic in the context of his infamous model-theoretic argument.

[3] There are two versions of mathematical structuralism: a realist view according to which mathematical structures exist independently of being instantiated by a concrete structure; and an eliminativist position according to which statements about mathematical structures are disguised generalizations about sets of objects that exemplify them (see Shapiro, 1997, pp. 149–50). For an excellent survey see Reck and Price (2000). The most well known advocates of realist structuralism in the philosophy of mathematics are Parsons (1990), Resnik (1997) and Shapiro (1997). Recent critiques include Hellman (2005) and MacBride (2005). Ontic structural realism was introduced by Ladyman (1998) in contrast with epistemic structural realism, and has since been elaborated by French and Ladyman (for example, 2003a, 2003b). Both are developments of ideas introduced into the contemporary literature by Worrall (1989) to defend scientific realism against the pessimistic meta-induction. Gower's (2000) historical survey of structural realism discusses how structuralism figures in the thought of Cassirer, Schlick, Carnap and Russell. Others who follow Ladyman (1998) in regarding structural realism as a metaphysical response to the ontological import of modern physics as well as a solution to the problem of theory change include: Bain (2004; MS), Esfeld (2004), M. Esfeld and V. Lam (forthcoming), Lyre (2004), Stachel (2002; 2006). The relationship between ontic structural realism and *ante rem* structuralism has been explored by Psillos (forthcoming), Busch (2003) and Pooley (2006). A full discussion of structural realism and further references can be found in chapters 2 and 3 of Ladyman and Ross (2007).

some importance that the range of possible positions on these issues be clarified.[4] Once this is done it is apparent that the arguments against the structuralist idea of what Stachel calls 'contextual individuality' collapse into expressions of prejudice. Esoteric posits such as tropes and bare particulars seem an embarrassment of metaphysical riches to a naturalistic philosopher interested in the metaphysics of mathematics and science (and self-individuating spacetime points are mismatched with the diffeomorphism invariance of General Relativity). Yet individuation by qualitative intrinsic properties is not an option for either mathematical or physical objects in general either. For both the *ante rem* structuralist and the ontic structural realist the identity and diversity of objects is dependent on the relational structure of which they are parts. Individuals need not have self-individuating elements, nor be individuated independently of the other individuals in the relational structures of which they are parts.

The next section explains briefly how intrinsic individuality fares in the context of contemporary physics. The following section explains how relations may be used to ground identity and diversity of objects in a structure. In section four some examples from graph theory illustrate the issues and show that even contextual individuality grounded in relations does not obtain in general in mathematics. Hence, it is argued that the *ante rem* structuralist must accept ungrounded or primitive contextual individuality. The relationship between primitive identity and haecceitism is then considered. The last section notes the key issues concerning the relationship between mathematical and physical structure.

II

Intrinsic Individuality. It is usually assumed that:

(i) The existence of an individual in spacetime is ontologically independent of other individuals (except for those that are

---

[4] Structuralism has also become popular in metaphysics recently in the form of causal essentialism. This is the doctrine that the causal relations that properties bear to other properties exhaust their natures. See Shoemaker (1980), Mumford (2004), which adopts a structural theory of properties, and Bird (2007), whose theory of dispositions is in some ways structuralist. Harte (2002) discusses an interesting Platonic form structuralism.

©2007 THE ARISTOTELIAN SOCIETY
Proceedings of the Aristotelian Society Supplementary Volume LXXXI

its proper parts).[5] Facts about the numerical identity and diversity of individuals are determined independently of their
relations to each other.
(ii) Each has some properties that are intrinsic to it.[6]

Haecceity, the property of primitive self-identity or primitive thisness, is posited to answer the general question as to what grounds
facts about the numerical identity and diversity of individuals.[7] If
each and every fundamental individual possesses such a property
then their individuality is intrinsic. However, many philosophers are
not inclined to invoke such metaphysical devices. The bundle theory
of individuation offers empiricists a way of accounting for individuality while only quantifying over properties that are within the
reach of natural science. If the identity and individuality of objects is
to be explained by the empirically accessible properties that they
possess, then it would seem that the Principle of the Identity of Indiscernibles (PII), restricted so that only qualitative and not identity
involving properties are in its scope, must be true. If so there are
some properties (perhaps including spatio-temporal properties) that
distinguish each thing from every other thing, and the identity and
individuality of physical objects can be accounted for in purely
qualitative terms.

Quantum Mechanics and General Relativity teach us that the nature of space, time and matter are not in keeping with a metaphysics
that describes the world as composed of self-subsistent distinguisha-

---

[5] Einstein in a letter to Max Born (Born, ed., 1971, pp. 170–1; quoted in Maudlin, 2002, p. 7 and Hagar, 2005, p. 757) says that the idea of independently existing objects comes from 'everyday thinking'. He also regards it as a necessary presupposition of physics. Sub-sequent developments seem to have proved him wrong in this second speculation. Ladyman and Ross (2007, ch. 1) call for the abandonment of such everyday thinking in metaphysics.

[6] It is also often claimed that all the relations between individuals other than their spatio-temporal relations supervene on the intrinsic properties of the relata (Humean superve-nience). Ladyman and Ross (2007, ch. 3) argue that contemporary physics undermines Humean supervience. It may also be argued that all the properties of fundamental physics seem to be extrinsic to individual objects.

[7] The notion of haecceity originates with Duns Scotus but in contemporary metaphysics it was revived in the guise of primitive thisness by Adams (1979). Positing haecceities may be thought to engender an infinite regress for what individuates each haecceity? If haecceities can be primitively the particular haecceities that they are, then why not allow that the indi-viduality of objects be primitive, dispensing with the need for haecceities in the first place? It is also reasonable to question whether such metaphysical posits ever genuinely explain or ground anything.

ble individuals. In the case of Quantum Mechanics the problem is that there are quantum states of many particles that attribute exactly the same properties to each of them. For example, the famous singlet state of two fermions, such as electrons, attributes to the pair the relation that their spins in any given direction are opposite to each other, but does not attribute a definite spin in any direction to either particle alone. Given that they may also be attributed exactly the same spatial wavefunction, as when they are both in the first orbit of an atom for example, then clearly such particles violate PII as usually formulated. This leads to a dilemma that was articulated by Steven French and Michael Redhead (1988); either quantum particles are not individuals, or they are individuals but the principle of individuation that applies to them must make reference to some kind of empirically transcendent haecceity, bare particularity or the like.

In the case of General Relativity the problem is more subtle. The general covariance of the field equations of General Relativity means that any spacetime model and its image under a diffeomorphism (a infinitely differentiable, bijective map of the model to itself) are in all observable respects equivalent to one another; all physical properties are expressed in terms of generally covariant relationships between geometrical objects. In other words, the points of spacetime are intrinsically entirely indiscernible one from another, and it makes no difference if we swap their properties around so long as the overall structure remains the same. This is made more apparent by the so-called 'hole argument', which shows that if diffeomorphic models are regarded as physically distinct then there is a breakdown of determinism. Carl Hoefer argues in response for the abandonment of the 'ascription of primitive identity to space-time points' (1996, p. 11). By 'primitive identity' he means intrinsic individuality.

Of course, these considerations from physics do not logically compel us to abandon the idea of a world of intrinsically individuated objects each possessing intrinsic properties. Transcendentally individuated quantum particles and spacetime points that essentially possess all their metrical properties (see Maudlin, 1990) are metaphysical possibilities. However, physics tells us that certain aspects of such a world would be unknowable in principle.

Frank Jackson (1998), Rae Langton (1998) and David Lewis (forthcoming) advocate a world of unknowable intrinsic natures. Jackson refers to 'Kantian physicalism' (pp. 23–4), Langton to 'Kantian Humility', and Lewis to 'Ramseyian Humility'. Jackson argues that science only reveals the causal/relational properties of physical objects: 'We know next to nothing about the intrinsic nature of the world. We know only its causal cum relational nature' (p. 24). Langton argues that science only reveals the extrinsic properties of physical objects. Both then argue that their intrinsic natures, and hence the intrinsic nature of the world, are epistemically inaccessible. Jackson points out that this inference can be blocked if the natures of objects and their intrinsic properties are identified with their relational or extrinsic properties, but argues that this makes a mystery of what it is that stands in the causal relations. To a naturalist unknowable intrinsic natures and things in themselves are merely philosophical toys; idle wheels in a metaphysical machine whose workings do not affect the observable world. Like Esfeld (2004, pp. 614–16), Ladyman and Ross (2007) take it that such a gap between epistemology and metaphysics is unacceptable.

Given that there is no a priori way of demonstrating that the world must be composed of intrinsically individuated objects with intrinsic natures, and given that our best physics puts severe pressure on such a view, it might seem that the naturalistic philosopher ought to deny that quantum particles and spacetime points are individuals.[8] I used to take this line and defend ontic structural realism as realism about structure combined with eliminativism about individual quantum objects and spacetime points. Simon Saunders' revival of the weak form of the identity of indiscernibles (see his 2003a, 2003b and 2006) convinced me that the defender of ontic structural realism ought not to insist that quantum particles are not individuals, but ought instead to emphasize that in so far as they are individuals it is the relations among them that account for this. Similarly, Oliver Pooley (2006) argues that eliminativism about individual spacetime points can be avoided without any tension with General Relativity, if it is accepted that the facts about their identity and diversity is grounded in relations they bear to each other. His

---

[8] In fact Jonathan Lowe (2005, p. 78) adopts this position despite his avowedly non-naturalist metaphysics.

'sophisticated substantivalism' allows that spacetime points be individuated relationally and not independently of the metric field. This means embracing contextual individuality grounded in relational structure.

III

Grounding Identity and Diversity in Properties and Relations. Critics of *ante rem* structuralism have claimed that the idea that facts about the identity and diversity of mathematical objects are determined by their places in structures cannot account for cases of mathematical objects which violate standard PII.[9] Examples of such objects are numerous the most well-known being that of i and $-i$. The field of complex numbers admits of a non-trivial automorphism, which is to say there is a structure-preserving bijective map of the complex plane onto itself other than the identity map. (Here a map, f, is structure-preserving just in case, for any objects, x and y in the domain, and for any operation between them, $*$, such that $x*y=z$, $f(x)*f(y)=f(x*y)=f(z)$, and for any relation between them, R, xRy implies that $f(x)Rf(y)$.) The map in question takes each complex number of the form $x+iy$ and replaces it by the complex number $x-iy$. So, i is mapped to $-i$ and $8-10i$ is mapped to $8-(-10)i=8+10i$, and so on.[10] The structure of the complex plane is completely preserved by this mapping so if the properties of the complex numbers are restricted to their relational mathematical properties then i and $-i$ possess all and only the same properties as each other. Hence, it is argued that the structuralist who is a realist about mathematical objects faces a dilemma; either apparently distinct but indiscernible mathematical objects are identical, or they differ only haecceitistically. If the latter horn is grasped then the idea that there is no more to mathematical objects than their structural properties must be abandoned and *ante rem* mathematical structur-

---

[9] This objection is due to Burgess (1999) and Keränen (2001) and is pressed by MacBride (2004; 2005).

[10] It is easy to check that this operation is structure preserving. Other examples of mathematical structures with non-trivial automorphisms (symmetries) include the group formed by the integers under addition with the map z goes to $-z$, and the set of points in Euclidean space which possess various symmetries including, for example, arbitrary rotations.

©2007 THE ARISTOTELIAN SOCIETY
Proceedings of the Aristotelian Society Supplementary Volume LXXXI

alism collapses into traditional Platonism. If the former horn is grasped then the mathematical structuralist is contradicting the practice of mathematicians which treats the mathematical objects in question as being distinct. As Fraser MacBride (2005, p. 582) puts it, is seems that *ante rem* mathematical structuralism is either old news or bad news.

The standard philosophical example of a structure that admits of a non-trivial automorphism, and hence violates standard PII, is that of Max Black's two intrinsically identical spheres that are a mile apart in empty space (1952). Permutation of the spheres results in the same world. Similarly, the singlet state of two fermions admits of the non-trivial automorphism that permutes the two particles. However, Simon Saunders (2003a; 2003b; 2006) challenges the claim that PII is false for fermions in such entangled states by re-introducing Quine's (1960, p. 230; 1976) distinction between three formulations of PII, namely absolute, relative and weak.[11]

Two objects are 'absolutely discernible' if there exists a formula in one free variable which is true of one object and not the other. For example, ordinary physical objects are absolutely discernible because they occupy different positions in space and time. Absolutely discernible mathematical objects include i and 1 since 1 is the square of itself and i is not.

Two objects are 'relatively discernible' just in case there is a formula in two free variables that applies to them in one order only. Moments in time are relatively discernible since any two always satisfy the 'earlier than' relation in one order only. An example of mathematical objects which are not absolutely discernible but which are relatively discernible include the points of a one-dimensional space with an ordering relation, $>$, since, for any such pair of points, x and y, if they are they are not the same point then either $x>y$ or $y<x$ but not both.

Finally, two objects are 'weakly discernible' just in case there is two-place irreflexive relation that they satisfy. Black's two spheres are obviously only weakly discernible. So too are two fermions in the singlet state and i and $-i$. All these examples have in common that the entities involved stand in some irreflexive (but symmetric)

---

[11] Ladyman (2005) deploys Saunders's version of PII to defend mathematical structuralism against the identity problem. For discussion see Ketland (2006) and MacBride (2006).

relation to each other.

The weak notion of individuality advocated by Saunders (according to which weak discernibility is sufficient for individuality) seems coherent. It would be question-begging to deny the sufficiency of weak discernibility merely because stronger forms of discernibility are sometimes available. Note however that while Saunders's view vindicates an ontology of individuals in the context of Quantum Mechanics, it is a thoroughly structuralist one in so far as objects are not assumed to be individuated independently of the nexus of relations in which they stand. Rather they are contextually individuated.

In the context of philosophy of mathematics, many philosophers have followed Russell in arguing that it is incoherent to suppose there could be individuals which don't possess any intrinsic properties, but whose individuality is conferred by their relations to other individuals:

> ... it is impossible that the ordinals should be, as Dedekind suggests, nothing but the terms of such relations as constitute a progression. If they are to be anything at all, they must be intrinsically something; they must differ from other entities as points from instants, or colours from sounds. What Dedekind intended to indicate was probably a definition by means of the principle of abstraction...But a definition so made always indicates some class of entities having... a genuine nature of their own. (Russell, 1903, p. 249)

The argument is that without distinct individuals that are metaphysically prior to the relations, there is nothing to stand in the asymmetric relations that are supposed to confer individuality on the relata. Contemporary philosophers of mathematics have been most influenced in accepting this insistence on intrinsic individuation by Paul Benacerraf (1965) who argued that objects to be properly so called must be individuals, and that therefore a structuralist construal of abstract objects like numbers must fail. According to Benacerraf, an object with only a structural character could be identified with any object in the appropriate place in any exemplary structure and could not therefore be an individual.

The metaphysical article of faith to the effect that objects and properties must have intrinsic natures prior to entering into relations is one that *ante rem* structuralists can simply reject. Charles

Parsons opposes Keränen (2001) and others who demand meta-physical accounts of objecthood in terms of haecceity, self-individu-ating elements, or intrinsic natures:

> There is a reason for my resistance, and this is that the structuralist view of mathematical objects coheres with a rather 'thin' conception of what an object is, that the most general concept of object derives from formal logic, that we are speaking of objects when we use the apparatus of singular terms, identity and quantification. This thin conception has a tradition behind it, whose principal representatives are Frege, Carnap and Quine; it is particularly Quine who has pressed its implications. It could be described as the view that the concept of object is a formal concept. (Parsons, 2004, p. 75)

Parsons includes the call for a principle of individuation, and PII, in the scope of what Keränen illicitly requests. On the other hand, the use of irreflexive relations to formulate a weak form of the identity of indiscernibles is repeatedly endorsed by Quine whom he cites as an authority here. However, the right conception of what an object is may turn out to be even thinner than Quine and Saunders argue.[12] Leitgeb and Ladyman (forthcoming) consider cases from graph theory that violate even weak PII.[13] The examples discussed in the next section suggest that, at least in the case of mathematics, the identity or diversity of objects or places in a structure is not to be accounted for by anything other than the structure itself. The identity and diversity of objects or places in a structure are relations that ought to be viewed as integral components of that structure in the same way as, for example, the successor relation is an integral component of the structure of natural numbers. Whether or not there are corresponding cases in physics is an open question briefly discussed in the final section.

---

[12] Quine has no problem with impredicative definitions while rejecting impredicative individuation in his critique of Davidson's theory of events. This is peculiar; insisting on predicativity is more plausible in epistemological rather than ontological contexts. See Horsten (forthcoming).

[13] Button (2006) mentions similar examples, while drawing dissimilar conclusions from them; his arguments are discussed in Leitgeb and Ladyman (forthcoming). Ketland (2006) arrives at similar conclusion to the latter as does Shapiro (forthcoming).

IV

Lessons from Graph Theory. Graphs are mathematical structures that contain only two kinds of entity, namely nodes and edges between nodes. Graphs may be *undirected* or *directed* depending on whether the relation between two nodes of their being joined by an edge is presupposed to be a symmetric or an asymmetric relation respectively. Graphs are *unlabelled* or *labelled*. In an unlabelled graph, different nodes are indistinguishable if considered in isolation (which is why unlabelled graphs are of special interest to structuralists). Labelled graphs are unlabelled graphs that come with an additional assignment of linguistic or numerical labels to their nodes, by which nodes become distinguishable by means of their labels even if taken in isolation.[14] However, it should be noted that if the labels of two nodes in a labelled graph with no edges are permuted the result is regarded as the same graph. Graphs are *symmetric* or *asymmetric* depending on whether or not there is a function that rearranges the nodes and leaves the graph structure unchanged, in other words, on whether or not there is a non-trivial graph automorphism.[15]

Graph theory clearly exemplifies the different versions of PII. Relative discernibility, without absolute discernibility, is exemplified by a directed graph with two nodes and one edge joining them. This example does not admit of a non-trivial automorphism. However, other directed graphs do such as the three node graph where each node has a directed edge coming towards it and going away from it, and where each node may be mapped to its downstream neighbour and the resulting structure is the same as the original. All the nodes in this graph are relatively discernible from each other, so the existence of a non-trivial automorphism is not sufficient for there being only weakly discernible objects in a structure. Note also that the nodes are not absolutely discernible and so if anything other than

---

[14] In the famous Black (1952) paper one of the two characters in the dialogue suggests distinguishing between the two globes by calling one 'Castor' and the other 'Pollux'; this case is directly analogous to the case of a labelled edgeless graph with order two. The other character points out that to use rather than mention these names one must presuppose that some way of fixing their reference is available which begs the question at issue. It is just assumed in graph theory that such labels can be deployed.

[15] Simple graphs, as characterized here, can be generalized to multigraphs, in which two nodes may be connected by more than one edge, or hypergraphs, where one edge may connect more than two nodes. It is also possible to consider graphs with edges that connect nodes to themselves (loops). These complications do not play any role in the following.

haecceities accounts for the facts about the identity and diversity of the nodes then it must be relations that do so. (The existence of a non-trivial automorphism is of course sufficient for the failure of absolute discerniblity.)

The case of weak discernibility, without absolute or relative discernibility, is exemplified by the following unlabelled graph G with two nodes and one edge. This is the graph-theoretic counterpart of Black's two-spheres universe (or the complex field substructure consisting of the imaginary units i and $-i$, or the singlet state of two fermions):

G obviously admits of a non-trivial automorphism and so is a symmetric graph. However, the two nodes in G are weakly discernible since they stand in the irreflexive (though symmetric) relation expressed 'x is connected to y by an edge (in G)'. Therefore, by the Indiscernibility of Identicals (which is not contentious), they are distinct.[16]

If the standard graph-theoretic operation of taking away an edge is applied to G the resulting graph G′ looks as follows:

For a graph theorist, G′ is just as much an unlabelled graph as G is.[17] Indeed, according to graph theory there are precisely two unlabelled (simple, loopless) graphs with two nodes, namely, G and G′. (A large part of graph theory is devoted to the enumeration of (classes of) unlabelled graphs.) G′ is of particular interest with respect to the debate about the identity and diversity of individual objects in a structure. Since permuting the two nodes of G′ obviously leaves the graph unchanged, G′ allows for non-trivial automor-

---

[16] The Distinctness of Discernibles is the contrapositive of the Indiscernibility of Identicals, and the contrapositive of PII is the Discernibility of the Distinct.

[17] Shapiro (1997, p. 115), considers patterns of 'small cardinal numbers'. His 2-pattern can be regarded as corresponding to the above graph G′, however, while in his case the corresponding reference class is the collection of cardinal numbers, in the present case the reference class of G′ is the collection of unlabelled graphs. While the possible occurrence of edges is constitutive of the latter, edges do no play any role whatsoever in the former. Hence, Shapiro's 2-pattern could just as well be identified with G rather than G′.

phisms. Yet there is no irreflexive relation that may be used to ground the identity or difference of the nodes in accordance with the weak version of PII, nor is there any need for one; to the graph theorist the two nodes in G' are perfectly respectable mathematical objects that are distinct from each other.[18] The fact that G' consists of two nodes is simply part of what G' is being part of its graph-theoretic structure. The analogue of the structuralist slogan about natural numbers (as stated, for example, in MacBride, 2005, p. 583): 'There is no more to the individual nodes "in themselves" than the relations they bear to each other' is true provided that identity and difference of nodes is included among the relations that the nodes in a graph bear to each other.

Graphs such as G' are not exceptional; all other unlabelled graphs that contain at least two isolated nodes (for example, 11 out of the 156 possible unlabelled graphs with 6 nodes) include nodes that are not even weakly discernible. Furthermore, an analogous point can be made about all unlabelled graphs which include at least two distinct but isomorphic and unconnected components, in other words, two isomorphic subgraphs for which there is no edge that leads from a node within one of the subgraphs to a node outside of it. Consider, for example, the following graph G'':

G'' is symmetric and there is no irreflexive relation, nor any other way of grounding the difference between its two components. It is a brute structural fact about this graph that it includes two components that are structurally indistinguishable if taken in isolation. In general, the identity and diversity of nodes in a graph cannot be accounted for by anything than the graph structure itself.

Before considering the details of this return to the idea of primitive identity, it is worth noting that the question of whether only weak PII is satisfied is not (as I used to think) the same as the question of whether the facts about the identity and diversity of individuals in a structure can be accounted for by and only by the (other) relations among them (excluding haecceities). As noted above, there

---

[18] There are many other examples of mathematical structures with elements that are not even weakly discernible that have a less trivial structure. Philip Welch (in correspondence) suggests the example of the Klein 4-group.

are directed graphs in which the nodes admit of relative but not absolute discernibility, and hence where only relations can account for the diversity of the nodes. On the other hand, there are also cases of absolute discernibility where relations can account for the identity and diversity of the nodes. The following undirected graph is asymmetric:

Each node satisfies a structure description that no other node does as follows. Let a node be described by a list of numbers, one for each node it is related to, and where the number assigned to that node is the number of nodes to which it is related.

$$(3), (134), (234), (34), (1233), (4)$$

Hence, each node in this graph is absolutely discernible from each of the others. Yet clearly in this example facts about the relations between the nodes determine the facts about the identity and diversity of the individual nodes. Absolute discernibility is not sufficient for intrinsic as opposed to contextual individuality, and contextual individuality is compatible with the traditional form of PII.

According to the above, individuality is primitive, rather than being grounded in qualitative properties or relations. The notion of primitive identity is associated with the theory of haecceity that was derided as purely metaphysical above. Worse, haecceities are associated with haecceitism (the claim that there are worlds differing solely in respect of the permutation of individuals[19]), and the latter doctrine causes problems in the interpretation of physics because of the permutation invariance of quantum states and the diffeomorphism invariance of models of General Relativity. Indeed, the need to avoid these problems is what motivated ontic structural realism in the first place (Ladyman, 1998). Recall also that MacBride (2005) argues

---

[19] See Lewis (1986).

that irreducible identity facts amount to 'old news' because they turn structuralism into traditional Platonism with haecceities.

However, primitive contextual individuality is different to primitive intrinsic individuality (whether or not the latter is construed in terms of haecceities), for only the latter and not the former implies haecceitism. If individuation is intrinsic, and not grounded in qualitative properties but is either ungrounded or grounded in haecceities, then the identity of an individual objects is determinate in other counterfactual situations, and permuting an object with another indiscernible object gives rise to another state of affairs. Indeed Kaplan (1975, p. 722) defines haecceitism as the doctrine that it makes sense to ask questions about the transworld identity of individuals independently of their properties and relations; he equates primitive intrinsic individuality and haecceitism. On the other hand, if individuality is contextual then there is in general no reason to regard talk of the same object in another relational structure as intelligible. In the mathematical case this is clear. Consider the three node edgeless unlabelled graph, and the operation of removing a node. The same graph results whichever node we remove.[20] Permuting exactly structurally similar individuals in a mathematical structure results in exactly the same structure. For example, permuting the two nodes in G' above does not result in a new graph (and as noted above, this is true even if the graph is labelled). In the physical case, as was remarked above, permutation invariance of individuals is a feature of both particle physics and spacetime physics. Physicists do not regard situations that differ only in virtue of the permuation of individuals as distinct. Contextual individuality is the only option for a naturalist, and primitive contextual individuality does not imply haecceitism and so is not old news.

---

[20] Also if we have a graph with two nodes and one is removed and then a node is added there is no fact of the matter about which of the nodes in the graph we end up with is the one that was removed and replaced and which was left on its own in the intermediary graph of one node. This makes unlabelled graphs a good model for discussing issues concerning diachronic as well as synchronic identity in quantum mechanics (see, for example, the discussion in Lowe, 2004).

V

The Relation Between Mathematical and Physical Structuralism. In sum, philosophical theories of the identity and diversity of individual objects in a structure, can be distinguished according to whether individuation is posited to be grounded or ungrounded, and intrinsic or contextual. Intrinsic individuation can be grounded in haecceities, or absolute discernibility based on intrinsic qualitative properties. Intrinsic identity, whether grounded or ungrounded, implies haecceitism. Contextual individuation can be grounded in relations but this is compatible with absolute, relative or weak discernibility. Contextual individuation whether grounded or ungrounded is compatible with the denial of haecceitism, and this is more harmonious with mathematical and physical theory. Structuralism in general implies contextual individuation. In the mathematical case contextual individuation is in general primitive in a structure. In physics contextual individuation may be grounded in relations via weak discernibility for fermions and spacetime points. The weak indiscernibility of elementary bosons is taken by Saunders to be sufficient for denying them the status of individual objects. The existence of mathematical objects that are not even weakly discernible may be one important difference between mathematical and physical objects, or it may be taken as a reason for disputing the claim that elementary bosons are not objects. After all, bosons, like fermions and like nodes in an unlabelled edgeless graph, can be aggregated (although not enumerated; see Teller, 1995, and French and Krause, 2006 for discussion and the development of a corresponding formal framework).

Another philosopher who has applied graph theory to the metaphysics of physical reality in defence of a broadly structuralist view is Dipert (1997). He advocates contextual individuality, but claims that the world is an asymmetric graph because he believes that facts about the numerical identity and diversity of objects must be grounded in absolute discernibility in the form of a unique structure descriptions, whereas in symmetric graphs there are nodes that admit of exactly the same structure descriptions.[21] In the light of the

---

[21] Bird (2007) also thinks that the absence of non-trivial automorphisms in the graph structure that represents the relationship between dispositions and their stimuli and manifestations is necessary to avoid 'the regress of pure powers'.

above it seems that the failure of all forms of discernibility is conceptually possible. Carnap (1928), in his famous example of a rail-track network (cf. §14 of his *Aufbau*), acknowledges the possibility that the world might present itself as allowing for non-trivial automorphisms, in which case there would be two places in the network which would have to be regarded as indistinguishable by all scientific means. It remains an open question whether the empirical world has such a structure.

The following worry now arises: If only the structure of mathematical theories is relevant to ontology in mathematics, and only structural aspects of the mathematical formalism of physical theories are relevant to ontology in physics, then there is nothing to distinguish physical and mathematical structure. In a paper first delivered in Leiden in 1999, van Fraassen argues that the heart of the problem with radical structuralism is this:

> It must imply: *what has looked like the structure* of something with unknown qualitative features *is actually all there is to nature*. But with this, the contrast between structure and what is not structure has disappeared. Thus, from the point of view of one who adopts this position, any difference between it and 'ordinary' scientific realism also disappears. It seems then that, *once adopted*, not be called structuralism at all! For if there is no non-structure, there is no structure either. But for those who do not adopt the view, it remains startling: from an external or prior point of view, it seems to tell us that nature needs to be entirely re-conceived. (van Fraassen, 2006, pp. 292–3)

The essence of van Fraassen's objection here is that the difference between mathematical (uninstantiated/abstract) structure, and physical (instantiated/concrete) structure cannot itself be explained in purely structural terms.[22] He reiterates the point (2006, pp. 293–4) in the context of Fock space formalism used in quantum field theory: all that there is cannot merely be the structure of this space, he insists, because then there would be no difference between a cell being occupied and a cell being unoccupied. However, just because our theory talks of occupation numbers does not imply that what is occupying the cell must be a non-structural object, individual or not.[23]

---

[22] There is an analogy here with the theory of universals and the problem of exemplification.

[23] A similar complaint is made by Cao (2003). Saunders (2003c) points out that there is no reason to think that ontic structural realists are committed to the idea that the structure of the world is mathematical.

Physical structure exists, but what is it? What makes the world-structure physical and not mathematical? Ladyman and Ross (2007) advocate a kind of neo-positivism according to which when questions like this arise it is time to stop; however, perhaps van Fraassen is right that I should have stopped earlier.[24]

REFERENCES

Adams, R. 1979: 'Primitive Thisness and Primitive Identity', *Journal of Philosophy*, 76, pp. 5–26.

Allaire, E. 1963: 'Bare Particulars', *Philosophical Studies*, 14, pp. 1–8.

——1965: 'Another Look At Bare Particulars', *Philosophical Studies*, 16, pp. 16–21.

Bain, J. 2004: 'Theories of Newtonian Gravity and Empirical Indistinguishability', *Studies in the History and Philosophy of Modern Physics*, 35, pp. 345–76.

——MS: 'Towards Structural Realism'. Available online at <http://ls.poly.edu/~jbain/papers/ SR.pdf>.

Benacerraf, P. 1965: 'What Numbers Could Not Be', *Philosophical Review*, 74, pp. 47–73; reprinted in P. Benacerraf and H. Putnam (eds.), *Philosophy of Mathematics: Selected Readings* (Cambridge: Cambridge University Press, 1983).

Bird, A. 2007: *Nature's Metaphysics: Dispositions, Laws, and Properties* (Oxford: Oxford University Press).

Black, M. 1952: 'The Identity of Indiscernibles', *Mind*, 61, pp. 153–64.

Born, M. (ed.) 1971: *The Born–Einstein Letters* (London: Macmillan).

Burgess, J. 1999: Review of Shapiro (1997), in *Notre Dame Journal of Formal Logic*, 40, pp. 283–91.

Busch, J. 2003: 'What Structures Could Not Be', *International Studies in the Philosophy of Science*, 17, pp. 211–25.

Button, T. 2006: 'Realistic Structuralism's Identity Crisis: A Hybrid Solution', *Analysis*, 66, pp. 216–22.

Cao, T. 2003: 'Structural Realism and the Interpretation of Quantum Field Theory', *Synthese*, 136, pp. 3–24.

Carnap, R. 1928: *The Logical Structure of the World* (Berkeley, CA: University of California Press).

---

[24] For discussions about the issues addressed in this paper I am heavily indebted to Alexander Bird, Jeremy Butterfield, Steven French, Øystein Linnebo, Fraser MacBride, Oliver Pooley, Simon Saunders, Bas van Fraassen, and most of all to Hannes Leitgeb.

Chappell, V. 1964: 'Particulars Re-Clothed', *Philosophical Studies*, 15, pp. 60–4.

Dipert, R. R. 1997: 'The Mathemtical Structure of the World: The World as Graph', *Journal of Philosophy*, 94, pp. 329–58.

Esfeld, M. 2004: 'Quantum Entanglement and a Metaphysics of Relations', *Studies in the History and Philosophy of Modern Physics*, 35, pp. 601–17.

Esfeld, M. and V. Lam forthcoming: 'Moderate Structural Realism About Space-Time', *Synthese*.

French, S. and D. Krause 2006: *Identity in Physics: A Historical, Philosophical and Formal Analysis* (Oxford: Oxford University Press).

French, S. and J. Ladyman 2003a: 'Remodelling Structural Realism: Quantum Physics and the Metaphysics of Structure', *Synthese*, 136, pp. 31–56.

——2003b: 'Between Platonism and Phenomenalism: Reply to Cao', *Synthese*, 136, pp. 73–8.

French, S. and M. Redhead 1988: 'Quantum Physics and the Identity of Indiscernibles', *British Journal for the Philosophy of Science*, 39, pp. 233–46.

Gower, B. 2000: 'Cassirer, Schlick and "Structural" Realism: The Philosophy of the Exact Sciences in the Background to Early Logical Empiricism', *British Journal for the History of Science*, 8, pp. 71–106.

Hagar, A. 2005: 'A Philosopher Looks at Quantum Information Theory', *Philosophy of Science*, 70, pp. 752–75.

Harte, V. 2002: *Plato on Parts and Wholes: The Metaphysics of Structure* (Oxford: Oxford University Press).

Hellman, G. 2005: 'Structuralism', in S. Shapiro (ed.), *The Oxford Handbook of Philosophy of Mathematics and Logic* (Oxford: Oxford University Press).

Hoefer, C. 1996: 'The Metaphysics of Space-Time Substantivalism', *Journal of Philosophy*, 93, pp. 5–27.

Horsten, L. forthcoming: 'Criteria of Identity: Predicative and Impredicative'.

Jackson, F. 1998: *From Metaphysics to Ethics: A Defence of Conceptual Analysis* (Oxford: Oxford University Press).

Kaplan, D. 1975: 'How to Russell a Frege-Church', *Journal of Philosophy*, 72, pp. 716–29.

Keränen J. 2001: 'The Identity Problem for Realist Structuralism', *Philosophia Mathematica*, 9, pp. 308–30.

Ketland, J. 2006: 'Structuralism and the Identity of Indiscernibles', *Analysis*, 66, pp. 303–15.

Ladyman, J. 1998: 'What Is Structural Realism?', *Studies in the History and Philosophy of Science*, 29, pp. 409–24.

——2005: 'Mathematical Structuralism and the Identity of Indiscernibles', *Analysis*, 65, pp. 218–21.

——and D. Ross 2007: *Everything Must Go: Metaphysics Naturalized* (Oxford: Oxford University Press).

Langton, R. 1998: *Kantian Humility: Our Ignorance of Things in Themselves* (Oxford: Oxford University Press).

Leitgeb, H. and J. Ladyman forthcoming: 'Criteria of Identity and Structuralist Ontology', *Philosophica Mathematica*.

Lewis, D. 1986: *On the Plurality of Worlds* (Oxford: Blackwell).

——forthcoming: 'Ramseyan Humility', in D. Braddon-Mitchell, R. Nola and D. Lewis (eds.), *The Canberra Programme* (Oxford: Oxford University Press).

Lowe, E. J. 2003: 'Individuation', in M. Loux and D. Zimmerman (eds.), *The Oxford Handbook of Metaphysics* (Oxford: Oxford University Press).

——2004: 'The Four-Category Ontology: Reply to Kistler', *Analysis*, 64, pp. 152–7.

Lyre, H. 2004: 'Holism and Structuralism in U(1) Gauge Theory', *Studies in the History and Philosophy of Modern Physics*, 35, pp. 643–70.

MacBride, F. 2004: 'Introduction', *Philosophical Quarterly*, 54, pp. 1–15.

——2005: 'Structuralism Reconsidered', in S. Shapiro (ed.). *The Oxford Handbook of Logic and Mathematics* (Oxford: Oxford University Press).

——2006: 'What Constitutes The Numerical Diversity of Mathematical Objects?', *Analysis*, 66, pp. 63–9.

Maudlin, T. 1990: 'Substances and Spacetimes: What Aristotle Would Have Said to Einstein', *Studies in the History and Philosophy of Science*, 21, pp. 531–61.

——2002: *Quantum Non-Locality and Relativity*, 2nd edition (Oxford: Blackwell).

Meiland, J. 1966: 'Do Relations Individuate?', *Philosophical Studies*, 17, pp. 65–9.

Mumford, S. 2004: *Laws in Nature: Routledge Studies in Twentieth-Century Philosophy* (London: Routledge).

Parsons, C. 1990: 'The Structuralist View of Mathematical Objects', *Synthese*, 84, pp. 303–46.

——2004: 'Structuralism and Metaphysics', *Philosophical Quarterly*, 54, pp. 56–77.

Pooley, O. 2006: 'Points, Particles and Structural Realism', in D. Rickles, S. French and J. Saatsi (eds.), *Structural Foundations of Quantum Gravity* (Oxford: Oxford University Press).

Psillos, S. forthcoming: 'The Structure, the Whole Structure and Nothing But the Structure?', *Philosophy of Science, Supplementary Volume*.

Quine, W. V. 1960: *Word and Object* (Cambridge, MA: MIT Press).

——1976: 'Grades of Discriminability', *Journal if Philosophy*, 73, pp. 113–16; reprinted in *Theories and Things* (Cambridge, MA: Harvard University Press, 1981).

Reck, E. and M. Price 2000: 'Structures and Structuralism in Contemporary Philosophy of Mathematics', *Synthese*, 125, pp. 341–87.

Resnik, M. 1997: *Mathematics as a Science of Patterns* (Oxford: Oxford University Press).

Russell, B. 1903: *The Principles of Mathematics* (Cambridge: Cambridge University Press).

——1911: 'On the Relations of Universals and Particulars', *Proceedings of the Aristotelian Society*, 12, pp. 1–24; reprinted in R. C. Marsh (ed.), *Logic and Knowledge* (London: George Allen & Unwin, 1956).

Saunders, S. 2003a: 'Indiscernibles, General Covariance, and Other Symmetries', in A. Ashtekar, D. Howard, J. Renn, S. Sarkar and A. Shimony (eds.), *Revisiting the Foundations of Relativistic Physics: Festschrift in Honour of John Stachel* (Dordrecht: Kluwer).

——2003b: 'Physics and Leibniz's Principles', in K. Brading and E. Castellani (eds.), *Symmetries in Physics: Philosophical Reflections* (Cambridge: Cambridge University Press).

——2003c: 'Structural Realism Again', *Synthese*, 136, pp. 127–33.

——2006: 'Are Quantum Particles Objects?', *Analysis*, 66, pp. 52–63.

Shapiro, S. 1997: *Philosophy of Mathematics: Structure and Ontology* (Oxford: Oxford University Press).

——forthcoming: 'Identity, Indiscernibility and *Ante Rem* Structuralism: The Story of i and $-i$'.

Shoemaker, S. 1980: 'Causality and Properties', in P. van Inwagen (ed.), *Time and Cause* (Dordrecht: Reidel).

Stachel, J. 2002: '"The relations between things" versus "the things between relations": The Deeper Meaning of the Hole Argument', in D. Malament (ed.), *Reading Natural Philosophy: Essays in the History and Philosophy of Science and Mathematics* (Chicago and LaSalle, IL: Open Court).

——2005: 'Structural Realism and Contextual Individuality', in Y. Ben-Menahem (ed.). *Hilary Putnam* (Cambridge: Cambridge University Press).

——2006: 'Structure, Individuality and Quantum Gravity', in D. Rickles, S. French and J. Saatsi (eds.), *Structural Foundations of Quantum Gravity* (Oxford: Oxford University Press).

Teller, P. 1995: *An Interpretative Introduction to Quantum Field Theory* (Princeton, NJ: Princeton University Press).

van Fraassen, B. C. 2006: 'Structure: Its Shadow and Substance', *British Journal for the Philosophy of Science*, 57, pp. 275–307.

Worrall, J. 1989: 'Structural Realism: The Best of Both Worlds?', *Dialectica*, 43, pp. 99–124; reprinted in D. Papineau (ed.). *The Philosophy of Science* (Oxford: Oxford University Press).

Scientific Structuralism
James Ladyman and Bas C. van Fraassen

II—Bas C. van Fraassen

Structuralism(s) About Science: Some Common Problems

Structuralist views of science can be realist or empiricist but face some of the same problems. *The identity of indiscernibles*: if not honoured in mathematics, nevertheless required to relate mathematics to the phenomena? *Metaphysics*: does Ladyman's 'radically naturalized metaphysics' still violate empiricist scruples? '*Structure is all there is*': can we accept the 'disappearance' of objects (things that bear structure but aren't themselves structure)? What could it mean to do without those sorts of entities in thinking about the world(-picture) of the physical sciences?

I also have a structuralist view of science, and although it is not one of the Structural Realisms, we run into some of the same problems.

Scientific theories provide representations of the phenomena in their domain. But what is a representation? A painting of, for example, Napoleon at Austerlitz is an artefact, of wood and canvas, with paint on it. That is not all there is to it: it has a referent, meaning, semantic content, something like that. It has that 'more' not because it is wood, canvas, covered with paint, but because of the role it plays for us.

Scientific representations are, in the main, models. A model is a mathematical structure. Just as for the painting, there is more to it: a given structure may not be a model, or equally, may be a model of one thing in one context and of another elsewhere—this has to do with the role it plays for us. Just for now, though, let us stay with the first answer. Then what can we read into the slogan that 'structure is all we know'? At the least, that in science only structure is represented:

I. Science represents the empirical phenomena as embeddable in certain *abstract structures* (theoretical models).

Our Common Problems. We face some of the typical problems structuralism encounters as soon as we add the important second point:

II. Those abstract structures are describable only up to structural isomorphism.

To connect with James Ladyman's paper, I will focus on two of these
problems, but I will need to put our different approaches in the context of our different takes on the role and value of metaphysics. So
the rest of my paper will have three parts.

The first will focus on problems relating to identity of indiscernibles. Then I will, in a sort of interlude, address the 'radically naturalized metaphysics' within which Ladyman works at present. The
third can then address the other slogan, 'Structure is all there is'.
That is, we can ask what view we can take about the 'disappearance' of objects, in the sense of things that bear structure but aren't
themselves structure. What could it mean to do without those sorts
of entities, or without that sort of concept at all, in thinking about
the world[-picture] of the physical sciences?

I

Identity and Individuation. The question of whether any entities can
be distinct yet indiscernible, or how that could make sense, arises at
many points: in ontology, in epistemology, in philosophy of mathematics, in the interpretation of physics.

Mathematics: Possibility versus Practice. Ladyman made a good
case for saying that in mathematics, the Principle of Identity of Indiscernibles (PII) is not a principle that is honoured in practice.
Leibniz would not have demurred: he explicitly exempted abstract
objects from this principle.[1] As examples he gave mathematical entities: lines, figures, curves, and contrasted them to concrete entities

---

[1] With thanks to Anja Jauernig for these citations: Letter to De Volder, June 1703 (Loemker,
1969, p. 859), 'People ... commonly use only incomplete and abstract concepts, ... which
nature does not know in their bare form; ... Such concepts men can easily imagine to be
diverse without diversity—for example, two equal parts of a straight line, since the straight
line is something incomplete and abstract, which needs to be considered only in theory. But
in nature every straight line is distinguishable by its contents from every other. Hence it cannot happen in nature that two bodies are at once perfectly similar and equal.' See further
Letter to De Volder, July 1701 (Loemker, 1969, p. 853) and Leibniz's fifth paper to Clarke
(Alexander, 1956, p. 63).

having such structures, which need to be individuated by specific differences.

Even for mathematics, and abstract entities in general, there have been arguments to uphold the PII. First of all there is the contention that mathematics can be construed, without even going to any special metaphysical thesis, in such a way that the PII is satisfied. I am thinking here of Gödel's suggestion that we take set theory as true, but that all the sets there are, are the constructible sets. These form a 'minimal' set-theoretic universe, and they are all mutually discernible.

The universe of constructible sets consists of the entities generated from the empty set by application of operations salient in the axioms: there is an empty set, it is unique, but every set has a unit set, so now we have two. For every two sets there is a pair, so now we have three. For every set there is a still larger one, its power set, ... and so on. The claim can be made, with good support, that classical mathematics, all the mathematics used in physics, can be reconstructed in this framework.

But mathematical practice shows no sign of deference to this conception. In practice, as Ladyman amply illustrated, there is no such tendency to stay within a well-defined PII-observing realm. We could dismiss this as ontological opportunism, but I think we would do better to follow the mathematicians' example.

Logical Arguments Against Violation of the PII? However, there are general arguments to rule out violations of the PII.[2] I'll mention some, and respect their air of plausibility, but I do think they are spurious.

Consider a set A with two elements, and suppose they are distinct but indiscernible—that graph with two nodes and no edges, if you like. Its power set exists, that is the set of its subsets, and of these there are four: A itself, the empty set, and two unit sets. The elements differ from each other, in that for each there is a unit set in which it belongs and the other does not. So, these elements are discernible after all.

---

[2] For an extended discussion of such arguments and the general conditions of possibility of individual discernibility see van Fraassen and Peschard (forthcoming).

The rebuke is obvious: if the elements are distinct but indiscernible, then their unit sets are distinct but indiscernible—hence belonging to distinct unit sets does not bestow discernibility.

Second argument about this set A: to say that it has two elements means that there is a well-defined permutation on it, a function f that maps A into A and whose values are distinct from its arguments. In fact, this function is unique. Doesn't it bestow discernibility on the elements? If they can be permuted they must be different, you'd think! But no, the image of A under this function is just A itself, no difference has been displayed. That this permutation exists follows from their distinctness, and implies no more.

Third argument: to say that A has two elements, that means in set theory that there is a one-to-one mapping of A onto the set $\{1, 2\}$. Call that mapping g; then one element of A is such that g of it is 1, and the other element such that g of it is 2—so they are discerned, so to speak, by this mapping.

Unlike the permutation, this function is not unique: there are precisely two of them. So as for the first argument, the retort can be: if the elements are distinct but indiscernible, so are those two functions!

The 'Master Argument': Individuation and Isomorphism. I think you can see the Master Argument driving these defensive moves against the PII. It resides in the simple but profound point that, as Hermann Weyl famously said, a mathematical science

> can never determine its subject-matter except up to isomorphic representation. The idea of isomorphism indicates the self-understood, insurmountable barrier of knowledge. (Weyl, 1934, p. 19)

'Isomorphic' is a context-dependent term: two structures can, for example, be isomorphic groups (they are related by a group isomorphism), although different in other respects. But that does nothing to take the bite out of Weyl's insight. For when a subject is represented by a mathematical structure, that representation determines the context, and we can't say that two subjects are represented respectively by that structure and by one isomorphic to it, yet represented differently.

Leaving Mathematics: The Phenomena. Although mathematical in form and theoretical practice, the mathematical sciences other than pure mathematics itself are meant to have, or be capable of having or acquiring, real empirical import. Given principles I and II above, how is that possible then?

Carnap, who was attempting to devise a structuralist view of science in the *Aufbau* came squarely up against this problem. Suppose all that a scientist tells us about something is its structure, and suppose something else has that structure as well ... shouldn't s/he be able to say which of the two s/he is talking about?

> Thus our thesis, namely that scientific statements relate only to structural properties, amounts to the assertion that scientific statements speak only of forms without stating what the elements and the relations of these forms are. Superficially, this seems to be a paradoxical assertion... in empirical science, one ought to know whether one speaks of persons or villages. This is the decisive point: *empirical science must be in a position to distinguish these various entities* ... (Carnap, 1928/1967, §12, p. 23)

Carnap tries a number of dodges, even at one point suggests that we could embrace an ontology according to which isomorphism implies identity. Amazing words for the author of 'Pseudo-Problems in Philosophy'!

Coordinate Systems, Coordinating Structure to Domain of Application. A mathematical space, such as Euclidean space or Minkowski space, has points, lines, subspaces that are related to each other in various ways. The points do not differ one from another, nor do the lines.

Remark on 'Weak Discernibiliy': It is true that for each point there is, for example, another one at a positive distance from it, while it is not at a positive distance from itself. This fact entails that there are distinct points, more than one—I would not use, as Ladyman and Saunders do, the term 'weak discernibility' for this. All the points have all the same properties, they are not discernible from each other at all. What is easily deduced, without assuming identity of indiscernibles (but rather its uncontroversial converse), is that given the irreflexive relations there must be more than one point. This is one way to establish distinctness *precisely in the absence of discernibility*.

In application to a specific practical problem, a specific phenomenon or empirical domain, how do we orient ourselves in, or with respect to, such a space?

The obvious answer would seem to be that we introduce a coordinate system, a frame of reference. But to understand how that is possible, we certainly need something that cuts across that 'insurmountable barrier to knowledge', isomorphism.

As an example to inspect, take the (at first blush so obvious) statement that the Euclidean unit sphere can be coordinatized by mapping into a set of *n*-tuples of real numbers. There are many ways to do that: we can coordinatize the sphere in various ways.

What I just said is irresponsibly sloppy. *We* can't do it at all. To pick out an origin or a pole in this space, we'd have to single out a specific point—but they are all the same, so we can't! What the sloppy language stood for is just this:

> There are functions, satisfying certain conditions, that map the Euclidean sphere into numerical coordinates.

But since the points are mutually indiscernible, so are those functions. We can't specify them either.

So much for that abstract object, the Euclidean unit sphere. Surely things go better with that more familiar (approximate) sphere, the Earth. It has differentiating amounts of snow and ice at the poles (for now at least anyway), it has an oriented magnetic field, there is a North Star to sight, and so forth.

But whatever practical problem we are trying to address, we will in the most scientific way begin with a model that represents the structure of this part of the universe. Now we can think that in this model, it is part of the very construction of the model, to locate the representation of the Earth's surface in, for example, Euclidean space, or to assign numerical coordinates. But the representation of the Earth's surface is itself a mathematical object, so don't we have the same problem as before? To assign numerical coordinates would seem to consist in specifying a function that maps that representation of the surface into a vector space over the real numbers. This is the *problem of coordination* vividly discussed by Schlick, Reichenbach, and Cassirer around 1920.[3]

Enter Common Sense? Ostension. Easy, I think, to get impatient at this point: we've gotten stuck in a truly scholastic problem. But if that is so, and if we had to get stuck in it, then that would seem to be an indictment of the structuralist view of science.

Carnap saw two possible solutions to the problem of relating the structures by which science represents to what it means thereby to represent. One he wanted to dismiss out of hand, as defeating the aim to fashion a structuralist view of science. That was recourse to *ostension*, to the user's reference to what s/he could identify in self-attributive acts or statements. The other solution, which he pursued, was to find a way to guarantee that everything has a uniquely identifying description or characterization.

Even if that second solution could be tenably maintained, it would leave a gigantic gap in our attempt to understand what happens in our own dealings with the world. For any description or characterization on which we rely applies, indexicals aside of course, quite possibly to something else in the universe. If a shorter description does uniquely identify, we would not be in a position to know that. The only certainty of uniqueness would even then reside in the form 'exists in a world that is thus and so', as Leibniz envisaged, and that is one not epistemically accessible to the finite mind.

So I will insist that the only good solution to the first problem the structuralist runs into, is to supplement the structuralist view of science with an *indexical* view of how scientific representations can have any genuine empirical content at all. 'A theory is true if it has a model that fits its domain'—yes, but the relation of fitting a specific domain has to be *specified*. In the end the idea of such a specification makes no sense if conceptually divorced from use and practice, from the context constituted by the user's self-orientation with respect to the theory's models. (*Mutatis mutandis* for empirical adequacy.)

Conceived in this way, the absolute need for *real* coordinate systems—the anchoring of theory to experience, as opposed to the mathematical construct—appears as what Weyl calls 'the unavoida-

---

[3] See Ryckman (2004, pp. 26–8 and 40 on Reichenbach and Cassirer; pp. 53–5 for Schlick; and his appendix, pp. 245–9 for a discussion of Michael Friedman's return to this problem); see also van Fraassen (forthcoming).

ble residuum of the ego's annihilation' in the sciences' objective representation of nature.[4]

A Defeat for Structuralism? Is this a defeat for structuralism? I say
not. The user's self-orientation with respect to a scientific model is
itself an event, that can be located in the world depicted by science.
That depiction would take the form of representation by means of a
mathematical structure, and could be, in principle, perfectly accurate, leaving out no relevant detail as far as the facts are concerned.

But to have that depiction of one's act of orientation is not the
same as orienting oneself with respect to the model. Just to give the
simplest example: imagine I am told that 12pm on 8 July is the moment at which BvF orients himself with respect to the University of
Bristol's campus map. Even if that is true, and even if I am told that
precisely at 12pm on 8 July, the information does not by itself suffice to make me aware of where I am or in what direction I must go.
To make it suffice, I need to realize something indexical, I have to
self-attribute the identity of BvF, and the time of hearing this as
12pm, 8 July.

II

What About Metaphysics? It will perhaps have been obvious that I
tried at every point to avoid intimations of either realist metaphysics
or scientific realism with respect to the empirical sciences, in how I
addressed the idea that 'structure is all we know'. Before going on
to the equally provocative 'Structure is all there is', I do need to face
this question of metaphysics, if only briefly.

'Radically Naturalistic' Metaphysics. Ladyman espouses a 'radically
naturalistic metaphysics' (Ladyman and Ross, forthcoming, ch. 1).[5]
As an empiricist I decry metaphysics—but this needs a quick qualifier. I am not against everything that comes under the heading of
metaphysics. As I've said before, I am against pre-Kantian meta-

---

[4] 'das unvermeidliche Residuum der Ich-Vernichtung', a phrase that occurs recurrently, with
minor variations, in Weyl's writings. See Ryckman (2004, pp. 128–31).
[5] Which Ladyman kindly made available in draft. The quotes in this section are from this
chapter.

physics, and then only if practised after Kant. To heed this, we need not be Kantians or transcendental idealists: empiricism today should equally take Kant's critique to heart, and not be enmeshed in the Illusions of Reason that he exposed. But that said, there are fuzzy borderlines to this cluster concept, metaphysics. What about the 'radically naturalistic' variant?

While rather similar in strategy to traditional metaphysical theorizing, this enterprise is motivated exclusively by attempts to unify hypotheses and theories that are taken seriously by contemporary science. It contrasts itself first of all to attempts at domesticating scientific discoveries so as to render them compatible with intuitive or 'folk' pictures of structural composition and causation.[6] Such domestication is typically presented as providing 'understanding', in the everyday sense of 'understanding' as 'rendering more familiar'. To this Ladyman and Ross (forthcoming, ch. 1) contrast a pursuit of explanation, which is at the same time a pursuit of truth, 'where an explanation must be true (at least in its most general claims)'. To which they add that in contrast, 'a given metaphysic's achievement of domestication furnishes no evidence at all that the metaphysic in question is true, and thus no reason for believing that it explains anything.'[7]

Strikingly, they themselves soon agree that this at first sight reasonably goal is set too high: 'Based as it is on incomplete science, this metaphysics probably is not true' (Ladyman and Ross, forthcoming, ch. 1). Yet in response to this doubt about the conditions of possibility for their success, they argue that because of their metaphysics' relation to science, it has a distinct advantage:

> However, if it is at least motivated by our most careful science at time *t*, then it is the best metaphysics we can have at *t*. (Ladyman and Ross, forthcoming, ch. 1)

---

[6] '[T]he attempt to domesticate twenty-first century science by reference to homely images of little particles that have much in common with seventeenth- and eighteenth-century mechanistic and materialist metaphysics is forlorn. ... Indeed, it is no longer helpful to conceive of either the world, or particular systems of the world that we study in partial isolation, as "made of" anything at all' (Ladyman and Ross, forthcoming, ch. 1).

[7] 'We, however, are interested in objective truth rather than philosophical anthropology. Our quarrel will be with philosophers who claim to share this interest, but then fail properly to pay attention to our basic source of information about objective reality' (Ladyman and Ross, forthcoming, ch. 1).

Question: what is the meaning of 'best' here? Given the doubt that science is already true, it cannot mean 'most likely to be true'. Perhaps it means most likely to become true in the long run, if this project is pursued in the same way by all later generations—assuming no extinction for the human race or scientific community.

Does it follow that the metaphysics grafted onto science in this fashion is also the most likely metaphysics to evolve into a true theory of the world? They themselves indicate why that does not follow: '[C]areful work by various philosophers of science has shown us that this task is not straightforward because science, usually and perhaps always, underdetermines the metaphysical answers we are seeking' (Ladyman and Ross, forthcoming, ch. 1).[8] But somewhat later they seem to ignore this, as they reply to Jonathan Lowe's critique of naturalism:

> [E]ven if naturalism depends on metaphysical assumptions, the naturalist can argue that the metaphysical assumptions in question are vindicated by the success of science, by contrast with the metaphysical assumptions on which autonomous metaphysics is based which are not vindicated by the success of metaphysics since it can claim no such success. (Ladyman and Ross, forthcoming, ch. 1)

If the metaphysical assumptions are underdetermined by the science to which they pay such attention, then no such assumptions can claim vindication from the success of science.

So, to sum up this quick critical look at their approach in metaphysics, I do not see that this enterprise, as they characterize it here, is genuinely a pursuit of truth. The understanding they seek, which requires explanation, must in actuality involve explanation without requiring any assurance of truth for its value or for the satisfaction of their requirements. This is not to deny value to the enterprise, but does ask for a different assessment of its value.

The Value One Can See in Metaphysics. If we portray this work not as a pursuit of truth but as *an attempt to arrive at interpretation*, we

---

[8] Compare: 'Even if we are able to decide on a canonical formulation of our theory, there is the further problem of metaphysical underdetermination with respect to, for example, whether the entities postulated by a theory are individuals or not ... We need to recognize the failure of our best theories to determine even the most fundamental ontological characteristic of the purported entities they feature' (Ladyman, 1998, p. 419).

immediately agree that the view we can construct is underdetermined by the science of which it is a view. Then we also have room for the possibility that other views, satisfying the same or similar requirements, can have equal value. Their requirements, enshrined in such principles as *Principle of Naturalistic Closure* (PNC) and *Primacy of Physics Constraint* (PPC), are formulated so as to bring the metaphysical theory close to the science to be understood. While these principles may also be contestable, contesting them need not be on the basis of what is more likely to be true, but of what is more likely to increase our understanding.

What is the point in that case? Well, what is the point of interpretations of *Finnegans Wake* or Milton's *Paradise Lost*, or a painting like *Red Square*? Each interpretation lets us see the work in a new light, helps us to navigate through it in a certain way, shows the internal coherence, may give us a firm grasp on it—and even aid in arriving at the sort of understanding that Dieks and de Regt characterize as what the working scientist aims at in his dealing with theory.[9]

In this way, radically naturalistic metaphysics has value in my eyes too, a value considerably greater than that of the domesticating and 'scholastic' varieties that both of us roundly reject.

III

A World Without Objects. The most puzzling aspect of Ontic Structural Realism is the insistence that we can, and should, conceived of the world as not consisting of objects, even in the very broad sense of bearers of structure which are themselves something other than structure(s). The motivation for this view should help to explain what is meant. I see this motivation as having two main parts:

(1) a very general response to a very general problem of 'equivalent descriptions', and

(2) a response to the specific problem of 'identical particles' in philosophy of physics.

---

[9] Dieks and de Regt (1998) and de Regt (1999) propose the following characterization of intelligibility: scientific theory *T* is intelligible (for scientist *S* in context *C*) if *S* is able to foresee qualitative (i.e. non-quantitative) consequences of *T* without entering into detailed calculations. See further de Regt (2004).

The latter is an instance of the former (and not the only salient instance) but takes the general problem out of the realm of purely logical possibilities. My plan for this last section is to concentrate on the general problem, with as specific case the earlier example of 'object language' versus 'event language', to see what morals we can draw for structuralism.

Equivalent Descriptions. Reichenbach comes back often to this problem, and consistently advocates a radical reaction. In the nineteenth-century, particle mechanics and rigid body mechanics had been giving way to continuum mechanics, phenomenological thermodynamics and field theories. There were many suggestions that the underlying ontology of physics had to be revamped. On the one hand the mechanics of bodies became more and more idealized; on the other there were suggestions that everything we classify as bodies are really wave disturbances in some underlying material continuum. Through the development of geometry it became clear that the same physical phenomena can be modeled in very different forms of space. William Clifford's *On the Space Theory of Matter* (1870) already argued that energy and matter are simply different types of curvature of space. However, it seemed also that such questions cannot be settled independently by experiment, and on the other hand, that physics cannot be formulated in a 'geometrically vacuous' format. As Poincaré and Reichenbach argued, it is only the combination of a physics and a geometry that has empirically testable content. But then, *possibly, different such combinations could represent nature equally well.* Suppose that is so; then we have in principle *equivalent descriptions* with no test against nature to favor one over the other.

While pragmatic factors may dictate a choice, the logically tenable reactions range from outright belief in a privileged fit to reality, to a deep agnosticism: either one of them is true, and we can't know which, **or** the very question of which is true makes no sense.

This possibility of relevantly equivalent descriptions continued to fascinate much philosophy of science in the twentieth century. As examples we can count Whitehead and Tarski's formulations of 'point-less' geometry, Carnap and Goodman's equal rights for a world constructed out of 'experiences', Quine's ontological relativity, and Putnam's arguments against metaphysical realism that challenge even the objectivity of cardinalities. None can be read as unqualified success, but there must be lessons in that.

Objects versus Events. Reichenbach (1956) provides a seminal example of how such an issue can be transposed from ontology to methodology. At the very fundamental level of persisting substantial objects versus event structures, he offered a duality between two forms of discourse which are roughly *though not completely* inter-translatable, but may offer distinct yet adequate representations of nature. A rough sketch, not entirely in Reichenbach's terms:

> Object X is F at t if and only if a case of *X's being F* occurs at t.
>
> Event Y is *an X's being F* if and only if Y *involves* X and Y *involves* F-ness.
>
> Events Y and Z are *genidentical* if and only if there is an object that both involve.
>
> The *history* of object X is the set of all events that involve it.
>
> An *object history* = a maximal class of mutually genidentical events.

In the event language we can envisage *pseudo-objects* (sequences of events that appear to occupy a spatio-temporal trajectory but are not genidentical) and allow as well for *individual events that involve no objects at all*—'mere happenings'. But perhaps at the level of microphysics, all apparent objects are just pseudo-objects. Perhaps 'histories' are sequences of events selected by criteria that have more to do with our conceptualizing than with anything connecting them ... Reichenbach explored this option precisely in his discussion of the problem of 'identical particles'.[10]

This would be metaphysics, if it made sense to ask which is the true description. Reichenbach's attitude, that it is only a matter of 'philosophical bookkeeping', is clearly expressed there:

> Neither interpretation is 'more true' than the other; the two are equivalent descriptions. (Reichenbach, 1956, p. 235)

Equivalence → *Common Structure?* If the two are really equivalent but different, it is reasonable to look for what is in common: some

---

[10] See further van Fraassen and Peschard (forthcoming).

underlying *structure* or skeleton fleshed out differently. But it is not easy, for two reasons.

First of all, none of the predicates that apply to the one sort of entities apply to the other, even if they have cognates, even in the case of space, time, space-time, before language is subjected to some procrustean regimentation. Objects exist for some time, an event lasts for a while; an object is in some region, an event occurs there; and so forth.

Secondly, each of the two languages have riches the other lacks. Object identity over time is grafted onto event language with the blatant neologisms mentioned above. There is logical room for events that involve no objects at all—lightning perhaps. Also for events that involve indefinitely many objects which do not together constitute some bigger object -- a storm, a wave.

Given this, can event language simply win out? Can objects, indeed any persisting substantial material basis for events, be simply discarded in favor of a 'pure' event world, in which persisting material is an appearance due to regularity in displayed patterns?

With this we arrive at a recent debate over Ontic Structural Realism.

IV

'Structure Is All There Is': The Impasse. I mentioned the 'identical particle' issue; it offers a quick introduction to how the above question relates quickly to the physical concept of a field.

The Salient New Example of 'Equivalent Descriptions'. Holding on to the feasibility of persisting object discourse has proved increasingly onerous. When Einstein published his study of the photo-electric effect, drawing on Planck's quantum theory, the picture of a light ray as a stream of particle-like photons seemed apt again. But Bose, with a quick addition by Einstein, showed that such an assembly of photons, formally rather like a gas ('photon gas') did not show the sort of gas behaviour modelled in classical (Maxwell-Boltzmann) statistical mechanics.

Immediately physicists spoke of 'loss of identity'. Maybe we have a violation of Leibniz's Identity of Indiscernibles here: the individual photons are many, but not different from each other in any way. This became more plausible when it turned out that the 'particles' in quantum theory are not there assigned specific locations or spatial trajectories. Logically, there is another option: that there are *individuating differences* between the photons, with Leibniz's principle not violated, but that these differences 'don't count' in their behaviour. In this sort of case Reichenbach claims that there is no rational or scientific basis for choosing between the two descriptions of what is happening.

The option to give up on the idea of light consisting of particle-like entities at all can look to quantum field theory. In general the simplest state of a ensemble of N particles would look like this:

$$\psi_1 \otimes \psi_2 \otimes \ldots \otimes \psi_N$$

But if there are no relevant differences between the particles in the case of a photon ensemble, the order does not matter, and the state should be described in a way that explicitly abstracts from this—it must be a *permutation-invariant* state. So the above formula gives way to a superposition of all its permutations. This makes possible a description of the state which is 'coordinate free'—'label free'—it can be specified simply by something like

$$N_1 \text{ of } \psi_1, \, N_2 \text{ of } \psi_2, \, \ldots, \text{ etc.,}$$

and the numbers N_i are called the *occupation numbers*. Now there is no logical implication at all that *whatever we are describing here* is an aggregate of distinct individuals. For we can read it in some such form as 'the nth cell is N_n-multiply occupied' while discarding some connotations of 'occupied'.

Ladyman versus Cao on Quantum Fields. This is, tellingly, the prime example for Ontic Structural Realism's slogan of 'structure all the way down'. Is it accompanied by Reichenbach's kind of methodological neutrality with respect to alternative conceptualizations? The passage I quoted in a note above continues:

> What is required is a shift to a different ontological basis altogether, one for which questions of individuality simply do not arise. Perhaps we should view the individuals and nonindividuals packages, like par-

ticle and field pictures, as different representations of the same structure. (Ladyman, 1998, p. 420)

This sounds like 'equivalent and having equal rights, but let us look
for the common structure as the objective core of both'. But that is
not what Ladyman's insistence elsewhere on 'structure all the way
down' would suggest. French and Ladyman (2003) write, in response to Tian Cao's insistence that structure must have a bearer:

> If we acknowledge the individuality/non-individuality underdetermi-
> nation then we're going to have to come up with a different under-
> standing of ontology. The question then is whether, without *objects*
> we can still retain a form of *objectivity* capable of satisfying the real-
> ists' demand for mind-independence. (p. 38)

> If all the 'observable' (in the physicist's sense) properties of an object
> can be represented in structural terms, then what is the nature of the
> ontological residuum? (p. 43)

Do these two sides have arguments? Each has a question that the
other can not answer, and each has reasons which carry no weight
at all for the other:

> If there is something to nature besides its structure, but struc-
> ture is all that science describes or can describe, then what is
> that *something*, that *undescribed and indescribable some-
> thing*...?

> But what sense does it make to try and conceive of structure
> that is not structure of something? *Structure of nothing is noth-
> ing*, isn't that so?

V

A Plea for a Change in View. Initially talk of objects and an object-
less ontology were held up as different but relevantly equivalent,
hence hiding some common structure that they flesh out in different
ways. If that vision could be sustained it would offer good support
for structuralism, with even a real clue to how to identify what is
structure and what is not.

Putnam, convinced that truly equivalent but different descriptions
of nature are possible, even feasible, for the physical sciences, opts
(at one point, I hasten to add) for pluralism in ontology rather than

structuralism. That would seem to be, in this context the natural opponent to structuralism within ontology.

But I sense at various points a distinct sympathy on Ladyman's side for Reichenbach's quite different option to transpose the issue from ontology to methodology—a better alternative at least for the empiricist philosopher.

REFERENCES

Alexander, H. G. (ed.) 1956: *Leibniz–Clarke Correspondence* (Manchester: Manchester University Press).

Carnap, R. 1928/1967: *The Logical Structure of the World*, trans. R. A. George (Berkeley, CA: University of California Press).

de Regt, H. W. 1999: 'Ludwig Boltzmann's *Bildtheorie* and Scientific Understanding', *Synthese*, 119, pp. 113–34.

——2004: 'Discussion Note: Making Sense of Understanding', *Philosophy of Science*, 71, pp. 98–109.

Dieks, D. and H. W. de Regt 1998: 'Reduction and Understanding', *Foundations of Science*, 3, pp. 45–59.

French, S. and J. Ladyman 2003: 'Remodelling Structural Realism: Quantum Physics and the Metaphysics of Structure', *Synthese*, 136, pp. 31–56.

Ladyman, J. 1998: 'What is Structural Realism?', *Studies in the History and Philosophy of Science*, 29A, pp. 409–24.

——and D. Ross, with D. Spurrett and J. Collier forthcoming: *Everything Must Go: Metaphysics Naturalized* (Oxford: Oxford University Press).

Loemker, L. 1969: *Leibniz: Philosophical Papers and Letters* (Dordrecht: Reidel).

Putnam, H. 1983: 'Equivalence', in *Realism and Reason: Philosophical Papers,* Vol. 3 (Cambridge: Cambridge University Press), pp. 26–45.

Reichenbach, H. 1956: *The Direction of Time* (Berkeley, CA: University of California Press).

Ryckman, T. 2004: *The Reign Of Relativity* (Oxford: Oxford University Press).

van Fraassen, B. C. forthcoming: 'Representation: The Problem for Structuralism', *Philosophy of Science*.

——and Isabelle Peschard forthcoming: 'Identity Over Time: Objectively, Subjectively', *Philosophical Quarterly.*

Weyl, H. 1934: *Mind And Nature* (Philadelphia: University of Pennsylvania Press).

EXPRESSIVISM AND EPISTEMOLOGY
JAMES LENMAN AND MICHAEL RIDGE

I—JAMES LENMAN

WHAT IS MORAL INQUIRY?

Considered moral judgements—or 'intuitions'—play a seemingly inelim-
inable role in moral inquiry, but it has proved difficult to arrive at a satisfying account of why we should take them as seriously as we do. The
difficulty is particularly vexatious for robustly realist understandings of
moral inquiry and its subject matter. It is more tractable for those who
understand moral inquiry as the pursuit of a form of self-understanding.
But the clearest and most satisfying picture of the proper role of intuitions emerges only, I argue, in the context of an expressivist, constructivist conception of moral inquiry as the pursuit of agreement on the moral
norms we are willing to accept.

I

Moral inquiry is an activity in which we all at some level engage.
And it's natural to think that some of us some of the time do it quite
well while others do it less well. And when we do it well it is natural
to think of it as a way of finding things out about how we and others ought and ought not to act. Only it's not very easy to understand
what this activity is and how it is meant to work. What exactly is it
we are supposed to be doing when we try to determine what we
ought morally to do?

Here is a natural and widely familiar story. We start out with a
bunch of *considered moral judgements*,[1] judgements we find attractive and plausible and of whose truth we are stably confident, judgements whose credibility is not compromised by the circumstances in
which we formed them being circumstances where we were in fear
or distress or stood to gain or to lose personally from forming certain judgements rather than others.[2] (Sometimes considered judgements so understood are referred to as 'intuitions' and I'll follow

---

[1] This is of course a technical term in Rawls's philosophy. See his (1951; 1972, rev. edn.
1999). What I say here broadly follows his (1972, pp. 47–8; 1999, p. 42).
[2] There is an interesting discussion of these 'filters' and how they may be motivated in
DePaul (1993, pp. 17–18).

that practice here though it's worth being clear that intuitions, so understood, are not 'gut reactions'.)

We then seek to impose theoretical unity and coherence on these judgements in ways that we hope will illuminate other moral questions where we are less confident what we should say. This we do by considering and comparing general principles and theoretical conceptions, themselves intuitively plausible, in whose light we seek to make sense of our more particular considered judgements. In the pursuit of coherence among these things, we 'work from both ends' (Rawls, 1972, p. 20; 1999, p. 18), looking for attractive general and theoretical ideas to which our considered judgements conform, while open to the possibility of revising the latter as our estimation of their credibility shifts in the light of modifications to our more general and theoretical understandings.

The standard name for this process is the pursuit of *reflective equilibrium*, a term most at home in ethics following its deployment there by John Rawls.[3] It is widely accepted among moral philosophers that the story of reflective equilibrium is roughly right as an account of how moral inquiry must proceed. Thus Shelly Kagan, in the opening chapter of *Normative Ethics*, urges that what we are seeking in normative ethics is a theory that fits as well as possible with our firmest intuitions and that enjoys an intuitively plausible rationale (1998, pp. 11–17). Brad Hooker, in *Ideal Code, Real World*, urges that in doing moral philosophy we are looking for theories with the virtues of internal consistency, coherence with the convictions we have after careful reflection, unification by fundamental and independently attractive principles and helpfulness in settling questions where we are uncertain or in disagreement (2000, ch. 1, esp. p. 4).[4] More recently still, Mark Timmons (2002, pp. 12–17) urges that we should evaluate moral theories with regard to the extent to which they are consistent, intuitively appealing, cohere with our considered moral judgements in particular by entailing and explaining them, as well as cohering with other non-moral beliefs and yielding determinate verdicts.

---

[3] See his (1951; 1972, esp. §§4, 9 and 87; 1993, esp. p. 8). As Rawls notes (1972, p. 51, n. 26; 1999, p. 45, n. 26), this is a conception of moral theorizing with a long pedigree, stretching back through Sidgwick to Aristotle.

[4] Hooker's desiderata also include, less relevantly to my present concerns, justification from an impartial standpoint.

Not everyone agrees. R. B. Brandt (1979, p. 22) famously dismissed the method of reflective equilibrium as a mere 'reshuffling of moral prejudices'. R. M. Hare was scathing, in several of his writings, about what he called with characteristically splendid magisterial scorn the 'Argument from Received Opinion' (Hare 1971).[5] Peter Singer (1974, p. 516) is troubled by any method that relies overmuch on confidently held particular judgements which he fears stem 'from discarded religious systems, from warped views of sex and bodily functions, or from customs necessary for the survival of the group in social and economic circumstances that now lie in the distant past'. And even Kagan (2001), writing more recently, acknowledges that it's hard to supply this way of proceeding with much in the way of any convincing rationale while also regretfully noting that it is equally hard to see how else we might proceed. Such bafflement about credible alternative methods is natural and widespread. Hare himself was immunized from it by a sanguine conviction that we could arrive at determinate answers to normative ethical questions relying on nothing more than a clear grasp of 'logic and the facts' (1981, pp. 6, 101 ff.). The pervasive acceptance of the method of reflective equilibrium largely reflects the fact that almost nobody now shares that conviction. That leaves us with no very credible story to tell except the story of reflective equilibrium, a story that seems only too vulnerable to what Michael DePaul (1993, ch. 1) has given the admirably self-explanatory name of the *No Contact with Reality Objection*.

Consider our empirical knowledge, both scientific and everyday, of the natural world. Here sensory observation divulges to us an immensely rich and complex picture, stable and shared, of a causally ordered natural world, recalcitrant to our will in certain dimensions, shaped by our agency in others. And the natural world so divulged is one in which we ourselves and our cognitive capacities feature as constituents. Scientific investigation of this world and our place in it, investigation itself controlled by and responsible to sensory observation, appears to vindicate in rich detail both the modest idea of a natural world constituted prior to and independently of our cognitive engagement with it and the presumptuous idea that we *can* so engage, that we are capable of forming true beliefs about it by our exercise of observational capacities responsive to the truth

---

[5] See further Hare (1989; 1981, §§1.3, 4.4).

of those same beliefs.[6] Of course we may sometimes be vexed by all kinds of sceptical or anti-realist challenges to this picture, or to parts of it, but in so far as we elect to place our trust in our capacities for empirical, perceptually mediated knowledge, we are guided by that trust to a rich—albeit certainly far from complete—understanding of how these same capacities work. But we look in vain in this naturalistic picture for any remotely comparable understanding of the operation of any capacity for intuiting an independently constituted domain of moral truths.

With moral inquiry, it's thus deeply unclear how intuition could play anything like the crucial role observation plays in science of hooking that inquiry up to some domain of facts putatively determined prior to and independently of that inquiry. Indeed it's unclear how *anything* could do this job. Some disagree. Thus Richard Boyd in 'How to be a Moral Realist' asks, 'What plays the role in moral theory that observation plays in science?' and boldly responds, *Observation* (1988, pp. 206–9).[7] But his thought seems to be just that, *if* homeostatic consequentialism, his favoured hypothesis according to which goodness and rightness are determined by whatever turns out to satisfy a set of homeostatically clustered goods conceived as satisfying human needs, is true, *then* moral inquiry is just a matter of investigating human needs and that is just a prosaically factual dimension of ordinary scientific inquiry. But of course we can so characterize moral inquiry only once we know that goodness and rightness are properly so conceived and the more interesting, philosophically perplexing bits of moral inquiry are the bits we would have to do to put us in that position in the first place. How *that* sort of inquiry hooks up with reality is a question to which I can't find a satisfying answer in Boyd.[8]

---

[6] I'm here echoing Wright (1992, pp. 1–2).

[7] Cf. his comparison between moral theory and automobile engineering in Boyd (2003b, pp. 41–3), elaborating briefer remarks in (1988, pp. 205–6).

[8] Boyd himself thinks we can vindicate his realist understanding of moral inquiry, along lines he takes to be analogous to the case of science, by seeing moral terms as referring to whatever candidate moral properties best explain the success of moral discourse in achieving its aims (1988; 2003a, esp. pp. 515–19). There are many problems here. For one thing, it is not at all clear that the parallel is convincing, that we really have in moral inquiry a narrative of achievement relevantly comparable to what we can point to in science. A lot has happened to be sure in the way of social and cultural change and some of what has happened has been shaped for better or worse by the work of moral theorists (French *philosophes*, English philosophical radicals, etc.) that clarified, focused and developed our central

I can't see how moral inquiry could credibly be represented simply as empirical inquiry governed by observation without an essential role for the considered judgements we find intuitively compelling. If we deny any standing to such things, any entitlement to play the role of evidence or something very like the role of evidence, then I don't think we have a credible story about what moral inquiry might be and how we might engage in it. So the question that comes into centre stage here is: What are moral intuitions that we should take them seriously as it seems, for moral inquiry to be possible, we must?

If moral inquiry isn't just science, then we can't see it as controlled by observation as science is. We also plausibly can't see moral intuitions playing the sort of role intuitions might perhaps play more

---

moral ideas. But plausibly nothing of a kind to make constructivist and other anti-realist understandings of ethics look simply quixotic in the way that like understandings of the causal order of physical nature look simply quixotic. For another, what is to *count* as success or as progress in the ethical case is so thoroughly theory-dependent (and in ways it is surely far from obvious are closely paralleled in the case of science) that a debilitating circularity threatens. The more so perhaps as Boyd (right-headedly to my mind) tends to characterize the aims of moral inquiry in practical, substantively moral terms (see e.g. Boyd 2003a, p. 517; 2003b, p. 36). Boyd strikes a rather modest note here, suggesting we may see ethical theory as in the business of offering hypothetical imperatives: 'Theories of the natures of the good, etc. have ... just the same hypothetical normative import as do our theories of the natures of chemical kinds. "If you want to achieve the aims of moral practice, classify things this way: ..."' (Boyd 2003a, p. 545). No doubt there could be many such classificatory schemes corresponding to many competing putative such aims. Intriguingly, these various schemes, on Boyd's account, may come to seem strikingly akin to the systems of thick concepts possessed by unreflective 'hypertraditional' societies as conceived by Williams (1985, pp. 142ff.). Williams allows that the application of concepts can yield real knowledge but distinguishes such knowledge sharply from anything that would address the reflective questions that arise when we stand back from these determinate conceptual structures and attempt to evaluate them and determine which furnish the best form of human life. But this reflective enterprise—about which Williams is somewhat pessimistic—is an essential aspect of what I here understand by moral inquiry. It's also the part where appeals to intuition appear to play the most pervasive and troublingly central role. The analogy is borne out by Boyd's rather deflationary take on the 'critical stance' that Robert Adams (1999, pp. 77–82) has alleged his naturalism is ill-suited to accommodate. Boyd's lengthy discussion of this objection concludes by suggesting (2003a, p. 546) a division of labour between 'investigations of the metaphysics of morals'—of which his naturalist metaethics are an account—and an in principle distinct process whereby we 'satisfy ourselves that the referents of "good" and similarly approbative moral terms are things we actually admire'. He doesn't tell us very much about this latter process but this robustly naturalistic characterization of it seems to place him rather firmly in the camp of the self-understanding model which I discuss in the following section. This limitation to the epistemic illumination shed by Boyd's classificatory hypotheticals likewise vexes, I suggest, David Brink's contention (1989, p. 110) that we need do no more than appeal to 'a distinctive way of seeing the world or a distinct set of conceptual categories' in order to put naturalistic puzzlement at intuitionist epistemology to bed.

generally in scientific and other non-moral contexts. Where this is concerned, an attractively modest story can be constructed from thoughts aired by Boyd (1988, pp. 192–3) and, more recently, Hilary Kornblith (1998). Both these philosophers reject, as good naturalists, the picture of intuitions as providing us with a priori noninferential knowledge and paint an alternative picture on which intuitions can be both a posteriori and as inferential as can be. What distinguishes them as intuitions is that while they are as inferential as can be, pervasively informed by an extensive background of experience and understanding, their inferential character is not, as it were, phenomenologically available. Think of the detective's hunch (you all know the sort of thing, 'I feel it in my bones, Sergeant Bloggs, …') or the scientist's intuitively compelling hypothesis. These may just come to their experienced scientist or detective subjects with no apparent inferential source, but they are things that should be taken seriously, as the intuitions you or I may have on matters of chemistry or of crime should not. For *our* intuitive thoughts about these matters do not feast subconsciously on the inferential sources supplied by years of expert engagement as those of such experts do. So the intuitions at least of experts have some authority, albeit of a largely preliminary kind: while what Inspector Blump feels in his bones may be good enough for Sergeant Bloggs in suggesting fruitful lines of inquiry, it properly cuts very little ice in a court of law. If he wants his conclusions taken seriously *there*, we expect him to come up with some proper evidence. None of this seems however really to help us. For while it's clear how intuitions might have this sort of authority in areas where observation plays a controlling role, it's not something we can help ourselves to in areas where it does not. We have only to look at the contemporary literature in normative ethical theory to see the inescapable controlling role played here by intuition itself. And in ways that, after two and a half millennia of ethical theorizing, are not looking terribly preliminary.

We would, of course, be home and dry if we had some credible reason to suppose our capacity for finding certain moral judgements intuitively acceptable were somehow relevantly akin to our capacity for perceptual knowledge. But that is a picture which seems fairly to invite a charge of epistemological bankruptcy. The huge and rich naturalistic understanding we have of how sensory knowledge is acquired, how physical features of the world impinge causally on our sensory receptors and issue in perceptual knowledge has no echo whatever in any available realist understanding of moral intuition, leaving talk of the latter looking like little else than an *ad hoc* postulate born of a desperation to offer our pretensions to moral knowledge some kind of vindicatory story.

Some intuitionists, perhaps recognizing the force of this worry, have preferred mathematical knowledge to sensory knowledge as a parallel (Prichard, 1968, p. 8; Ross, 1930, pp. 29–30), but this is surely a case of *obscurum per obscurius*, getting us almost nowhere. For if there was ever a field even more vexed by occasion for epistemological puzzlement than is metaethics it is surely the philosophy of mathematics. More recently, Derek Parfit's invocation (2006, p. 331) of modal knowledge as a companion in guilt seems similarly ineffectual. It is all too easy to imagine a complementary invocation of moral knowledge addressed to anyone tempted by sceptical or anti-realist understandings of modality completing a very small circle of philosophical complacency.

There is an obvious way to try to overcome the difficulty which I shall be concerned in what follows to explore. I asked just now if anything plays the crucial role observation plays in science of hooking that inquiry up to some domain of facts putatively determined prior to and independently of that inquiry. And a natural answer is that *nothing* does but this is not a problem. It is not a problem because there simply is no domain of such facts determined prior to and independently of that inquiry. That sounds like an invitation to an error theory but needn't be if we can make perfectly good sense of moral inquiry without supposing it to be in the business of investigating any such domain. Indeed perhaps it is only by some such anti-realist turn that we can hope to make sense of the authority we impute to the method of reflective equilibrium and in particular to the intuitions on which it ultimately rests.

II

I shall first consider a relatively modest retreat from metaphysical ambition. One appealing way of understanding moral inquiry is to view it not as a means by which we learn about some features of the world that are prior to and independent of our moral sensibilities, but as a means by which we learn about our moral sensibilities themselves. I'll call this the *self-understanding model*. The considerable attraction of such a view in this context is that it allows us to understand how moral intuitions might somehow be authoritative for moral inquiry, might get to carry something like evidential weight, without supposing them to be an exercise of some mysterious capacity whereby we are somehow placed epistemically in rapport with some prior domain of moral facts.

A suggestive analogy here might be with the study of grammar. In seeking to characterize in general terms which English sentences are grammatical, which not, we take the linguistic intuitions of native speakers as enjoying evidential status. But this is not because we take ourselves thereby to be brought into contact with some external domain of grammatical facts determined prior to and independently of those intuitions about which the holders of those intuitions how somehow successfully contrived to find out a whole lot. The relationship between those intuitions and the grammatical facts is a considerably more intimate one. In investigating the grammar of the language I speak, we are in effect studying a complex feature of my psychology and my intuitive dispositions to judge sentences grammatically acceptable or otherwise stand in expressive, causal and indeed, to some extent, constitutive relations to that same feature that earns them a clear evidential status when our inquiry is a grammatical one. Similarly we might understand moral inquiry to be simply the study of our moral sensibilities, sensibilities of which our intuitive moral judgements are an expression.

This is an approach clearly in tune with the view of Rawls in *A Theory of Justice*. There he characterizes moral theory as 'the attempt to describe our moral capacity' (1972, p. 46; 1999, p. 41) and, a couple of pages on, characterizes a theory of justice of the sort he is after as 'a theory of the moral sentiments ... setting out the principles governing our moral powers, or, more specifically, our sense of justice' (p. 51; p. 44).[9] And of course Rawls (1972, p. 47; 1999, pp. 41–2) himself famously rehearses (though he did not invent[10]) the analogy

---

[9] It is important to register that the former characterization is qualified 'at first'; the latter (in the revised edition only) 'in its initial stages'.

[10] Mikhail (2000, p. 7) cites *inter multos alios* Pufendorf, Hale, Hutcheson, Hume, Rousseau, Smith, Reid, Bentham, Mill and Pareto.

with grammar.

The linguistic analogy suggests a particularly strong version of the self-understanding model of moral inquiry, one which views at least key features of our moral sensibility as both innate and universal in line with the understanding of grammar which characterizes the mainstream of contemporary linguistics since Chomsky.[11] But there are weaker versions of the self-understanding model that regard, or are consistent with regarding, the aspects of the self we seek to understand as less deep, more cultural, less biological. This is characteristic of the later Rawls of *Political Liberalism*, who has nothing to say about analogies with linguistics but who takes himself to be articulating an understanding of justice that expresses and develops an ideal of the reasonable he takes to be implicit in the public political culture of western liberal democracies.[12] Others such as Michael Walzer (1987) still more explicitly espouse a cultural version of the self-understanding model.

Now if this is what moral inquiry is, we have little difficulty making sense of the method of reflective equilibrium and the authority of intuition. But it can seem rather implausible that this is what moral inquiry is. Thus here is Gilbert Harman:

> A moral philosopher who tries to find general principles to account for judgements about particular cases, hoping eventually to get principles and cases into 'reflective equilibrium' is studying common sense ethics. The results of such a study are results in moral psychology. Just as a study of common sense physics is not a study in physics, the study of common sense ethics is not an investigation of right and wrong unless what it is for something to be right and wrong can be identified with facts about moral psychology. (Harman, 1986, p. 61)[13]

The worry at work here is clear enough. There are, we might say,

---

[11] This kind of moral nativism is defended in Dwyer (1999) and Mikhail (2000). An impressive critique is Prinz forthcoming. (It is, I think, a misreading to take Rawls's use of the linguistic analogy as placing him squarely in the nativist camp. Thus, in chapter 7 of *A Theory of Justice*, Rawls compares 'empiricist' and 'rationalist' models of moral learning, and notes undogmatically: 'I shall not try to assess the relative merits of these two conceptions of moral learning. Surely there is much that is sound in both and it seems preferable to try to combine them in a natural way' (1972, p. 461; 1999, pp. 403–4).)

[12] See Rawls (1993, pp. 8–9, 13–15, 24–5 n.27, 43, 175).

[13] More recently Harman has written very sympathetically about the kind of moral nativism defended by Mikhail; see Harman (2000).

©2007 THE ARISTOTELIAN SOCIETY
Proceedings of the Aristotelian Society Supplementary Volume LXXXI

two projects here. There is, firstly, a descriptive project of correctly characterizing our moral sensibility. Secondly, there is the normative project of identifying which moral commitments are *correct*, of *justifying* such commitments. These projects are distinct and should not be confused.

Fair do's. But we should first note that, as John Mikhail (2000, ch. 4) has stressed, Rawls himself is certainly not guilty of confusing these projects. Rather he suggests in *A Theory of Justice* that making progress with the descriptive project may be the most fruitful way at our immediate disposal to make progress with the normative project. '[I]f we can find an accurate account of our moral conceptions,' Rawls writes, 'then questions of meaning and justification may prove much easier to answer' (1972, p. 51; 1999, p. 45).

That seems plausible and right, at least up to a point. There can be a difference between getting you to understand why I do what I do and justifying my behaviour to you. In some cases, where what I do is simply rotten and corrupt, the former project may be possible and the latter impossible. But where what I do makes good sense the two enterprises do not look so different. In seeking self-understanding I try to bring to the surface what reasons I may have for acting or being disposed to act in certain ways and, having done so, to discover whether my disposition so to act is robust in the light of this understanding. This is to echo T. M. Scanlon in 'The Aims and Authority of Moral Theory', where he claims that that the aim of moral theory is less to provide a justification of morality than 'to explain more clearly the kind of reasons those who accept morality have for doing so' (1992, p. 14). 'The aim of moral inquiry,' he goes on to write, 'is not to justify "considered judgments" with reference to some new and independent standard but to clarify the reasons we already had for believing them to be correct and to determine whether in the light of reflection we still find them persuasive' (1992, p. 16). What moral inquiry offers us, he suggests, are 'useful exercises in self-understanding, the results of which can alter our moral thinking' (1992, p. 13). What seems plausible and right then is that the descriptive project, fully carried through, may be expected not just to make clear what I think, morally speaking, but also what my reasons are for thinking it. And where those reasons are compelling reasons, that may leave exponents of the normative project feeling there is little they need to add. Except of course that the status of such compelling reasons as such remains moot, if by so calling them we mean something more robustly normative than the psychological fact about ourselves that we are disposed to be compelled by them.[14]

III

I think we should indeed grant that the descriptive project of self-understanding and the normative project of justification are intimately connected in the kinds of ways Rawls and Scanlon have proposed. But while we should indeed grant this, we should also, I wish to urge, keep hold of the thought that the projects are after all distinct. Trying to get clear about ethics can only be helped by a clearer understanding of the psychology of our dispositions to form moral intuitions. But we can only go so far in this inquiry without asking ourselves what we take these intuitions to be. Are they beliefs, or are they better construed as propositional attitudes of some distinct non-cognitive kind? And if they are beliefs, what are they beliefs about? For, whatever they are about, moral inquiry had better be about that too. No credible account of my moral sensibility will understand the judgements that express it simply as judgements about *itself*. To echo Simon Blackburn (1984, p. 219), my thought that the Holocaust was wrong is a thought about the Holocaust, not a thought about me. Certainly my moral sensibility is *reflective*, pervasively critically engaged with its own workings and contents. But it is not *reflexive*: the thoughts that drive that engagement and those that issue from it look, in large measure, outward to the world in which my moral life is lived. And if we think of this outward looking sensibility in robustly cognitive terms, as a form of receptivity to moral aspects of the world, we're stuck back where we started with the kind of realist take on moral intuition I urged in the opening section is desperately questionable.

It may help to forget about controversial issues like abortion, euthanasia, human cloning or the vexed ethics of redirecting trolleys. Let's stick with moral intuitions of the most clear-cut and platitudi-

---

[14] Scanlon himself, I should stress, certainly does mean something more robustly normative that that; see Scanlon (2003). I hope in work in progress to engage more fully with Scanlon's work on metaethics.

nous kind. Think of the most clear-cut and obviously appalling instances of such crimes as murder, torture or rape. Now of course we
all think it's just a no-brainer that behaviour like this is wrong. This
is a judgement in which our confidence is both very strong and
highly robust, stronger and more robust surely, for most of us, than
such confidence as we may invest in any metaethical stories anyone
has cooked up to make sense of it. And the question I'm asking here
about this judgement—a question which is much less of a no-
brainer—is: *What sort of thought is this?* I don't think it's plausibly
the thought that a loving God is dismayed by such actions though if
there is a loving God I am sure he is. Partly that's implausible because our confidence in this thought is surely highly robust vis-à-vis
changes in our beliefs about whether or not there is a God. And I
don't think it's the thought that this sort of behaviour has some sort
of non-natural property because I don't think there are any non-natural properties. And indeed, as with the God case, even if I did think
there were non-natural properties, I don't think you would need to
agree with me about that rather rarefied metaphysical claim to agree
with me that this sort of behaviour was morally wrong. And I'm dis-
inclined to think it's the thought that these actions had some natural
property or other, as it seems to me you might well agree with me
about the natural properties such actions had and none the less coherently, albeit viciously, disagree with me about their wrongness.[15]

Here I propose an expressivist turn. Think of my considered
judgement that actions such as these are morally wrong not, strictly
speaking,[16] as a kind of *belief* at all, but as a kind of *desire*. More
exactly, in cases such as these, I'd like to suggest, we may think of it
as a kind of *unwillingness*. I'm unwilling to accept any set of rules
for the regulation of my community that permit members of that
community to murder, rape torture and so on. So when we deliberate together about what the terms of our moral community should
be, this is one of the basic commitments I bring with me to the table.

I think that helps, and I'll try to explain why. It's not quite right to

---

[15] This is perhaps the most questionable of these assertions and I don't pretend anything I
say here amounts to an adequate defence of it. For such a defence see Gibbard (2003, ch. 7).
The observations made in this paragraph are all variations of what Gibbard (2002, p. 49),
calls the '*What's at issue*' argument.

[16] It is a delicate issue just what 'strictly speaking' amounts to here. For my two-pennyworth
see Lenman (2003); cf. Sinclair (2006).

say moral inquiry is what *I* do when I try to bring my moral judgements into reflective equilibrium. That's certainly part of it, but only a preliminary part. Moral inquiry, when it's serious and for real, is something we do *together*. It's an attempt by us to bring *our*—and not merely *my*—moral judgements into a harmonious state of reflective equilibrium. Robinson Crusoe can, to be sure, go in for moral inquiry. But it is distinctive of at least a core part[17] of moral as opposed to other forms of normative or ethical inquiry that it's a bit idle for Robinson to do this (just as it's a bit idle—if quite good fun—for me to spend time thinking about what, were I immensely rich, I would do with all the money).

Moral inquiry is what we do when we try—as we constantly do—to constitute a moral community together. And in the light of that fact, we can make progress with the problem of what authority might attach to my moral intuitions, say, for definiteness, to the considered judgement I have that murder, torture and rape are morally wrong. What that signals, as I have suggested, is that, if you want to join me in constituting a moral community, that is something you have to deal with when we deliberate together about how that community should be morally ordered.[18]

Moral inquiry is, in large measure, the attempt by the members of a community—or of what aspires to be one—to arrive by co-deliberation at agreement on what might be an acceptable set of moral standards for the conduct of that community. It is an attempt to determine what moral norms we might, at our best, stably agree in endorsing as a basis for governing our lives together, but where by 'determine' I mean not so much *discover* as *settle*. To put it a little

---

[17] Of course Robinson might worry, far from idly, about, for example, what might morally constrain his dealings with non-human animals he encounters, but I take it that plausibly the central part of morality concerns the proper mutual responsibilities of fellow members of human moral communities; cf. Scanlon (1998, pp. 171–87).

[18] And if the intuitions I bring to the table are silly or appalling? What if I'm unwilling to accept norms which don't forbid the wearing of grey trousers or which don't mandate the extermination of Jews. Then of course you will say I am being unreasonable. It's important to be clear that the expressivist take on intuitions I'm defending doesn't deny that intuitions are responsible to reason. Indeed my account of intuition is motivated, remember, by a desire to make sense of the method of reflective equilibrium where that is precisely an account of how moral reasoning operates. That's not inconsistent with saying our conceptions of that operation accords moral intuition an indispensable role. But that in turn is not inconsistent with saying that, as members of an already existing moral community with a fair measure of existing stable agreement on what we deem reasonable, we may simply reject certain intuitions as silly or plain monstrous.

provocatively, *moral inquiry is politics*.[19] As such, it is a project properly and inevitably shaped by those confidently held commitments and aspirations that we the parties to it bring to the co-deliberative table. Or, to put it another way, it is shaped by our moral intuitions.

Of course, it would be wrong to say that all moral judgements express our desires about what standards we would wish to inform a moral community. For moral community is always already (albeit more or less imperfectly) in place. And where moral community is in place, moral standards are in place, and many of the moral judgements we make simply serve to affirm and to apply these. Moral argument and moral inquiry can thus be addressed to two issues: firstly, how our own moral standards should be interpreted and applied—here the self-understanding model comes into its own—and secondly, what these standards ought to be. And in practice, of course, these things too are frequently deeply entangled, the more so as our engagement with the latter issue is never *ex nihilo*, always a matter of rebuilding a ship on which we remain afloat.

Moral inquiry is the attempt to reach and sustain certain kinds of agreement, shared understandings of what should be the moral terms of our life in community together. It is the business of seeking to build and sustain the moral commonalities that make human community and human relations possible. And that in large measure is the business of getting clear about which moral commitments and aspirations we share and which we can be brought to share. That is the currency in which our talk of moral intuition trades.

My earlier focus on the morally platitudinous is shared by Russ Shafer-Landau (2003, p. 248) when he reports: 'It seems to me self-evident that, other things equal, it is wrong to take pleasure in another's pain, to taunt and threaten the vulnerable, to prosecute and punish those known to be innocent, and to sell another's secrets solely for personal gain.' Notice how the expressivist understanding I here propose is well placed to explain the phenomenology whereby we find these judgements so compelling without recourse to the decidedly murky notion of self-evidence. Thoughts to the effect that such cruel, unjust or mean actions are wrong are indeed highly psy-

---

[19] Riposte to an imaginary uncharitable reader: *you* think I have a cynical and pessimistic picture of what moral inquiry must be; *I* think I have an idealistic and optimistic conception of what politics can be.

chologically compelling to most people, thoughts it is hard for us to envisage significantly revising. But this deep-seated confidence is just what we should expect if these thoughts expressed—as plausibly they do—deep-seated features of our emotional constitution.[20] When we switch from a realist to an expressivist understanding of the confidence to which Shafer-Landau's invocation of self-evidence owes its limited appeal, we can reach an understanding of that same confidence that is clear and straightforward where talk of self-evidence was murky and doubtful.[21]

DePaul's *No Contact with Reality Objection* fails because, ultimately, securing contact with moral reality is not the point. DePaul himself (1993, esp. chs. 2 and 3; 1998) takes us a long way to this insight in stressing as he does that coherence serves rationality where rationality is itself an epistemic virtue independently of truth-conduciveness. But from a robustly realist perspective it remains puzzling why that should be so. We certainly don't want simply to rest the whole business, as DePaul ultimately appears to,[22] on an unsupported intuition that coherence—or rationality conceived as involving it—is a good. And we don't need to. Here my proposed expressivist, constructivist approach comes into its own. Moral inquiry, as I propose conceiving it, is, fundamentally, a *practical* activity addressed to *practical* problems. There are innumerable such problems, but the basic one is simply that of bringing the desires, aspirations and commitments we bring with us to the enterprise into desirable forms of coherence, where that is understood both intrapersonally and—crucially in the case of moral inquiry—interpersonally. The pursuit of coherence through reflection and co-deliberation is desirable because they are the means by which we ad-

---

[20] Cf. Frankfurt's rich discussion of 'volitional necessities' in the second lecture of his (2006).

[21] Just to clarify. I think the notion of self-evidence is murky when it is plugged into a robustly realist metaethics of the sort Shafer-Landau espouses. But it maybe doesn't need to be. Thus Audi's influential discussion in his (1996) plugs it into a 'reflectionist' account of moral methodology intended to be neutral between various metaethical positions including 'non-cognitivism' (see esp. p. 123). Indeed, as Blackburn (1984, chs. 5 and 6; 1993, esp. chs. 1, 8 and 9; 1998, esp. chs. 3 and 9) and Gibbard (2003, esp. ch. 2) have urged, there is much in a realist understanding of ethics that expressivists can reconstruct in a quasi-realist spirit. This might even extend to the notion of self-evidence (cf. Audi, 1996, p. 135, n.43). That said, while it is a notion for which the realist has real need to give some credibility to his questionable faith that our intuitions put us in contact with some independently constituted moral reality, it's less clear that the expressivist has any particular need for it.

[22] Most explicitly in his (1998, pp. 306–7).

dress the most basic practical problem of all: the problem of deciding what to do.[23] And what makes deciding what to do a *problem* is
that the huge plurality of desires, aspirations and commitments that
we bring to it are liable to *conflict*. They don't conflict with the way
things independently are, but simply and pervasively *with each other*. That's the problem that gives reflection and co-deliberation their
most basic point: the point of resolving that conflict by reaching a
set of normative understandings that we can stably agree in reflectively endorsing.

At the *intra*personal level, conflict is of course inescapable. The
project of arriving at a set of desires that are comprehensively free of
it is not a possible project for anything we would be likely to recognize as a human being. First-order desires, in particular, can hardly
do otherwise than conflict pervasively. But the project of reaching
and reflectively endorsing an adequately coherent set of higher-order reflective commitments about which of my desires should constitute my will, while never complete, is one in which we can and
constantly do readily engage. (That's why the authority of higher-
order volitions is neither mysterious nor arbitrary.[24]) At the *inter*personal level conflict is again pervasive. Sometimes of course it doesn't
much matter: if you and I can't come to agree about what is and is
not funny, that may be no big deal. But moral norms express aspirations for fair terms of social cooperation and community, structured
by relatively clear, stable and shared understandings of the normative expectations to which it is appropriate we should hold each
other responsible for meeting or failing to meet, aspirations that
cannot be satisfactorily met except where there is a substantial
measure of agreement over what norms these should be. Hence the
special urgency attaching to our efforts to reach and sustain shared
moral understandings.

Understood as I here propose, moral inquiry looks both outward
to the world and inward to the soul of the inquirer, but the world it
looks out to is not a world of independently constituted moral facts,
but one of prosaically natural facts with which we deliberate and re-

---

[23] Reflection and co-deliberation do not perhaps represent the only way to address this
problem. But for creatures who care to the extent we do about autonomy and democracy
they are surely the only credibly acceptable way.

[24] The *locus classicus* for concern on this score is Watson (1975). For similar thoughts on
how to meet it, illuminatingly elaborated, see Bratman (2004).

flect together how best morally to engage. Seeing things in this way makes clearer what is right as well as what is not quite right about the self-understanding model. Trying to think in a theoretical way about what sort of set of shared moral commitments can prove acceptable to creatures such as ourselves as a basis for moral community and trying actually to agree together on a set of such commitments are categorically different sorts of activity, the one theoretical, the other practical. But the intimacy of the mutual relevance relation between these projects is not, I hope, hard to see.[25]

REFERENCES

Adams, R. M. 1999: *Finite and Infinite Goods: A Framework for Ethics* (New York: Oxford University Press).

Audi, R. 1996: 'Intuitionism, Pluralism and the Foundations of Ethics', in W. Sinnott-Armstrong and M. Timmons (eds.), *Moral Knowledge? New Readings in Moral Epistemology* (New York: Oxford University Press), pp. 101–36.

Blackburn, S. 1984: *Spreading the Word: Groundings in the Philosophy of Language* (Oxford: Clarendon Press).

——1993: *Essays in Quasi-Realism* (New York: Oxford University Press).

——1998: *Ruling Passions: A Theory of Practical Reason* (Oxford: Clarendon Press).

Boyd, R. 1988: 'How to Be a Moral Realist', in G. Sayre-McCord (ed.), *Essays on Moral Realism* (Ithaca: Cornell University Press), pp. 181–228.

——2003a: 'Finite Beings, Finite Goods: The Semantics, Metaphysics and Ethics of Naturalist Consequentialism, Part I', *Philosophy and Phenomenological Research*, 66, pp. 505–53.

——2003b: 'Finite Beings, Finite Goods: The Semantics, Metaphysics and Ethics of Naturalist Consequentialism, Part II', *Philosophy and Phenomenological Research*, 67, pp. 24–47.

Brandt, R. 1979: *A Theory of the Good and the Right* (Oxford: Clarendon Press).

[25] This research was supported by an award in the academic year 2006–7 under the UK Arts and Humanities Research Council's Research Leave Scheme and complementary leave from the University of Sheffield. I'm grateful too for feedback to Chris Bennett, George Botterill, Aisling Crean, John Divers, Lisa Fuller, Bob Hale, Ulrike Heuer, Jules Holroyd, Chris Hookway, Rob Hopkins, Stephen Laurence, Stephen Makin, Eric Olson, David Owens, Mike Ridge, Jenny Saul, Bob Stern, Yonatan Shemmer, Valerie Tiberius, Leif Wenar, Richard Woodward and audiences at Birmingham and Leeds, as well as the home crowd at Sheffield.

Bratman, M. 2004: 'Planning Agency, Autonomous Agency', in J. S. Taylor (ed.), *Personal Autonomy: New Essays on Personal Autonomy and Its Role in Contemporary Moral Philosophy* (Cambridge: Cambridge University Press), pp. 33–57.

Brink, D. 1989: *Moral Realism and the Foundations of Ethics* (Cambridge: Cambridge University Press).

DePaul, M. R. 1993: *Balance and Refinement: Beyond Coherence Methods of Moral Inquiry* (London: Routledge).

——1998: 'Why Bother With Reflective Equilibrium?', in M. R. DePaul and W. Ramsey (eds.), *Rethinking Intuition: The Psychology of Intuition and Its Role in Philosophical Inquiry* (Lanham, MD: Rowman and Littlefield), pp. 293–309.

Dwyer, S. 1999: 'Moral Competence', in K. Murasugi and R. Stainton (eds.), *Philosophy and Linguistics* (Boulder, CO: Westview), pp. 169–90.

Frankfurt, H. 2006: *Taking Ourselves Seriously and Getting It Right* (Stanford, CA: Stanford University Press).

Gibbard, A. 2002: 'The Reasons of a Living Being', *Proceedings and Addresses of the American Philosophical Association*, 76, pp. 49–60.

——2003: *Thinking How to Live* (Cambridge, MA: Harvard University Press).

Hare, R. M. 1971: 'The Argument from Received Opinion', in his *Essays on Philosophical Method* (London: Macmillan), pp. 117–35.

——1981: *Moral Thinking: Its Levels, Method and Point* (Oxford: Clarendon Press).

——1989: 'Rawls's Theory of Justice', in Norman Daniels (ed.), *Reading Rawls: Critical Studies on Rawls's* A Theory of Justice (Stanford, CA: Stanford University Press), pp. 81–107.

Harman, G. 1986: 'Moral Explanations of Natural Facts: Can Moral Claims Be Tested Against Moral Reality?', *Southern Journal of Philosophy*, 24 (supplement), pp. 57–68.

——2000: 'Moral Philosophy and Linguistics', in his *Explaining Value* (Oxford: Clarendon Press), pp. 217–26.

Hooker, B. 2000: *Ideal Code, Real World* (Oxford: Clarendon Press).

Kagan, S. 1998: *Normative Ethics* (Boulder, CO: Westview Press).

——2001: 'Thinking About Cases', in *Social Philosophy and Policy*, 18, pp. 44–63.

Kornblith, H. 1998: 'The Role of Intuition in Philosophical Inquiry', in M. R. DePaul and W. Ramsey (eds.), *Rethinking Intuition: The Psychology of Intuition and Its Role in Philosophical Inquiry* (Lanham, MD: Rowman and Littlefield), pp. 129–41.

Lenman, J. 2003: 'Disciplined Syntacticism and Moral Expressivism', *Philosophy and Phenomenological Research*, 66, pp. 32–57.

Mikhail, J. 2000: *Rawls's Linguistic Analogy: A Study of the 'Generative Grammar' Model of Moral Theory Described by John Rawls in* A Theory of Justice (PhD Dissertation, Cornell University).

Parfit, D. 2006: 'Normativity', in R. Shafer-Landau (ed.), *Oxford Studies in Metaethics*, Volume 1 (Oxford: Clarendon Press), pp. 325–80.

Prichard, H. A. 1968: *Moral Obligation and Duty and Interest: Essays and Lectures* (London: Oxford University Press).

Prinz, J. forthcoming: 'Is Morality Innate?', in W. Sinnott-Armstrong (ed.), *Moral Psychology, Volume 1: The Evolution of Morality* (Cambridge, MA; MIT Press, 2007).

Rawls, J. 1951: 'Outline of a Decision Procedure for Ethics', *Philosophical Review*, 60, pp. 177–97; reprinted in his *Collected Papers*, ed. S. Freeman (Cambridge, MA: Harvard University Press, 1999), pp. 1–19.

——1972: *A Theory of Justice* (Oxford: Clarendon Press; rev. edn. Oxford: Oxford University Press, 1999).

——1993: *Political Liberalism* (New York: Columbia University Press).

Ross, W. D. 1930: *The Right and the Good* (Oxford: Oxford University Press).

Scanlon, T. M. 1992: 'The Aims and Authority of Moral Theory', *Oxford Journal of Legal Studies*, 12, 1–23.

——1998: *What We Owe to Each Other* (Cambridge, MA: Harvard University Press).

——2003: 'Metaphysics and Morals', *Proceedings and Addresses of the American Philosophical Association*, 77, pp. 7–22.

Shafer-Landau, R. 2003: *Moral Realism: A Defence* (Oxford: Clarendon Press).

Sinclair, N. 2006: 'The Moral Belief Problem', *Ratio*, 19, pp. 249–60.

Singer, P. 1974: 'Sidgwick and Reflective Equilibrium', *Monist*, 57.

Timmons, M. 2002: *Moral Theory: An Introduction* (Lanham, MD: Rowman & Littlefield).

Walzer, M. 1987: *Interpretation and Social Criticism* (Cambridge, MA: Harvard University Press).

Watson, G. 1975: 'Free Agency', *Journal of Philosophy*, 72, pp. 205–20.

Williams, B. 1985: *Ethics and the Limits of Philosophy* (London: Fontana/Collins).

Wright, C. 1992: *Truth and Objectivity* (Cambridge, MA: Harvard University Press).

Expressivism and Epistemology
James Lenman and Michael Ridge

II—Michael Ridge

Epistemology for Ecumenical Expressivists

In this paper I defend a version of expressivism about epistemic discourse. The version of expressivism I defend is a species of what I have elsewhere called 'Ecumenical Expressivism'. I argue for three main theses. First, I argue that at least some of the most powerful arguments for metaethical expressivism carry over nicely to provide arguments for expressivism about epistemic discourse. Second, I argue that existing expressivist accounts of epistemic discourse are problematic. Third, and finally, I argue that Ecumenical Expressivism can evade some of those problems and provide a more plausible version of expressivism about epistemic discourse.

There is a rich tradition of defending and refining so-called 'expressivist' theories of moral discourse, and James Lenman's contribution to this symposium falls within this tradition, broadly construed. This tradition now spans several decades, going back at least to A. J. Ayer's *Language Truth and Logic* (1946). By contrast, expressivist theories of epistemological discourse have received far less attention. Only recently has there been an attempt by leading expressivists (most notably Simon Blackburn and Alan Gibbard) to extend their theories to cover epistemological discourse. Understandably, this work has itself been highly programmatic, leaving many key questions unanswered.

In my view, the historical asymmetry between the philosophical resources devoted to metaethical expressivism, as opposed to epistemological expressivism, is not entirely warranted. At least some of the same considerations which make metaethical expressivism seem plausible extend fairly easily to epistemological discourse. I begin my discussion by explaining both why expressivists have become more interested in epistemological expressivism and why what I take to be some of the best arguments for metaethical expressivism carry over to the epistemological case (section one). I then turn my attention to Gibbard's (section two) and then Blackburn's (section three) efforts on behalf of epistemological expressivism. After explaining why I think these accounts run into trouble, I develop an alternative account which builds on what I take to be insightful in Gibbard's and Blackburn's accounts, but without being open to the objections lodged against their accounts (sections four and five). This form of epistemological expressivism I defend is, as I explain below, a species of a view I have defended elsewhere, and which I call, 'Ecumenical Expressivism'.[1]

I

In its earliest and crudest forms, metaethical expressivism maintains that normative sentences express desires rather than beliefs, and that because desires are neither true nor false, neither are normative sentences. Later expressivists have been less keen to discard such seeming platitudes as 'It is true that torturing babies for fun is wrong'. In my view, they have been right to do so. Most notably, Simon Blackburn has developed a form of expressivism he calls 'Quasi-Realism', and Alan Gibbard has developed and defended an alternative species of the quasi-realist genus. The quasi-realist aims to make sense of the realist-sounding things ordinary folks say within a broadly expressivist framework. So, unlike traditional expressivists, Blackburn and Gibbard want to make sense of talk of moral truth and indeed moral knowledge in a way that is consistent with their metaethical expressivism.

Blackburn's considered strategy for accommodating talk of moral truth has been to invoke deflationist accounts of the truth predicate. One of the main inspiration for deflationist accounts of truth stems in part from the deep problems facing more robust theories of truth, perhaps most notably, so-called 'correspondence theories'. In light of the apparently grave difficulties facing more robust conceptions of truth, the deflationist begins with the hypothesis that saying (or thinking) p is true is really no different from saying (or thinking) that p.[2]

---

[1] See Ridge (2006; forthcoming a; forthcoming b).

[2] Deflationism is suggested by some of Wittgenstein's remarks, though Wittgenstein himself would probably not have found it useful to develop a philosophical theory of truth. For an early defence of deflationism as a philosophical theory, we should instead turn to F. P. Ramsey (see Ramsey, 1978). More recently, the idea has been developed in some detail by Paul

It is easy to see how deflationism might seem like a powerful tool for quasi-realists like Blackburn. For suppose there really is nothing more to saying that it is true that charity is good than there is to saying that charity is good. This suggests that the expressivist can indeed allow that normative utterances are truth-apt. The point will simply be that in saying that it is true that charity is good one is expressing one's attitude in favour of charity in just the same one that one does when one says that charity is good.

I am myself not entirely satisfied with this strategy. While I have considerable sympathy for deflationism about truth, that view faces certain technical difficulties.[3] It is not clear whether these difficulties are soluble. It would therefore be unfortunate if expressivism's fortunes were too tightly tied to those of deflationism about truth. For this reason I have myself elsewhere defended a rather different way for expressivists to make sense of talk of moral truth.[4] However, I shall not here rehearse this alternative, as doing so would require a lengthy excursion from the main line of argument here.

For simplicity, let us assume that Blackburn is right, and that the expressivist can reasonably invoke a deflationist account of truth to accommodate the truth-aptness of moral discourse. Even granting this much,[5] Blackburn's lofty quasi-realist ambitions are not entirely fulfilled. For a thoroughgoing quasi-realist would vindicate not only talk of moral truth, but of moral knowledge. In later work, Blackburn and fellow quasi-realist Alan Gibbard have turned their attention to just this challenge. For those familiar with their work, it is perhaps no surprise that they defend a form of expressivism about knowledge attributions in order to accommodate the very idea of moral knowledge given metaethical expressivism.

I am not here going to argue for metaethical expressivism, nor do I need to do so. For my aim in this section is not to convince you that epistemological expressivism is actually correct, but that it has as about as much going for it as metaethical expressivism does. In

---

Horwich (1990, p. 7), who maintains that there is nothing more to understanding the truth predicate than there is to understanding the equivalence schema, 'It is true that p if and only if p'. This schema is taken from the important work of Alfred Tarski (1958) on truth in formal languages, and is usually referred to as the 'T-schema'.

[3] See Ketland (1999) and Shapiro (1998).

[4] See Ridge (forthcoming a).

[5] And granting that the expressivist can solve the notorious 'Frege-Geach problem', for that matter. For my own attempt to solve that difficult problem, see Ridge (2006).

this context, I am simply going to take metaethical expressivism as a given, and ask whether anyone convinced by the standard arguments for metaethical expressivism should not also be an expressivist about epistemological discourse.[6]

The first reason to favour an expressivist account of knowledge claims is that such an account can, as I explain in section four, accommodate and explain the pre-theoretical intuition that attributions of normative knowledge *even if* normative judgement itself is understood in terms of metaethical expressivism. All else being equal, we should aim for an analysis which preserves the intelligibility of judgements which pre-theoretically seem perfectly intelligible. So in so far as metaethical expressivism is itself secure, we have some reason to favour an expressivist account of knowledge attributions too.

The second argument for expressivism about knowledge attributions is more direct. Knowledge claims are normative. To say someone knows that *p* is, *inter alia*, to say that the person is *justified* or, as it is sometimes put, *warranted* in judging that *p*.[7] Having a justified true belief is not sufficient for knowledge, as Edmund Gettier's (1963) classic arguments showed quite conclusively, but it is plausibly necessary for knowledge.

Gettier invites the reader to consider cases in which someone's belief is justified and true, but where the justification and the explanation of the truth of the proposition believed are not connected in the right way. One of Gettier's frequently cited examples involves someone traveling through what we might call 'fake barn land', where there are lots of barn façades along the highway. Driving through fake barn land, I look out the window and see what looks like a barn, and judge that it is a barn. It looks like a barn, and I have no reason to doubt my perceptual faculties, so I have a justification for my belief. Moreover, I happened to get very lucky—what I was looking at actually was a barn, and not one of the many barn façades I might have instead seen. Intuitively, although my belief is justified, the justification does not connect with the truth of what I

---

[6] For another recent argument for expressivism about epistemological discourse, see Chrisman (2007). I discuss Chrisman's arguments elsewhere (in work in progress).

[7] This is not entirely uncontroversial. Some epistemologists deny that knowledge requires justified belief. I lack the space to address these concerns here, but in my view it is clear that in at least one important and central sense, knowledge does require justified belief.

believe in the right way for my belief to count as knowledge. My belief is true, but its truth has nothing to do with my reasons for believing it, so it is in a sense simply an accident that my belief is true.
Intuitively, we do not think knowledge is accidental in this way.
Hence justified true belief is not sufficient for knowledge.

Gettier's counterexamples to what had been the standard analysis
of knowledge poses some very deep problems for philosophers who
have tried to analysed knowledge by taking the formula of Justified
True Belief (or JTB, for short) and adding some suitable additional
condition in order to rule out so-called 'Gettier cases'. That said,
having a justification for one's belief is plausibly at least necessary
for knowledge (though even this is not entirely uncontroversial),
and this is one sense in which knowledge attributions are normative. I return to the Gettier problem in a few paragraphs and again
in section three.

In fact, knowledge claims are normative in another respect. To
tell someone that you know that p is a way of reassuring them that
they can safely rely on your testimony with regard to the question of
p—that they can trust you. To say that you know that p is at least
sometimes a way of reassuring your interlocutor that he can be sure
enough that p for practical purposes in the context at hand. Saying
that you know that p can in this sense (among other things) serve
the same function as one's saying, 'p—you can count on it!' This is
why people are prone to say that they know that p in a very emphatic way when their interlocutor has expressed uncertainty about
whether it is reasonable to act on the assumption that p. Moreover,
this is why we find it so natural to speak of knowing that p 'to a
moral certainty'. Such a claim is apt when our knowledge of p is
sufficiently robust that it would, in our view anyway, be reasonable
to act on the assumption that p even if something of moral significance hangs in the balance.

So claims of the form 'S knows that p' are normative in at least
two ways. First such attributions of knowledge indicate that S is
epistemologically justified in judging that p. Second, such attributions of knowledge at least imply that your interlocutor would be
well advised to trust S's judgement that p, if forced to form an opinion with regard to p one way or the other, anyway.

The fact that epistemic claims are normative in these two respects
gives us some reason to think that such claims are well understood

in terms of the same sort of semantics we think is correct for other kinds of normative discourse. In so far as we are expressivists about practical normative judgement, this provides at least some reason for thinking expressivism might well be true about epistemic judgements as well.

The third reason to favour some form of expressivism about knowledge attributions builds on the second. At this stage it is useful to return to the problems generated by Gettier's counterexamples to the view that knowledge just is justified true belief.

Despite decades of ingenious attempts to deal with the 'Gettier problem', very few philosophers indeed would claim that great progress has been made. Simon Blackburn (1993, p. 37) at one point characterized this literature as the 'Gettier salt mine'. Timothy Williamson summarizes these metaphorical salt mines as follows:

> Experience confirms inductively what the present account implies, that no analysis of the concept *knows* of the standard kind is correct. Indeed, the candidate concepts turn out to be not merely distinct from, but not even necessarily coextensive with, the target concept. Since Gettier refuted the traditional analysis of *knows* as *has a justified true belief* in 1963, a succession of increasingly complex analyses have been overturned by increasingly complex counterexamples. (Williamson 2000, p. 30)

The concept of knowledge is both normative and seems to resist traditional conceptual analysis. In a way, this point parallels G. E. Moore's complaint about attempts to analyse 'good', though here the point goes even further. Not only can we question any given analysis of 'knows' without betraying conceptual confusion; all analyses to date seem open to direct refutation by counterexample. If this is correct, then we could take knowledge to be a conceptually basic mental kind, which is what Williamson suggests. Alternatively, though, we could understand knowledge attributions in expressivistic terms. Either of these approaches would accommodate the idea that it is impossible to provide a reductive analysis of the concept of knowledge. Indeed, historically expressivists used G. E. Moore's arguments against the analysability of 'good' to argue for metaethical expressivism as opposed to Moore's anti-reductionist realism. Similarly, I am proposing to use Williamson's point about the unanalysa-

bility of 'know' to argue for expressivism about 'know' as opposed
to Williamson's anti-reductionist realist account.[8]

Williamson does not actually consider the possibility of an expressivistic analysis of knowledge claims. He instead proposes
(2000, p. 2) his own anti-reductionist descriptivist account which he
suggests can be judged by the theoretical fruits that it bears. I shall
here return the favour and not argue directly against Williamson's
anti-reductionist view. Following Williamson's methodology, to
some extent at least, I suggest that the reader judge the proposed expressivistic account of knowledge attributions by the theoretical
fruit that it bears.[9]

In any event, this third argument, which we might call 'the argument from unanalysability' gives us some reason to take an expressivistic view of knowledge attributions. At this stage, in light of the
three arguments so far discussed, we have enough reason at least to
try to see what an expressivistic account of epistemological discourse might look like.

II

Alan Gibbard (2003) proposes an expressivist account of knowledge attributions, according to which such attributions are in Gibbard's terms 'plan-laden'. The avowal of a plan-laden judgement
expresses a speaker's contingency plans, rather than her descriptive
beliefs about the way the world is. Plan-laden judgements differ
from judgements of 'prosaic fact', which are constituted by ordinary
descriptive beliefs about the way the world is. According to Gibbard, knowledge attributions are like judgements about what one
ought to do. Both are normative, and the mark of the normative is
on Gibbard's account being plan-laden.

More specifically, Gibbard suggests that saying something of the
form '*S* knows that *p*' expresses a plan to rely on *S*'s judgement with

---

[8] See also Chrisman (2007), which independently makes a very similar point.

[9] I forgo a detailed critique of Williamson's view not because I think it does not merit discussion. Far from it; Williamson's position is original and he makes a very impressive case
for it. In fact, it is because the issues raised by Williamson's view are so complex, and the
debate over his view has already moved so far along, that it would take us too far afield to
discuss the key issues in the depth they deserve here.

regard to p. Concluding that Joe knows that p is concluding that Joe's judgement with respect to p is to be relied upon. On Gibbard's account, to judge that something is to be relied on just is to plan to rely on it.

Gibbard later qualifies this account in an important way. He suggests that to judge that to attribute knowledge to somebody is to plan to rely on that person's judgement that p in a specific way. First, one's plan to rely on the person's judgement in circumstances C is itself grounded in one's plan to judge in C that the person in question does himself judge that p.

Second, one judges that in the situation in which the person upon whom one plans to rely finds himself when judging that p, there are no 'defeaters' (Gibbard, 2003, pp. 226–7). A defeater is a consideration which blocks the proper and otherwise reliable functioning of the person's judgement. In this way the notion of reliably tracking the facts (whether descriptive or normative) enters into Gibbard's account as well. Note that Gibbard here must rely heavily on the appeal to a deflationist account of the truth predicate to make sense of talk of normative facts which might be tracked within a nonetheless expressivist framework.

Third, when we attribute knowledge to S about p, we plan to rely on that person's judgement about p, but do so while focusing entirely on S and his situation. We do not therefore, decide whether to rely on S in virtue of idiosyncratic features of our own situation. Instead, we focus on S alone, 'shifting those of us who might rely on him into the background and abstracting away from our features' (Gibbard, 2003, p. 227). This condition is meant to preserve the important idea that ascribing knowledge to S is to make a judgement about S and S's situation, and not to make a judgement primarily about oneself and one's own situation.

There are a number of delicate questions one might now ask about the details of Gibbard's account. For example, when we are discussing purely normative judgements, what is it to judge that there are 'no defeaters' present? Gibbard himself allows that his account is, 'rough and inexact, in spite of its complexity' (Gibbard, 2003, p. 229). Fair enough; as I noted in the introduction, it is early days for expressivist accounts of knowledge attributions. Here, though, I want to raise a worry which in my view cut to the heart of Gibbard's proposal, so that delicate questions of detail may be irrelevant.

Any approach which analyses a speaker's attribution of knowledge to S in terms of plans to defer to S's judgement faces a dilemma. Either, like Gibbard, these plans must abstract from the speaker's own circumstances or not. On the first horn of the dilemma, someone might reject Gibbard's requirement that my attribution of knowledge to S about p is constituted by my deferring in a way that abstracts from the peculiarities of my own circumstances. Instead, they might allow that my plans to defer can indeed take into account peculiarities of my own circumstances. As Gibbard's discussion implies, this approach seems to make my judgement that S knows that p turn out to be too much of a judgement about me, as opposed to S. Moreover, any such approach seems vulnerable to straight counterexamples. For example, suppose I judge that S is reliable with respect to p, and not subject to defeaters. I do not, however, plan to rely on S with regard to p because I judge it to be morally distasteful even to take a view about whether p is true. Moreover, I do not even form contingency plans for what to believe should I come to abandon this moral evaluation (of taking a view with respect to p), because I believe that making plans for what to do should I become so corrupt is itself a sign of moral corruption. Intuitively, this should be consistent with my judging still judging that S knows whether p is the case, for I might know that S is in as good a position as anyone to form a reliable judgement about p. However, on the view I am now considering, I cannot count as attributing this knowledge to S; in so far as I do not plan to rely on S (or indeed, anyone, under any circumstances) specifically with regard to p, I cannot on Gibbard's account count as attributing knowledge to S.

Gibbard implicitly takes the second horn of this dilemma, and casts the issue in terms of whether the speaker plans to rely on S with regard to p *when focusing on S alone, and abstracting from the speaker's own peculiar features.* This avoids the counterexample just pressed against a hypothetical version of the reliance-expressive account of knowledge attributions. For now we ask about the speaker's plans in isolation from the peculiarities of her circumstances, and hence in isolation from her belief that she is friends with S^*, who is a better judge, etc.

However, Gibbard's approach therefore faces another objection. For it is not at all obvious that ordinary speakers as much as form plans of the sort Gibbard has in mind. After all, there is no practical need to plan for circumstances in which I have abstracted from all the peculiarities of my own situation. Nor is the case here like our musings on what to do in various fictional or historical circumstances—there, at least, it is clear enough pre-theoretically that we do indeed think about what to do in such circumstances, even though we know we will never be in them. Planning for what to do while abstracting from all of the peculiarities of my own specific situation seems a bit different. Such planning behind a sort of 'veils of ignorance' might serve a useful theoretical role in certain contexts, but it does not seem to be part of our ordinary everyday planning about on whom we shall rely. It is, however, obvious that ordinary speakers do regularly attribute knowledge to others. Therefore, knowledge attributions are not constituted by the weird sorts of contingency plans Gibbard says they are.

The preceding objection is very swift. Perhaps he has a reply I have not been able to anticipate, or perhaps I have simply misunderstood his account. I do not have much more to say about this, though, so for now I shall leave the ball in Gibbard's court and move on to Simon Blackburn's expressivist account of knowledge attributions.

III

Blackburn takes the idea of reliably tracking the facts as his starting point, and argues (contra the 'reliabilist' school of epistemology) that this is at most necessary, and not sufficient for knowledge. Like Williamson, he also despairs of any reductive analysis of knowledge attributions. Instead, he argues that knowledge attributions are irreducibly normative, and that the mark of normative judgements, whether the norms in question are epistemic or practical, is that they are best understood in expressivist terms.

More specifically, Blackburn argues that attributing knowledge of p to S is not only to judge that S's judgement that p is in some sense reliable. It is also to judge that there is no chance that an improvement in S's acquaintance with the facts would *justify* S in abandoning his judgement that p.[10] Because the notion of justification here is clearly normative, we should therefore understand knowledge attributions in expressivist terms.

One advantage of Blackburn's approach which he does not discuss is that it helps avoid the Gettier problem. For Gettier cases are always such that there are some epistemic improvements which would justify abandoning the belief in question. The structure of Gettier cases ensures this. For the structure of such cases is always one in which the reasons for which an agent believes that p turn out not to have anything to do with why p is true. Learning that your putative justification does not bear on the truth of a proposition in the right way itself plausibly constitutes an improvement in one's epistemic perspective (that is, better acquaintance with the facts), and it also plausibly justifies abandoning the belief in question—so long as one has no further and independent grounds for holding the belief, anyway.

It may help to go through an example. Recall the example I used to illustrate the Gettier problem, which I justifiably and truly believe that what I have just seen out my window is a barn (see section one). Quite clearly in that case there were epistemic improvements which would have justified my abandoning the belief, even though further epistemic improvements would have justified my accepting the belief again. Specifically, suppose I learned that we were in fake barn land. That sounds like an epistemic improvement with respect to my judgement, and it also sounds like it would justify my giving up the belief that what I had just seen was a barn.

Blackburn's account is fine as far as it goes, but it does not go far enough. As an expressivist about knowledge attributions, he is committed to taking attributions of knowledge to express distinctive attitudes. Precisely what kinds of attitudes are involved here, though? What is it, on Blackburn's account, for a speaker to take a certain improvement in his acquaintance with the facts to *justify* abandoning a given belief? More to the point, what it is it for a speaker to judge that no such improvements would justify abandoning a given belief? Without answers to these questions, it is hard to know just how plausible an expressivist account of knowledge attributions really is. Unfortunately, Blackburn does not address this question; in fairness, it is not clear that defending a fully worked out expressivist

---

[10] See Blackburn (1996, p. 87).

account of knowledge attributions was his main aim in the paper in question. To this significant extent, Blackburn's account is incomplete. Because I think Blackburn's basic approach was on the right track, I shall try to remedy this incompleteness. First, though, I need to take a slight detour from the main line of argument in order to introduce my own version of expressivism, which I call 'Ecumenical Expressivism' (in section four). With that account in hand, I finally turn my attention to how an Ecumenical Expressivist might plausibly develop the kernel of an expressivist theory we find in Blackburn's discussion into a more fully worked out account (in section five).

IV

Much of the debate between cognitivists and expressivists stems from the rather Janus-faced character of normative judgement.[11] In some respects, normative judgements seem like ordinary beliefs. We call them 'beliefs', as when we say things like, 'Britney believes that she ought to spend more time at the tanning salon.' Most pertinently for present purposes, we do not hesitate to classify them as true or false or even as constituting knowledge.

In other respects, though, normative judgements seem more like desires. Normative judgement is practical; it reliably guides action. Changes in normative view reliably track changes in motivation. We tend to question the sincerity of someone who claims that she really ought to do something but shows no signs whatsoever of being motivated to do it, feel bad about not doing it, etc. Failure to act on one's all things considered normative judgement about what one ought to do is irrational.[12] This contrasts with acting contrary to what one believes is required by merely conventional norms like those of etiquette.

These competing characteristics of normative judgements have led to the formation of two diametrically opposed philosophical camps—the cognitivists and the expressivists. Cognitivism is traditionally defined as the doctrine that normative utterances express

---

[11] In the next few paragraphs, I draw heavily on Ridge (forthcoming b).

[12] This is not uncontroversial, but this is not the place to discuss the controversy. For a contrasting view, see Arpaly (2000).

beliefs rather than desires. Expressivism, by contrast, is traditionally defined as the doctrine that normative utterances express desires rather than beliefs. This definition does fit well with Ayer's early form of expressivism. Unfortunately, the terms of this debate mask the following logical space:

> *The Ecumenical View*: Normative utterances express *both* beliefs and desires.

On the traditional way of carving up the metaethical territory, the Ecumenical View seems to imply that neither expressivism or cognitivism is correct. In that case, one of the central metaethical debates of the past century has been a tempest in a teapot. This might be a welcome conclusion to those weary of apparently interminable debates about those doctrines. However, the issues at stake in that debate remain live ones even if the Ecumenical View is correct. We can usefully redraw the terms of that debate within an ecumenical framework as follows:

> *Cognitivism:* For any normative sentence M, M is conventionally used to express a belief such that M is true if and only if the belief is true.

> *Expressivism:* For any normative sentence M, M is not conventionally used to express a belief such that M is true if and only if the belief is true.

The distinction is exclusive but not exhaustive. There is logical space for hybrid views according to which some but not all normative utterances express beliefs which provide their truth conditions. For present purposes I put such views to one side. Also, expressivism as characterized here does not include the positive thesis that normative utterances function to express proattitudes. I have not included this in my definition of expressivism simply because I want to emphasize the ecumenical idea that this thesis can be common ground between expressivists and cognitivists. For it should be clear enough that, characterized in these terms, there can be both cognitivist and expressivist versions of the Ecumenical View. The Ecumenical Cognitivist and the Ecumenical Expressivist agree that normative utterances express both beliefs and desires. They disagree about the connection between the truth of the belief expressed and the truth of the sentence.

Here there is a divide between expressivists like Ayer and more quasi-realist expressivists like Blackburn. The former will claim that normative utterances are not truth-apt and so trivially do not inherit the truth conditions of any belief they express. Quasi-realists, though, want to insist that normative utterances *are* truth-apt. The difficult question then becomes how to maintain that normative utterances conventionally function to express beliefs, are truth-apt (contra Ayer) and yet do not automatically inherit the truth conditions of the belief they express in the way that ordinary assertions seem to do. Before we can usefully explore this question, though, we must first develop Ecumenical Expressivism in just a little more detail.

On the version of Ecumenical Expressivism I favour, normative utterances express the following two states of mind:

(1) A suitable state of approval to actions in so far as they would garner the approval of a certain sort of advisor, and

(2) A belief which makes suitable anaphoric reference back to that advisor.

The basic idea is best illustrated through examples. Suppose I am a utilitarian. In that case, my claim that charity is right expresses my perfectly general attitude of approval to actions in so far as they would garner the approval of a certain sort of advisor, which in this case is an advisor who approves of actions just in so far as they promote happiness. My claim *also* expresses a belief which makes anaphoric reference back to that advisor (the one which figures in the content of the attitude I expressed). In this case, the belief is that such an advisor would approve of charity.

Fully working out this approach actually requires the articulation of two senses of 'belief'. Since I have addressed this issue at length elsewhere,[13] I shall here be brief. First, there is a strict and philosophical sense of 'belief', and in this sense beliefs are a natural kind

---

[13] See especially Ridge (forthcoming a).

with a particular function, namely to represent the world as it is. In at least one important sense, beliefs in this sense have what is often called a mind-to-world direction of fit. It is in this strict sense of 'belief' that the belief expressed by a normative utterance might not thereby be guaranteed to provide the truth conditions for that utterance.

There is, however, a weaker sense of belief. In this sense, whatever state of mind or combination of states of mind is expressed by an ordinary declarative sentence that p thereby constitutes the belief that p. In this sense, belief might well not form a natural kind. If the form of expressivism I am defending is correct, then this will indeed be the case. For in this sense the utilitarian's belief that charity is right is actually constituted by something like a belief (now in the strict natural kind sense of 'belief')–desire pair—a desire of some sort to adhere to the prescriptions of a utilitarian advisor and a belief that such an advisor would insist on charity. Such belief–desire pairs are themselves very unlikely to turn out to be genuine natural kinds, and they certainly do not have a single direction of fit.

Once we allow that there is this weaker and deflationist sense of 'belief', though, we must be very careful in how we understand the central tenets of Ecumenical Expressivism. When the Ecumenical Expressivist asserts that the belief expressed by a normative utterance need not thereby provide the truth conditions for the utterance, he must be understood as meaning 'belief' in the strict natural kind sense. For in the deflationist sense, the judgement, for example, that charity is right just expresses the belief that charity is right. The Ecumenical Expressivist is decidedly not advancing the implausible view that 'charity is right' is not true if and only if the belief that charity is right is true. The point is instead that the particular belief (in the strict sense) that might constitute a given speaker's judgement that charity is right might not provide the truth conditions for 'charity is right'.

With this all too brief summary of Ecumenical Expressivism, we are now in a position to see how the machinery of Ecumenical Expressivism might help turn Blackburn's proto-theory into a more fully worked out expressivist account of knowledge attributions.

V

Ecumenical Expressivism is especially helpful in dealing with what are sometimes 'thick' evaluative concepts—concepts which have some characteristic descriptive component. So, for example, 'courageous' is a thick evaluative concept, whereas 'good' is a thin one. Ecumenical Expressivism allows that normative utterances express beliefs as well as pro-attitudes, and the relevant descriptive component of the thick evaluative concept in question can therefore be built right into the content of the belief expressed. So, for example, take the judgement that an action was courageous. On my account, to characterize an action as courageous is best understood in terms of expressing something along the lines (getting the details just right is not essential for my basic point) of the following two states of mind:

(1) A suitable state of approval to actions in so far as they would garner the approval of a certain sort of advisor.

(2) The belief that such an advisor would approve of the action in question *because of the specific way in which it involved standing fast in the face of danger.*

By contrast, Non-Ecumenical Expressivists have to understand the characterization of thick evaluative concepts simply in terms of the expression of non-cognitive attitudes. Of course, there can be constraints on the contents of these attitudes, so I do not mean to suggest that such approaches are hopeless. Rather, my point is that Ecumenical Expressivism may provide a more elegant and intuitively promising way of accommodating thick evaluative concepts. In fairness, I should add that even those who defend Non-Ecumenical Expressivism about thin normative concepts (like 'ought' and 'good') often seem implicitly to favour a form of what I am calling Ecumenical Expressivism about thick normative concepts.[14]

I emphasize the point about Ecumenical Expressivism and thick concepts because in so far as 'knows that' is a normative or evalua-

---

[14] See, for example, Gibbard (1990, pp. 112–13). Thanks to Matthew Chrisman for useful discussion here.

tive concept, it is clearly a 'thick' one, with all sorts of descriptive components. To characterize something as knowledge is not simply to approve of it, but also to take it to be a certain sort of belief, etc. If I am right about Ecumenical Expressivism being especially well suited to dealing with thick evaluative concepts, then it might therefore provide an especially promising way to give an expressivist account of 'knows that' and its cognates.

Indeed, in the case of knowledge attributions, Gibbard and Blackburn presumably agree that such attributions at least involve the purely descriptive belief that the subject believes the proposition putatively known. In which case, they are actually implicitly committed to what I am calling Ecumenical Expressivism about knowledge judgements. In this sense, my disagreement with them is in part about how the details of an Ecumenical Expressivist account should go in the case of knowledge, rather than about whether expressivists should be ecumenical in this particular case. In any event, with this methodological motivation in hand, let us now see what such an Ecumenical Expressivist account of knowledge attributions might look like.

Putting Williamson's idea that knowledge is an irreducible state of mind to one side, it should be relatively uncontroversial that to say that S knows that p is to express at least the following two beliefs:

(1) The belief that S believes that p.

(2) The belief that S's belief that p is true.

To be fully general, we must read 'belief' and 'believes' in the broader of the two senses articulated in section four. As noted earlier, I am here simply assuming for the sake of argument that some deflationist account of the truth-predicate will allow expressivists to make sense of (2) even if 'p' ranges over normative contexts. With these qualifications and caveats in hand, there should be no problem with this.

So far, so good, but this is obviously incomplete. The hard and distinctively expressivist part of the account comes in how we understand the judgement that S has epistemic justification for his belief with respect to p, and Blackburn's idea that no improvement in .

S's acquaintance with the facts would justify *S* in abandoning *S*'s belief with respect to *p*. Moreover, the account of justification must somehow distinguish epistemic from pragmatic justifications. The fact that my holding a belief would cause great harm might be a kind of justification for doing so, but not ruling out such facts hardly undermines the status of my judgement as knowledge.

Gibbard seems right about this much. In addition to planning what to do, we do in some sense plan to revise our beliefs in certain ways rather than others. We can, after all, in some sense shift our epistemic standards from one context to another, a point recently emphasized by contextualists.[15] In the epistemology class, one might temporarily come to the view that her ordinary standards of belief formation are too loose, and decide to abandon the belief that the external world exists. It seems that we can exert some control over what we believe by focusing on suitable sceptical hypotheses. In the case of the radical sceptic, one might remind oneself that there is no way to rule out the hypothesis that you are not really just a brain in a vat, and in this way at least for a time abandon the belief that there is an external world. David Hume emphasized that we cannot maintain such high epistemic standards for very long, but then this is an extreme case. There are more ordinary and sustainable ways in which we might shift our standards. For example, someone might be convinced that he has in the past been too reliant on anecdotal evidence for generalizations, and set himself against being so credulous in the future.

There is of course a huge debate over the extent to which our beliefs are under our direct voluntary control, and the preceding paragraph will be unlikely to convince someone with a worked out view in that debate. To clarify, though, I am not defending the radically voluntarist view that we can adopt any given belief at will. That does seem to me to be incoherent, at least for purely descriptive beliefs. I cannot simply stare at a bright red wall with my eyes wide open in ordinary light and genuinely believe that it is blue. This presumably is because belief formation is in some sense constitutively regulated by an aim to represent the world as it is. However, the most I am committed to is the much weaker thesis that somebody might stare at a bright red wall in this way and remain agnostic

---

[15] See, for example, Lewis (1996).

about whether it is really red, and might do so by focusing on suitably sceptical hypotheses. Actually, I am not even committed to quite this much, as here we have a rather extreme sort of scepticism which is hard to maintain. Rather, all I am really committed to is that we can form plans about how to go about revising and updating our beliefs, and that these plans can, perhaps indirectly, have a bearing on what beliefs we come to abandon or adopt. Here I agree with Gibbard, who made much use of the idea of our plans to rely on others in forming our beliefs.

However, for reasons rehearsed in my discussion of Gibbard, I do not think we should understand knowledge attributions as expressions of plans to rely on the person to whom knowledge is attributed. Instead, I want to suggest, to a first approximation, that knowledge attributions express a speaker's commitment to certain procedures of belief formation and revision. The commitment in question must not be one that is the result of a compulsion or other functional disorder. In Gibbard's (1990, pp. 60–1) useful terms, we might say that the speaker must genuinely accept the procedures in question, and not merely be 'in their grip'.

Not any old commitment will do here, though. To partially constitute a knowledge attribution, the commitment in question must be an epistemic one. Whether a commitment is epistemic, in turn depends on the motives for that commitment. In order for a commitment to a set of such procedures to count as epistemic, that commitment must be taken on at least in part because the speaker takes it that following such procedures will reliably (how reliably may vary from speaker to speaker) track the descriptive truth. Other motives for taking on the commitment must also be recognizably epistemic.

Importantly, though, I take the concept of the epistemic not to be entirely exhausted by the idea of tracking the truth. For example, endorsing a procedure of belief revision in part because it leads to simpler generalizations in some suitable sense of 'simpler' is a recognizably epistemic motive *even if* simplicity is not taken to enhance the speaker's ability to track the truth. In making moral judgements, someone may think it is important to be suitably dispassionate. This too can count as a recognizably epistemic motive for adopting a procedure for belief formation and revision. So too might the opposite, as in some cases a speaker may feel emotional engagement of certain sorts, as opposed to being dispassionate, is essential to sound moral judgement.

I do not think it is possible to give a reductive analysis of what makes a motive count as epistemic. I am inclined to think the concept is perhaps well understood as a Wittgensteinian 'cluster concept'. A cluster concept cannot be analysed into necessary and sufficient conditions, but anything falling under that concept must satisfy a sufficient number of the cluster of conditions which make up the concept, but there may be no saying in general terms just what counts as 'a sufficient number'. Also, the conditions may for these purposes be implicitly weighted, and some of them may even be necessary conditions. In the preceding paragraph I have articulated some of the elements of the cluster which make up that concept, and reliably tracking the truth is an essential component. If someone's commitment to follow a set of procedures for belief formation and revision were not at all motivated by an aim to track the truth reliably then that commitment simply would not count as epistemic.

In making an epistemic judgement, it is plausible to suppose that one is deploying, or at least adverting to epistemic standards. I want to understand this in expressivist terms—in terms of expressing one's epistemic endorsement of procedures for belief formation and revision. Epistemic endorsement is just a commitment to follow those procedures where that commitment is grounded in what I have called epistemic motives. I think we all do in fact give our epistemic endorsement to some such procedures, and then we try our best to deploy those procedures in making up our minds.

We do not, however, necessarily suppose that the procedures we have adopted are ideal. I am willing to allow that someone else's procedures for belief formation and revision might track the truth better than my own; indeed, this is almost certainly the case. I might think this, but still think that following my own standards will be good enough for knowledge. This also needs to be reflected in our account of knowledge attributions.

Similarly, I might think that someone else's epistemic procedures might be epistemologically better than my own in other respects—not simply in terms of tracking the truth. For example, I might find someone else's procedures simpler than my own, and my own epistemic procedures might place a premium on simplicity. Interestingly, in making this sort of judgement I must in effect deploy my own epistemic standards (that is, the procedures for belief formation/revision that I currently endorse) upon themselves, in light of what I take to be the relevant facts. For in the broad sense of 'belief' my epistemic endorsement of a procedure for belief adoption and revision is itself a belief—a belief about how to go about forming and revising one's beliefs. Hence, that procedure falls within its own scope.

I want to propose that in characterizing someone as knowing that p, we characterize them as *either* deploying the epistemic procedures we currently endorse *or* procedures which are 'close enough' for purposes of deciding whether p, *or* procedures which are even better than our own at tracking the truth and otherwise just as good, *or* a procedure which is (in a sense defined below) a successor to our current procedure. The idea of being 'close enough' is vague, and I know of no way of making it more precise, but the basic idea is that the procedures tend to be equally reliable in tracking the truth of p if p is a matter of fact, anyway. The idea of being a 'successor' to a procedure is a technical one. One epistemic procedure is a successor to another if the former would, in light of all relevant facts, require one to move from it to the latter.

Return to our account of the states of mind expressed by a sentence of the form 'S knows whether p':

(1) The belief that S believes that p.

(2) The belief that S's belief that p is true.

I now want to add the following additional components to this account:

(3) Epistemic endorsement of certain procedures for deciding what to believe.

(4) The belief that S's judgement that p is causally regulated by either (a) those procedures [anaphoric reference back to those procedures the speaker endorses in (3)] *or* (b) procedures which are close enough to those procedures, so far as p goes *or* (c) more fully informed successors to those procedures.

(5) The belief that no further acquaintance with the descriptive facts is such that acquaintance with those facts is sufficient for those epistemic procedures (the ones causally regulating his belief that *p*) to instruct him to abandon the belief that *p*.

The account on offer is complex, but then knowledge is by all accounts (well, apart from Williamson's anti-reductionist one) a complex concept. Notice that the structure now mirrors the structure of the account given for practical normative judgement in section four. There we had the expression of a non-cognitive state (the endorsement of a certain sort of advisor) and a belief which made anaphoric reference back to the content of that non-cognitive state (a belief about that sort of advisor). Here we have the same structure, as (3) is a non-cognitive state (a commitment, based on certain kinds of epistemic motives, to follow certain procedures), and (4) is a belief which makes anaphoric reference back to the content of that non-cognitive state (a belief which is in part about *those* sorts of procedures). (5) involves a more indirect form of anaphoric reference to the speaker's epistemic commitments, in that adverts to the procedures mentioned in (4), and those procedures are themselves characterized via anaphora to the speaker's epistemic commitments. Let me now explain the account in more detail.

(3) represents a speaker's current epistemic standards. To avoid hubris, though, the speaker's attribution of knowledge that *p* to *S* does not presume that *S* uses exactly those procedures. The belief expressed in (4) holds that *S*'s judgement that *p* is causally regulated by either those procedures, *or* ones which are 'close enough', *or* ones which are even better (by the lights of those very procedures). This last clause is very important. I might have no idea what procedures the physicist uses to determine that the material is radioactive. Whatever procedure he uses, though, I judge to be more reliable at tracking the truth than my own methods (if any I have!) would be for such purposes (putting to one side the possibility of my just asking the physicist, which is itself parasitic on his own methods anyway). Because I view procedures which track the truth (with respect to *p*) as better than my own (with respect to *p*, anyway), I can on the proposed account still attribute knowledge to the scientist without the absurd suggestion that he uses my own primitive methods of belief formation to answer his scientific questions.[16]

Finally, (5) is meant to capture Blackburn's useful (and hopefully Gettier-proofing) idea that no improvement in the putative knower's acquaintance with the facts would justify him in abandoning p.

The idea of 'causal regulation' deployed in (4) must be further cashed out. I have deliberately not said that the speaker must have used these procedures to form the belief that p. Often, we form our beliefs immediately, in response to sensory inputs, testimony, etc., without any or much thought at all, much less the self-conscious deployment of an epistemic procedure. Other of our beliefs might even be innate. Rather, the point is that the adoption of the belief in question is causally regulated by the knower's epistemic standards, in the sense that if those standards, in conjunction with the speaker's other beliefs, would require that the speaker not believe that p then she would not believe that p—at least, she would not continue to believe it if she had a moment to reflect.[17]

With this account in hand, we can see why knowledge attributions are normative. Such attributions are partly constituted by a speaker's epistemic standards—the procedures upon which the speaker intends (for epistemic reasons) to rely in forming and revising his beliefs. In Gibbard's terms, then, such judgements are 'plan-laden'. Thus far, then, I agree with Gibbard.

One interesting consequence is that sometimes our epistemological disagreements might be something like what Gibbard calls 'disagreement in plan'. You and I might agree about all the descriptive facts concerning S's judgement that p. I might, however, endorse procedures for belief formation and revision which lead me to deny that S knows that p, while you endorse procedures which lead you to the opposite conclusion. This might well simply turn out to reflect different epistemic standards, and our disagreement might be a disagreement not about how the world is, but about how to revise one's beliefs in the face of new information. This mirrors the way in which, on a metaethical expressivist account, moral disagreement might sometimes turn out to be disagreement in plan rather than disagreement in belief about how the world actually is.

---

[16] Thanks to James Lenman for useful discussion of this point.

[17] Thanks to Matthew Chrisman for useful discussion of the fact that our beliefs are not always or even usually the result of following some procedure. In an earlier draft, I fell prey to this overly intellectualized conception of belief formation and revision. No doubt this is a prejudice about how we form our beliefs to which philosophers are especially prone!

Unlike Gibbard, though, I do not characterize knowledge attributions as intentions to rely on the judgement of the person to whom knowledge is attributed. That runs into problems articulated in section two. Instead, I understand them as expressions of the speaker's endorsement of his own epistemic procedures, and beliefs which make anaphoric reference back to those procedures in a certain way. The account on offer has the virtue of explaining what is plausible in Gibbard's idea, though. For if we judge that someone knows that p, on this account, then all else being equal we will rationally inclined to plan to rely on his judgement. For if we judge that he knows that p then we will judge that he came to believe that p on the basis of procedures which are by our own lights at least as good as our own, at least with respect to p. However, sometimes all else is not equal, as when we view having a belief about p (or even planning to under any circumstances) as morally corrupt. So the account on offer can explain the seductive appeal of Gibbard's account, but without falling prey to an objection to which his own account seems vulnerable.

Like Blackburn, I hold that to characterize someone as knowing that p is to judge that no epistemic improvement would justify abandoning the judgement that p. Unlike Blackburn, though, I do not leave this judgement unanalysed, but instead give it a distinctively Ecumenical Expressivist gloss in terms of the expression of the speaker's own epistemic standards and a belief which makes anaphoric reference back to those very standards.

Moreover, I add a further element to my analysis not found in Blackburn's account. For on my account it is not enough that no further improvement would justify the putative knower in abandoning the belief. It must also be the case that the belief was in fact causally regulated by procedures with suitable epistemic credentials; otherwise it might still just be a matter of luck that the putative knower formed the belief he did. The account of what it is to judge the putative knower's epistemological procedures to have suitable epistemic credentials is itself then glossed in Ecumenical Expressivist terms—in terms of whether those procedures are close enough to the ones on which the speaker intends to rely, or some successor (in a sense articulated above) to those standards.

VI

Conclusion. I have in this paper tried to do three main things. First, I have argued that anyone tempted by metaethical expressivism should also and for similar reasons be tempted by epistemological expressivism. Second, I have argued that existing expressivist accounts of knowledge attributions (Gibbard's and Blackburn's) are problematic. Third, I have argued that my own form of Ecumenical Expressivism can blend what is plausible in both Gibbard's and Blackburn's accounts into a novel account that avoids the objections raised against their own accounts, and which has a number of further distinctive advantages of its own.

I end on a modest note, though. The debate over Epistemological Expressivism is still very much in its infancy, and I have no doubt that there are further moves to be made here. The exact details of the account I have offered here are, therefore, likely to be open to objections I have not yet anticipated. These objections may in turn suggest further revisions of the basic idea. I therefore offer the account in the spirit of an attempt to build on the insights of Blackburn and Gibbard, but without any illusion about this being the last word about what an expressivist account of knowledge attributions should look like. I do hope, however, at least to have given some reason for supposing that an Ecumenical Expressivism provides new and powerful resources for understanding a thick evaluative term like 'knows that' in expressivist terms, and that these resources are not readily available to non-Ecumenical forms of Expressivism. Whether I have made the best use of the resources provided by Ecumenical Expressivism in the details of my analysis, though, is a separate question, about which I await further fruitful discussion.[18]

REFERENCES

Arpaly, N. 2000: 'On Acting Rationally Against One's Best Judgement', *Ethics*, 110 (2), pp. 488–513.
Blackburn, S. 1984: *Spreading The Word* (Oxford: Oxford University Press).

[18] Many thanks to Matthew Chrisman and James Lenman for very helpful comments on earlier drafts of this material.

——1993: *Essays in Quasi-Realism* (Oxford: Oxford University Press).

——1996: 'Securing the Nots', in Sinnott-Armstrong and Timmons (1996, pp. 82–100).

——1998: *Ruling Passions* (Oxford: Oxford University Press).

Chrisman, M. 2007: 'From Epistemic Contextualism to Epistemic Expressivism', *Philosophical Studies*.

Gettier, E. L. 1963: 'Is Justified True Belief Knowledge?', *Analysis*, 23, pp. 121–3.

Gibbard, A. 1990: *Wise Choices, Apt Feelings* (Oxford: Oxford University Press).

——2003: *Thinking How to Live* (Cambridge, MA: Harvard University Press).

Horwich, P. 1990: *Truth* (Oxford: Oxford University Press); 2nd edn. 1998.

Ketland, J. 1998: 'Deflationism and Tarski's Paradise', *Mind*, 108, 69–94.

Lewis, D. 1996: 'Elusive Knowledge', *Australasian Journal of Philosophy*, 74, pp. 549–67.

Ridge, M. 2006: 'Ecumenical Expressivism: Finessing Frege', *Ethics*, 116 (2), pp. 302–37.

——forthcoming a: 'The Truth in Ecumenical Expressivism', in D. Sobel (ed.), *Reasons for Action* (Cambridge: Cambridge University Press).

——forthcoming b: 'Ecumenical Expressivism: The Best of Both Worlds', *Oxford Studies in Metaethics*, Vol. 2 (Oxford: Oxford University), pp. 302–36.

Shapiro, S. 1998: 'Truth and Proof—Through Thick and Thin', *Journal of Philosophy*, 95, pp. 493–521.

Sinnott-Armstrong, W. and M. Timmons 1996: *Moral Knowledge?* (Oxford: Oxford University Press).

Williamson, T. 2000: *Knowledge and Its Limits* (Oxford: Oxford University Press).

Aristotle on Action
Ursula Coope and Christopher Shields

I—Ursula Coope

Aristotle on Action

When I raise my arm, what makes it the case that my arm's going up is an instance of my raising my arm? In this paper, I discuss Aristotle's answer to this question. His view, I argue, is that my arm's going up counts as my raising my arm just in case it is an exercise of a certain kind of causal power of mine. I show that this view differs in an interesting way both from the Davidsonian 'standard causal account' of action and from accounts put forward by recent critics of Davidson, such as Hornsby, Alvarez and Hyman.

I

Aristotle and Modern Philosophy of Action. Aristotle holds that when I raise my arm, my action of raising my arm is the same event as my arm's going up.[1] We can, then, ask of Aristotle a question that is often posed in modern philosophy: when I raise my arm, what makes it the case that my arm's going up is an instance of my raising my arm? His answer, I shall claim, is that my arm's going up counts as my raising my arm just in case it is an exercise of a certain kind of causal power of mine.[2]

This combination of views distinguishes Aristotle's position from each of two opposed lines of thought in modern philosophy of action. On the one hand, Aristotle would disagree with what is often called the 'standard causal account of action', the view that my arm's going up counts as an action of mine in virtue of being caused in some appropriate way by my beliefs and desires.[3] On the other hand, he would also disagree with those critics of the standard causal account who insist that the action of raising my arm cannot be

---

[1] Aristotle, *Physics* III.3. I defend this interpretation of this chapter in Coope (2004).

[2] It is an *action* in virtue of being an exercise of a certain kind of causal power. It is an action of *mine* in virtue of the fact that the power in question is a power of mine.

[3] The standard view has its origin in the work of Davidson. See for instance Davidson (1971; 1963).

the same event as my arm's rising.[4] In this essay, I shall explain why
Aristotle would object to both of these modern positions and shall
discuss to what extent his own view presents an attractive alternative.

Aristotle's view might, at first sight, seem to have much in common with the standard causal account. The standard causal account, like Aristotle's, identifies my action of moving my body with
my body's movement. So according to both accounts, when I raise
my arm, my arm's going up is same as the event of my raising my
arm.[5] Moreover, Aristotle, like the proponents of the standard account, holds that human and animal actions must be caused, in
some sense, by a combination of the agent's desire and the agent's
being in some cognitive relation to the object of this desire.[6] But
there the similarity ends. For according to the standard causal account, what makes the movement the agent undergoes an action of
the agent's is the fact that it is caused in some appropriate way by
the agent's beliefs and desires: my arm's rising counts as my raising
my arm just because it is caused by my beliefs and desires. In contrast, though Aristotle thinks that human actions are explained by
desires and beliefs, it is not *because they are explicable in this way*
that they count as actions. On Aristotle's view, what makes a particular change *an action* is the fact that it is the exercise of a certain
kind of causal power: it is a *causing* of something. My arm's going
up counts as an action of mine (that is, it counts as my raising my
arm) only because it is the exercise of one of my causal powers.

This feature of Aristotle's view allows him to escape a certain
powerful criticism that has been levelled against the standard causal
account. The criticism is that the standard account fails to be an account of action or agency at all. On the standard account, when I
raise my arm, all that happens is that my beliefs and desires cause
my arm to go up. But in that case, so the criticism goes, I don't really *do* anything: I am merely an arena in which some events (my be-

---

[4] The objections I shall consider here are those raised by Alvarez and Hyman (1998) and by
Hornsby (2004a; 2004b).

[5] Or at least, on Davidson's account, this is *typically* the case when I raise my arm. Davidson
only defends this view in relation to 'primitive actions' (those actions we do not do by doing
something else). He has a different story about what happens when, for example, I raise my
right arm by manipulating a pulley with my left (Davidson, 1971, p. 49).

[6] At least, he says that the actions he calls self-movements must be caused by desire and *nous*
(and that '*nous*' in this context includes imagination). See *De Anima* III.9–11.

liefs and desires) cause others (the movements of my body). What the standard account fails to recognize (on this view) is that an action is *an agent's* bringing something about. This is not something that can be reduced to one event's causing another. The standard account assumes that the only sorts of things that can be causes are events and states. Because of this, it cannot make sense of a person's doing something. As Hornsby (2004a, p. 22) complains, on the standard account of action, 'the fact that the person exercises a capacity to bring something about is … suppressed'.

It should be obvious why Aristotle is not vulnerable to this criticism. He does not share the assumption that the only things that do any causal work are events and states. On the contrary, for Aristotle, what it is to be an action is to be an exercise of one of the agent's causal powers. However, from a modern perspective, it can seem very puzzling that anyone could hold this view, while maintaining that the action of moving X is the very same event as the movement that X undergoes. How *can* my action of raising my arm be the exercise of a causal power, if it is itself a movement my arm undergoes?

There are three different reasons why this is puzzling. The first reason is that the views I have attributed to Aristotle seem, when taken together, to have an implausible consequence. Alvarez and Hyman have argued that if an action is the exercise of a causal power of the agent it cannot be the same event as the movement that the agent's body undergoes. Their argument is very simple. The event of causing a movement could not, they say, be the same event as the movement caused:

> My raising my arm is my causing my arm to rise. Hence, if my raising my arm is an event, it is the same event as my causing my arm to rise. And hence, if my raising my arm and my arm's rising are one and the same event, then my causing my arm to rise and my arm's rising are one and the same event. But it cannot be plausible that causing an event to occur is not merely an event itself, but the very same event as the event caused. (Alvarez and Hyman, 1998, p. 229)

This argument poses a challenge to Aristotle (at least as I have interpreted him). It suggests that the two views I have attributed to him have, when taken together, the absurd consequence that causing a certain event is one and the same event as the event caused.

There is also a second reason why the position I have attributed to Aristotle might seem flawed. I have claimed that on Aristotle's view what makes an event an action is that it is an exercise of a certain kind of causal power: it is a *causing* of something. However, some modern philosophers maintain that causing is not itself an event. This, for instance, was von Wright's (1963, pp. 35–6) reason for denying that actions are changes: 'An act,' he said, 'is not a change in the world. But many acts may quite appropriately be described as the bringing about or effecting ("at will") of a change.' Alvarez and Hyman endorse this view that actions are not events. They suggest that the doctrine that actions are events should lose its allure once one realizes that an action is the causing of an event: 'It is, after all, far from obvious that a causing, like the event caused, is itself an event' (Alvarez and Hyman, 1998, p. 229). Given that Aristotle, like these modern philosophers, holds that an action is a causing, what is his reason for maintaining that it is nevertheless a kind of event (a change)?

The third source of puzzlement is over what reason anyone could have for identifying the action of moving one's body with the body's motion, if the reason is not a commitment to something like the standard account. Hornsby (2004a, p. 20), who holds that my action of moving my body is an event that causes my body's movement, asks rhetorically, 'Would anyone be inclined to think of someone's moving her foot as a foot's movement unless they imagined that a person's activity could be dissolved into the goings-on of states and events?' As we have seen, the answer to this is 'Yes: Aristotle would'. But Hornsby's question helps to bring out how odd Aristotle's position seems from a modern perspective. We need to explain why Aristotle thinks that the agent's action of moving (or changing) X is the same event as X's movement (or change), given that this view is not based on a commitment to the picture of causation that Hornsby is criticizing.

As I shall explain, Aristotle's discussion of agency provides us with the materials to answer each of these points. To the charge that he is committed to identifying a change with the action of causing that change, he can reply that an action is the causing of a state, rather than the causing of a change. On his view, my action of raising my arm is the same change as my arm's going up; but my action is a causing of my arm's being up (not of my arm's going up). To the objection that a causing is not a change, Aristotle can reply by pointing to certain characteristic features of change that are shared by actions (or at least, are shared by those actions, such as building a house and raising one's arm, that he identifies with changes). Finally, we can extract, from Aristotle's discussion of agency in *Physics* III.3, an argument that the action of moving (or, in general, changing) X is one and the same event as the movement (or change) that X undergoes.

II

Causing and What Is Caused. The first of these objections is that Aristotle seems to be committed to identifying a change with the action of causing that change. To answer this on Aristotle's behalf, we need to know more about what it is, on his view, that we are causing when we engage in an action of moving or changing something. A difficulty here is that the word 'causing' has no obvious equivalent in Greek. When I say that, on Aristotle's view, an action is a causing of something, what I mean is that it is an exercise of a certain kind of power (or potential): an active power rather than a passive power. In exercising an active power, one brings something about (*building a house* and *moving something* are exercises of active powers); in exercising a passive power one undergoes something (*getting hot* and *being moved* are exercises of passive powers).[7]

Aristotle's view, I shall argue, is that the power that is exercised in an action of *moving X* is a power to produce the *end* of X's movement: a power to produce a state, rather than a movement. In this sense, what I am causing when I move X is the state that X's move-

---

[7] When I move myself (e.g. when I walk from one place to another), I exercise both an active power (a power to bring something about) and a passive power (a power to be affected in a certain way). (As we shall see, Aristotle's view is that one part of me exercises the active power and another exercises the passive power.) The fact that actions like walking from place to place involve the exercise of an active power as well as a passive power explains, I think, why Aristotle describes them as self-changes. Waterlow (1982, p. 216) objects that ordinary discourse 'applies the language of "self-change" to movements and actions that are actually contrary to nature or inclination, not to those which are not, even when these are in the agent's power to control'. But Aristotle is, I think, onto something right here. The point is that walking to B (even when doing so is effortless and accords with my wishes) is something I *do*, and hence is an exercise of an active power; it is not merely a change I undergo.

ment is directed towards.[8] For example, when I raise my arm, what I am causing is *my arm's being up*, rather than *my arm's going up*. More generally, the action of changing something towards being F is, for Aristotle, a particular kind of causing of the state *being F*.

Aristotle never endorses this view of action explicitly. However, I shall claim that if we attribute this view to him, we can explain what would otherwise be a puzzling argument in *Physics* VIII.5. The argument concerns self-movement. Aristotle claims that something that moves itself must have distinct agent and patient parts: the only way it is possible for something to change itself is for one part of it to be the agent of the change and another part of it to undergo the change. As we shall see, his argument depends crucially on the view that when an agent changes something, what it is producing or causing is the state the change is directed towards, rather than the change itself.

Here is the argument:

> Movement is an incomplete actuality of the moveable. But the mover is already in actuality, e.g. it is the hot thing that produces heat, and in general, that which produces the form possesses it. So that the same thing in respect of the same thing will be at the same time both hot and not hot … Therefore, when a thing moves itself, one part of it is the mover and another part is moved. (*Physics* VIII.5.257b8–13)

Aristotle seems to be reasoning as follows:

(i) If something is changing (or moving) towards being F, then it is not (yet) F.

(ii) What changes (or moves) something towards being F must itself be F (e.g. something that heats must be hot).[9]

So: what changes (or moves) something towards being F must be distinct from what undergoes the change (or movement) towards being F (otherwise the same thing would at the same time both be F and not be F).

---

[8] 'The state the movement/change is directed towards' rather than 'the state in which the movement/change results': there are circumstances in which, because of interference, a change that is directed towards *being F* does not in fact result in the changing thing's being F. (An acorn that is becoming an oak will not end up being an oak if it is eaten before it reaches maturity.)

The claim that if something is changing towards being *F*, then it cannot yet be *F* is uncontroversial. The premiss in this argument that cries out for some support is premiss (ii). Why does Aristotle think that what changes something towards being *F* must itself be *F*?

One obvious thing to say is that Aristotle is appealing to some principle of *like causes like*, or to (what in this context amounts to the same thing) a *giving* model of causation. I cannot give you something I don't myself possess. Similarly (so the thought goes) an agent cannot make something else *F* unless it is (in some sense) already *F* itself.[10]

But this cannot be the whole story. The principle that like causes like does not, in itself, provide us with any reason for adopting Aristotle's premiss:

(ii) What changes something towards being *F* must itself be *F* (since it is causing something to be *F*),

---

[9] This claim needs to be qualified in two ways. (i) In order to accommodate obvious counterexamples, Aristotle needs to say that the agent of a change to *F* is something that is *F in a certain special sense*. The housebuilder changes the bricks and mortar into a house, but the housebuilder is not himself a house. Aristotle's view is that the housebuilder's soul contains the form of a house. In this very special sense, the housebuilder's soul can be said to 'have' the form that the bricks and mortar are acquiring. (A more difficult question is how the claim can be true of the agent of a spatial movement. The end state of a movement from *A* to *B* is: *being at B*. But surely Aristotle cannot hold that anything that is the agent of such a movement must already be at *B*. Perhaps in reply he would appeal to his view that, at least in the case of *self*-movement, there must be some object of desire that is the goal of the movement. A movement from *A* to *B* to reach an apple at *B* could be thought of as having *an apple*, as its end. Aristotle might claim, then, that it is because the self-mover has a representation of the apple as something desired that he is able to be an agent of this movement. To have a representation of the apple is (according to Aristotle) to have a part of one's soul that is (in a sense) an apple. In that sense, the self-mover has the form that his movement is towards.) (ii) The view that what changes something towards being *F* must itself be *F* does not, presumably, apply to those moved movers that are mere instruments. Aristotle says that such movers change together with, and in the same respect as, the thing that is moved (*Physics* VIII.5.256b17–18). This suggests that an instrumental mover that is changing something towards being F is itself (in a certain sense) changing towards being F. Such an instrumental mover cannot, then, already be *F*. If this is right, then Aristotle's view depends on a distinction between instrumental movers, which merely transmit agency, and true agents, which change something towards being *F* by themselves being *F*. (For more on instrumental movers, see n.31 below).

[10] Aristotle defends this view of causation in *Generation and Corruption* I.7. He explains there that for an agent to change a patient the two must initially be unlike each other. The agent, in acting, assimilates the patient to itself. The agent (which is already *F*) makes the patient (which was formerly not *F*) *F*: 'Fire heats and cold things cool, and generally what is active makes the patient like itself' (I.7.324a9–11). See also *Physics* III.2.202a9–12. (On Aristotle's use of the principle of 'like causes like', see Makin, 1991; on the 'giving' model of causation see Waterlow, 1982.)

as opposed to the alternative:

> (Cii) what changes something towards being F must itself be
> changing (since it is causing a change).

I shall argue that in our passage, Aristotle's primary concern is to
oppose a Platonic view of self-movement. The Platonic view he opposes is a view that assumes principle (Cii): it assumes that an agent
that changes something must itself be undergoing change. Hence
Aristotle needs some justification for holding his premiss (ii) as opposed to the alternative (Cii). In order to provide this justification, I
shall claim, it is necessary to invoke the view that an action of
changing something towards being F is a causing of the state *being
F*, not a causing of a change.

Aristotle claims that within a self-mover there must be some
agent part (a part that is the mover) and that this part does not itself
undergo the motion of which it is the agent. In saying this, he is rejecting Plato's account of self-movement. This becomes clear if we
look at the discussion of self-movement in Plato's *Laws*. There are
striking similarities between the line of thought sketched out by the
Athenian in the *Laws* and Aristotle's account of self-movement in
the *Physics*. Plato's Athenian, like Aristotle, distinguishes between
things that move themselves and moved movers (things that move
other things while, in their turn, being moved by something else).
And in both Plato's *Laws* and Aristotle's *Physics*, we get an argument that it is impossible for a chain of moved movers to go on for-
ever; any such chain must terminate in a self-mover:

> When we find one thing producing a change in another, and that in
> turn affecting something else, and so forth, will there ever be, in such a
> sequence, an original cause of change? How could anything whose
> motion is transmitted to it from something else be the first thing to ef-
> fect an alteration? It is impossible. In fact, when something which has
> set itself moving brings about an alteration in something, and that in
> turn brings about something else, so that the motion is transmitted to
> thousands upon thousands of things one after another, the entire se-
> quence of their movements must surely spring from some initial prin-
> ciple. (*Laws* 894e–95a)[11]

---

[11] Here I follow, with modifications, Trevor Saunders's translation in Cooper (1997).

But the Athenian's view about the nature of this initial principle is quite different from Aristotle's. The initial principle, we are told, 'can hardly be anything except the change brought about by self-generated motion' (895a). It is, in other words, a *change* that causes itself.

What we need to understand, then, is the reason for this disagreement about the initial principle. The assumption in Plato's *Laws* seems to be that a change must always be produced by a change. This is, at least, a plausible reason for supposing that a change that is not produced by *another* change must be a change that is causing itself. Aristotle agrees that it is impossible to have infinite chains of changes, each produced by the one before, but he rejects the assumption that a change can only occur if it is produced by a change. Indeed, he claims that it is impossible for something to be changing itself in Plato's sense. It is impossible for one thing, in one and the same part, to be undergoing a change and to be causing the very change that it is undergoing. Our question, then, is why Aristotle rejects this part of Plato's view. Why does he think that, in a self-mover, there must be some agent part that is responsible for the self-mover's motion but does not itself undergo this motion?

We cannot answer this by appealing to a principle of like causes like, or to a 'giving' model of causation. The reason is that the Athenian of Plato's *Laws* seems to base his argument on an appeal to a principle, or model, of the very same sort. As we have seen, the Athenian's argument is based on the assumption that a change must be produced by something that is changing. That is why he holds that a change that is not produced by another change must be produced by itself. But this Platonic assumption can itself be seen as an instance of the principle that like causes like (or of the giving model of causation): *change* can only be produced by *change*; an agent must itself be changing, if it is to *give* change to something else. Aristotle and his Platonist opponent agree about endorsing some principle of like causes like, or some version of the 'giving' model of causation.[12] What we need to ask, then, is why Aristotle thinks that this principle should be applied in the way he applies it (why, that is, he concludes that an agent that changes something towards being F

---

[12] Indeed, there is reason to think that Plato also endorses this principle elsewhere. See, for instance, David Sedley's discussion (1998, esp. pp. 123–7) of causation in the *Phaedo*.

must itself be *F*), rather than in the way that the Platonist does (to support the conclusion that a change must be produced by something that is changing). In other words, we need to ask why Aristotle endorses what I earlier called premiss (ii), as opposed to the alternative (Cii).

My suggestion is that the reason why Aristotle claims that what changes something towards being *F* must itself be *F* (instead of claiming that the agent must be something that is changing) is that he thinks of the action of changing something towards being *F* as a kind of causing of the state *being F* (rather than a causing of a change). If what is caused is the state *being F*, and if the agent must be like what it causes, then the agent must itself be *F*.

I have argued that, on Aristotle's view, the action of changing something towards *F* is a causing of the state *being F* (and not a causing of a change). Attributing this view to him enables us to understand why he thinks that an agent that changes something towards being *F* must itself be *F*. But this, of course, raises a further question. If he holds this view, is it simply an arbitrary stipulation? What would he say to a Platonist (or indeed, to anyone else) who insisted that an action of changing something was an action of producing a change?

Aristotle's answer, I think, would be to appeal to his account of change, and in particular to his view that change is an 'incomplete actuality'.[13] He describes change in this way at *Physics* III.1–2: 'Change seems to be a kind of actuality, but an incomplete one. This is because the potential, of which it is the actuality, is incomplete' (201b31–33). He returns to this point about the incompleteness of change in the lines leading up to the argument that we have been discussing:

---

[13] It is worth noting here that Aristotle may think that the Platonist himself is committed not only to the 'giving' model of causation but also to the view that change is in some sense incomplete. After all, when Aristotle introduces his view about the incompleteness of change in *Physics* III.1–2, he boasts that this captures the truth his predecessors were gesturing at when they described change as 'difference', 'inequality' and 'that which is not' (201b20–33). It is likely that one of the predecessors he has in mind is Plato. (The reference to inequality recalls *Timaeus* 57e–58c; the description of change as that which is not recalls *Sophist* 256d–e.) If so, then Aristotle is arguing that the Platonist, by his own lights, ought to accept that what changes something towards being *F* must be something that is itself *F*. The claim is that if the Platonist were to put together his view that like causes like and his view about the incompleteness of change, then he would see that a self-changer must have an unchanging part.

What changes [or is changed, *kineitai*] is the changeable. But this changes in virtue of potentiality, not in virtue of actuality.[14] That which is potentially such and such progresses to actuality, and the change is the incomplete actuality of the changeable. (*Physics* VIII.5.257b6–9)

What, then, does he mean when he says that change is an actuality that is incomplete? In *Physics* III.1, he defines change in terms of potentiality and actuality: change is the actuality of what is potentially, *qua* such (*Physics* III.1.201a10–11). How to interpret this definition is a matter for debate. The debate centres on how to understand the phrase 'what is potentially'. Two alternatives have been defended in the literature. Aristotle could mean: (i) change is the actuality of what is potentially changing, *qua* such, or he could mean (ii) change is the actuality of what is potentially in some end state, *qua* such.[15] The second of these alternatives makes best sense of the claim that change is an 'incomplete actuality'. The thought would be this. A change towards being *F* is a kind of fulfilment (or actuality) of the changing thing's potential to be *F*. The changing thing's potential to be *F* is completely fulfilled (or actual) when it is *F* (and the change is over). But its potential to be *F* is also fulfilled in a way, though incompletely, when it is in the process of becoming *F*. Its change is the incomplete fulfilment (that is, the incomplete actuality) of its capacity to be in this new state. Consider, for instance, an acorn that is growing into an oak tree. The acorn is potentially an oak tree. Before the acorn has begun to grow, this potential is not, in any sense, fulfilled. When the acorn has finally become an oak tree, its potential to be an oak tree is completely fulfilled, and it can no longer be described as 'changing into an oak'. The acorn is becoming an oak just when its potential to be an oak is *incompletely* fulfilled. A

---

[14]For a defence of this translation see Waterlow (1982, p. 244, n.27). The most obvious translation would be 'This is potentially, but not actually, changing.' But this cannot be right. When it is changing, the changing thing is actually changing. Moreover, the next sentence refers to the progression to actuality. If the actuality in question here were the state of changing, then the relevant progression would be a progression to the state of changing. But on Aristotle's view, there is no progression to a state of changing: there cannot be a change that is towards another change.

[15] For a defence of interpretation (i), see Heinaman (1994). For a defence of (ii), see Kosman (1969) and Waterlow (1982). According to a third interpretation, Aristotle is defining change as the *actualization* of what is potentially F, *qua* such. For this interpretation see Kostman (1987). I discuss these different interpretations and defend interpretation (ii) in Coope (forthcoming).

change, on Aristotle's view, is essentially a going towards some state. In defining change as the incomplete actuality of a potential to be in some end state, he is saying that changing to F is an incomplete way of fulfilling a potential to be F.

For our purposes, the important point here is that change is *only* an incomplete actuality. There is no potential that is a potential for *changing* towards F. In other words, a change towards F is not the complete fulfilment of any potential. It is, instead, the incomplete fulfilment of a potential for being F.

Consider now the agent that changes something towards being F. Since a change is not a complete actuality, the only complete actuality that is produced in the patient[16] is the state *being F*. If the agent must have, in actuality, whatever it is bringing about in the patient, this suggests that the agent must itself be F, not that the agent must (like the patient) be changing.

Moreover, just as the patient does not have a potential for *changing* towards being F, so also (on Aristotle's view) the agent does not have a potential for producing a *change* towards being F. The potential that an agent exercises in changing something towards being F is a potential that is completely fulfilled when the patient is in the state *being F*. It is a potential for producing this state, not a potential for producing the change towards this state.[17] The teacher is exercising a potential for producing understanding, not for producing the process of learning. According to Aristotle, the process of learning that occurs is not something that the teacher's action is causing; rather, it is itself one and the same as the teacher's action of producing understanding. Similarly, in moving my hand towards P I am causing my hand to be at P. My hand's motion towards P is not what I am causing; it is, rather, one and the same event as my action of causing my hand to be at P.

We can now return to the challenge with which we began. The charge was that Aristotle's account had an absurd consequence. Alvarez and Hyman argue that it is not plausible to claim both (i) that the action of moving X is the same change as the movement X undergoes and (ii) that the action of moving X is an exercise of a causal power of the agent. For taken together, these views seem to imply

---

[16] By 'the patient', I mean the thing that is acted upon by the agent.

[17] I say a little more about Aristotle's reasons for thinking this in section four below (discussion of premiss (ii)).

that the causing of an event and the event caused are one and the same. And that, surely, is absurd.

We are now in a position to see that, though Aristotle holds both (i) and (ii), he is not, in fact, committed to the view that the causing of an event and the event caused are one and the same. This is because, as his argument about self-change shows, he holds that *what I am causing*, when I change X towards being F, is X's *being F*. It is a mistake to call this action an action of producing (or causing) *the change to F*. It is, rather, an action of producing *the state, being F*. His claim, then, is that a certain kind of causing of being F, the kind that is an action of changing something towards being F, is one and the same event as that thing's coming to be F. To return to our earlier example, he holds that my raising my arm is my causing my arm to be up, and my causing my arm to be up is one and the same event as my arm's going up.

This explains why it is *possible* for Aristotle to hold both (i) and (ii), but it does not yet explain *why* he holds these views. I have already said something about the attractiveness of (ii). An action is a doing: it is the exercise of one of the agent's causal powers. But this leaves the question of why Aristotle is committed to (i), why, that is, he thinks that my action of moving X is the same change as the movement that X undergoes. To understand this, we need to see why he rejects alternative possible views. Among modern philosophers who emphasize that an action is an exercise of a causal power, there are at least two alternative views about the relation between an action and a change. Some philosophers hold that the action of moving X is not a change (or even an event) at all. Others think that the action of moving X is an event that causes the change that X undergoes.[18] In the next two sections, I shall explain why Aristotle would reject these modern positions.

III

Aristotle's View that the Action of Moving X is Itself a Movement. In modern philosophy, those who hold that an action is a bodily movement are sometimes accused of being misled by a quirk of the

---

[18] For the first view see Alvarez and Hyman (1998); for the second see Hornsby (1980).

English language. The word 'movement' can be used either in a transitive or in an intransitive sense. Clearly, my raising my arm is a movement in the transitive sense: it is my movement of my arm. But this does not imply that my raising my arm is a movement in the intransitive sense: that it is a movement that I undergo.[19] Aristotle gives no argument that an action is a change or a movement. We might wonder, then, whether he is subject to a similar confusion. In Greek, the transitive and the intransitive uses of the verb move (*kinein, kineisthai*) are distinct, the transitive being active and the intransitive middle. But there is no corresponding difference in the noun, *kinêsis* (change/movement). Moreover, Greek words for actions of changing something often have distinctive *êsis* endings, like the ending of the word for change itself, *kinêsis*. The word for housebuilding, for instance, is *oikodomêsis*; curing is *iatreusis*. Has this similarity of ending simply misled Aristotle into assuming that actions like housebuilding and curing are themselves changes?

There is, I think, no need to suppose that Aristotle is confused in this way. Though he does not give an argument that actions, such as housebuilding and arm-raising, are changes, there are two points we can make on his behalf. Both points also provide reason to reject the modern view that an action of changing something is not an event at all.

The first is that one can build a house, raise one's arm and, in general, move or change something *slowly or quickly*. Aristotle elsewhere uses this as a test of whether or not a certain candidate is a change. He claims that taking pleasure in something cannot be a change because it cannot be slow or quick. Being slow or quick is, he says, thought to be proper (*oikeion*) to every change.[20] A change, as we have seen, is a progression towards some definite end. It is the incomplete fulfilment of a potential to be in some particular end state. A sign that something is a progression of this sort (and hence is a change) is that we can ask how quick or slow it is: we can ask how much time was needed to reach the end in question. This is a

---

[19] The point is made, for instance, in Hornsby (1980, ch. 1).

[20] *Nicomachean Ethics* X.3.1173a32–1173b4. To say that being slow or quick is *oikeion* to every change is to say, not merely that being slow or quick is a necessary feature of change, but also that anything that is slow or quick must be a change. (Compare the claim, in *Metaphysics* X, that male and female are proper (*oikeia*) attributes of animal (1058b21–2). This means, not just that any animal is male or female, but also that anything that is male or female is an animal.)

question that can be asked not only about changes that we undergo, but also about our actions. Because building a house is a progression towards an end, we can ask how long it took to reach the end in question; that is, we can ask how quick or slow the action of building was. Similarly, I can raise my arm more or less quickly. This suggests that the actions of building a house and raising my arm are both changes.

The other sign that such actions are changes is that they can be interrupted before they are over. For instance, it makes sense to say, 'He was building a house, but got interrupted before he had finished.' Again, this is an indication that an action is a progression towards an end. Something that is not a progression of this sort cannot be cut off before it is 'over'. If you disturb me while I am gazing at the sky, you might prevent me from gazing for as long as I wanted to, but you do not cause me to leave my gazing *unfinished*. If you restrain my arm when it is only half way up, you have acted in such a way as to prevent my action of arm raising from being completed. Arm-raising (and in general, any action of changing or moving something) is—in a way that gazing at the sky is not—the sort of thing that can be unfinished or incomplete. According to Aristotle, this shows that actions like arm-raising and housebuilding (actions of changing or moving something) must themselves be changes.

IV

Aristotle's View that the Action of Raising My Arm is the Same Change as My Arm's Going Up. Given that my action of raising my arm is itself a change, why does Aristotle think that it must be identical with the change that is my arm's going up? Why, for instance, would be reject Hornsby's view that my action of raising my arm is an event that causes my arm to go up (or, more generally, that my action of changing X is an event that causes the change that X undergoes)?

Aristotle never gives a direct argument for his view. But it is, I think, possible to construct an argument on his behalf by making use of his discussion of agency and patiency in *Physics* III.3.[21] In this chapter, he discusses a puzzle about agency. The puzzle arises when we ask whether an agent's action and the change that occurs in the patient are, or are not, one and the same change. Absurd consequences seem to follow both from the assumption that they are two different changes and, equally, from the assumption that they are one and the same. Aristotle resolves the puzzle by attacking the arguments that purport to derive absurd consequences from the assumption that the action and the patient's change are one and the same.

We can, then, piece together his reasons for holding this view that the agent's action and the patient's change must be one and the same change, by looking at the half of the puzzle that contains an argument that they cannot be two different changes. The argument that emerges is as follows:

(i) There cannot be two distinct changes, both in one and the same thing and both directed towards the same end.

(ii) The action of changing something towards being F must itself be a change towards being F.

(iii) The agent's action must be in the thing acted upon (that is, in the patient).

Hence: the agent's action of changing the patient towards being F and the patient's change towards being F are both in the same thing (the patient) and directed at the same end (being F).

Hence (by (i)) they are one and the same change.

It will be helpful to look at each of these premisses in turn.

Premiss (i):
Aristotle makes this claim explicitly, in laying out the puzzle. He asks: 'How can there be two changes in one subject towards one form?', and replies: 'It is impossible' (202a35–6). He never justifies

---

[21] For a fuller defence of my interpretation of this chapter see Coope (2004).

this claim and it might seem open to an obvious objection: couldn't something be progressing, in two different ways, towards one and the same end? For instance, couldn't a sapling be simultaneously undergoing two changes towards being an oak: putting out longer roots and getting thicker about the trunk? Aristotle must hold that in a case like this the sapling would be undergoing one, albeit complex, change. Perhaps he thinks this follows from his account of change as the incomplete fulfilment of a potential to be in some end state. A thing either is, or is not, incompletely fulfilling a potential to be in a certain end state: it cannot, somehow, be incompletely fulfilling such a potential twice over.

Premiss (ii):

Aristotle does not explicitly say that the action of changing something towards being *F* is itself a change towards being *F*. However, this point is presupposed by the argument he presents in *Physics* III.3. He assumes that, if he can show that the agent's action is a change in the patient, he can use premiss (i)—the claim that there cannot be two distinct changes towards the same form in the same thing—to draw the conclusion that the agent's action and the change in the patient must be one and the same change. He assumes, that is, that the agent's action and the patient's change are both changes 'towards the same form'. Why does he think this?

We have already seen that, on Aristotle's view, the action of changing something is itself a change. According to his account, then, an action of changing something must be the incomplete fulfilment of a potential for some end state. But what, in the case of such an action, is the relevant end state? What potential, for instance, is incompletely fulfilled in the act of teaching or in the act of housebuilding?

The potential in question cannot itself be a potential for changing. Housebuilding cannot, for instance, be the incomplete actuality of a potential for the coming to be of a house. Aristotle insists that it is impossible for a change to have, as its end, some further change.[22] By defining change as an incomplete actuality, Aristotle is contrasting it with the complete actuality that is its end. The potential in

---

[22] See *Physics* V.2. Why Aristotle thinks that there can be no change towards another change is well explained in Waterlow (1982, pp. 156–7).

terms of which a change is defined, is incompletely fulfilled in the
change, but completely fulfilled in the end-state towards which the
change is progressing. Hence, the end must itself be a complete actuality. It cannot be a further change. A change that had as its end *a
change towards being F* would have to be *a change towards a
change towards being F* and that can be nothing other than *a
change towards being F.*

But nor can the potential in question be a potential for the *agent*
to be in some new state. There is no new state that an agent is typically in, as a result of successfully changing something. We can say,
of course, that the housebuilder, when he has completed his task, is
in the state of *having built* and that the teacher, at the end of the
day, is in a state of *having taught.* But it is misleading to think of
these as new states of the housebuilder or of the teacher. Of course,
if a housebuilder is still learning his craft, then when we describe
him as *having built something* we may be attributing to him new
properties (such as the possession of a certain amount of expertise
and experience). But the fully qualified housebuilder does not acquire any new causal powers, when it becomes true of him that he
has built another house. This suggests that *having built such and
such a house* is not a new property that he acquires, when he finish-
es building.

Even if *having built* were a state the housebuilder acquired, it
would be very odd to think that building was an action directed at
this state, or that the action of teaching was a change towards being
in a state of having taught. The point of housebuilding is to produce
a house. The point of teaching is to produce *understanding.* An action of housebuilding is over when there is a house; an action of
teaching, when the pupil understands the thing that is being taught.
The new states towards which these actions are directed are, in other words, states in the things acted upon: the bricks in the one case,
the pupil in the other.[23]

According to Aristotle, the action of building a house is (like the
change that is a house's coming to be) a change towards there being
a house; the action of teaching is (like the change that is the pupil's
acquiring understanding) a change towards the pupil's having un-

---

[23] As Aristotle says (*Metaphysics* IX.8.1050a17–19), 'teachers think they have achieved
their end when they have shown their student at work'.

©2007 THE ARISTOTELIAN SOCIETY
Proceedings of the Aristotelian Society Supplementary Volume LXXXI

derstanding. The action of changing something towards being F is the incomplete actuality of a potential that the agent has; this potential of the agent is a potential for something else (the thing acted upon) to be in the state F. Hence, the agent's action of changing something towards being F is (like the change in the thing that the agent is acting upon) a change towards being F.

Premiss (iii):
Aristotle might have argued that premiss (iii) follows directly from premiss (ii). If an action is a change towards being F, then it must be a change in the thing that (barring interference) ends up being F (that is, it must be a change in the thing acted upon). Interestingly, he does not argue in this way. Instead, in presenting the puzzle, he tries to establish that the action of changing something cannot be a change that is *in the agent*. His argument is that, if the agent's action were a change in the agent, then either (a) every agent would, when it acted to change something, itself be changed or (b) there would be an agent that had change in it but was not changed (202a30–1). He takes it as obvious that neither of these consequences is possible. As Aristotle understands it, (b) is clearly absurd: what would be the sense of saying that a certain change was *in* a thing, if that thing were not changed?[24] Why, though, does Aristotle take it for granted that (a) should be rejected? Why is it so obviously a mistake to suppose that every agent, when it changes something, is itself changed? The answer must be that Aristotle is assuming here that there are (or at least, can be) unmoved movers: things that change other things without themselves being changed.

To understand why Aristotle thinks he can assume this, we must recall our earlier conclusions about self-change. As we saw, Aristotle thinks chains of changes must end in something that moves itself. And he thinks that a self-mover must have a part that is an unmoved mover: a part that is a mover but does not itself undergo movement.

---

[24] I assume that *kinêsetai*, here, is a future middle, not a passive, form. Thus, Aristotle's objection is to the claim that something could have change in it but not undergo that change. If *kinêsetai* were passive, then he would be objecting to the claim that something could have change in it but not be changed by something. He would, in fact, object to either claim, but if his target here were the latter, one would expect to find some defence of his view that any change must have an agent.

In fact, Aristotle could have provided a more direct argument for this conclusion. He could, for instance, have appealed to his view that an agent must have the form that it is producing in the patient. An agent that is changing something towards being F must, in some sense, be F. As we have seen, this claim plays an important role in his argument about self-movement. He uses it there to show that the agent of a change to F must, in some sense, be distinct from the thing that undergoes the change to F. However, if (as premiss ii claims) the action of changing something towards being F is itself a change directed towards being F, the very same consideration will show that the action cannot be in the agent either: the agent is already F, but the agent's action (being a change towards being F) cannot be in something that is already F.

This shows how Aristotle could defend the claim that the agent's action is not in the agent. It is worth noting, though, that this is not yet premiss (iii). If he is to arrive at the conclusion that the agent's action and the patient's change are one and the same, he needs to show that the agent's action is in the patient. In the puzzle he presents in *Physics* III.3, he simply assumes that if the action is not in the agent, it must be in the patient. However, given that he himself allows, elsewhere, that it is possible for an agent to move a patient using an instrument,[25] it is not at all clear that this assumption is justified. If the agent moves the patient by means of an instrument, why couldn't the agent's change be a change in the instrument, and hence a change that was distinct from the change that occurred in the patient?[26] Aristotle never considered this. If he had done, it might have led him to modify his claim that an agent's action is the same change as the change that occurs in the patient. Per-

---

[25] See, for example, *Physics* VIII.5.256b14–15.

[26] Since the action of changing something towards being F is itself a change towards being F, this would imply that the instrument must itself undergo a change towards being F. There are obvious difficulties with this view, since typically the instruments by which we change something towards being F do not themselves become F. The housebuilder's tools do not become a house (note, though, that a pan transmits the stove's heat to the water by becoming hot itself). However, there is reason to believe that Aristotle must, in any case, accept something like this view about instrumental changes, on pain of being committed to the possibility of a certain kind of action at a distance. For if the instrument by which something changes towards being F is itself something that is neither F nor becoming F, how can it transmit agency to the patient? As we have seen, Aristotle thinks that the agent of a change towards being F must itself be F, but how is the agent's F-ness relevant to the change that occurs in the patient, if the agent and the patient are separated by intermediaries that are themselves neither F nor changing towards F?

haps he should have made this claim only with regard to cases in which an agent changes something directly, without making use of instruments.

V

Aristotle's Account as an Alternative to Modern Accounts: Some Advantages and Disadvantages. I have explained why Aristotle would disagree with certain modern accounts of action. Many of his arguments, though, depend upon assumptions that modern philosophers would reject: the assumption that like must be caused by like, for instance, or the view that change is, by definition, an incomplete fulfilment of a potential. Does Aristotle's account have anything to recommend it, independently of these assumptions?

As we have seen, Aristotle has a distinctive combination of views about the nature of action. On the one hand, he holds that the action of changing X is the same event as the change that X undergoes. Thus, on his view, my raising my arm and my arm's rising are one and the same event. But on the other hand, he also holds that this event counts as an action in virtue of being an exercise of a potential of mine to bring something about. My arm's going up is the event of my raising my arm because it is an exercise of a potential I have for making it the case that my arm *is* up. My question, then, is whether this combination of views constitutes an attractive alternative to modern accounts of action.

I have already touched on one reason for preferring Aristotle's view to a view like Davidson's. This is the central role that Aristotle assigns to an agent in his account of action. On Davidson's view, what makes my arm's rising an action of arm raising is just that it is caused by certain other states or events. My arm's rising counts as my raising my arm in virtue of being caused, in an appropriate way, by my beliefs and desires. But this leaves out of account the role *I* play in raising my arm. My beliefs and desires could cause my arm to move without my doing anything at all. Accounts of this sort miss a crucial feature of actions: the fact that an action must be an action *of an agent*. Aristotle's account is not vulnerable to this criticism. On Aristotle's view, what makes a particular event an action is not the fact that certain further events are its causes; rather, an event counts as an action because it itself is the exercise of an agent's potential for bringing something about.

However, by claiming that the action of raising my arm is the same event as my arm's going up, Aristotle retains something that is attractive about Davidson's view. For one thing, Aristotle is not committed to denying that an action is an event. Though he thinks that the action of changing something is an exercise of the agent's causal power, he claims that this exercise is itself a change. Because of this, he has no difficulty accounting for the fact that an action of this sort can (like other changes) occur more or less quickly. Similarly, he can accommodate the fact that it is possible to interrupt an action of changing something before it is over: this, again, is a feature that the action of changing (or moving) something shares with other kinds of change.

In addition, because he identifies the action of moving my body with my body's motion, Aristotle avoids some of the drawbacks of views, like Hornsby's, on which these are two separate events. On Hornsby's view, my action of moving my body is an event that causes my body to move. But this makes it hard to avoid the conclusion that actions (such as raising my arm) are invisible: we see their effects (since we see my arm's rising), but we do not see the actions themselves (the events that cause the arm rising or other bodily movement).[27] Moreover, if an action is a distinct event that causes my body's motion, then (at least according to a common view of causation), it must occur before my body moves. But do we really want to say that I raise my arm before my arm goes up? Aristotle is not vulnerable to either of these objections. On his view, to see my arm rising is to see my action of raising it (since these are one and the same event), and for the same reason, my action of raising my arm does not precede my arm's going up.

However, there is one objection sometimes leveled at Hornsby's view that can be brought, with at least equal force, against Aristotle. Hornsby is sometimes accused of alienating the agent from her body. The charge is that the view on which an agent's action is an event that causes her body to move represents the agent's relation to her body as being too like her relation to other objects. Thus Adrian Haddock (2005, p. 161) complains that:

---

[27] For her response to this objection see Hornsby (1997, ch. 6).

> [On Hornsby's view,] our bodies are pictured as entities whose powers
> are wholly distinct from our powers of agency, as entities that we can
> (at best) only cause to move—and in this respect they are the same as
> any other worldly object. Jane moves her body just as she moves (say)
> a glass of water.[28]

If it is a mistake to think our actions are no more closely related to
our bodies than to other worldly objects, then this is a mistake that
Aristotle makes too. In a sense, Aristotle is committed to this view
for reasons opposite to Hornsby's. Though Aristotle (unlike Hornsby) identifies my movement of my body with my body's motion, this
is not (for him) a sign that there is anything special about my relation to my body. As we have seen, he holds that, quite generally, an
action of changing X is the same event as the change that X undergoes. Thus, he would also identify my action of moving a glass of
water with the motion of the glass of water, and he would identify
my action of building a house with the change that the bricks and
mortar undergo in becoming a house. For Aristotle, my action is
only the same event as *my body's* motion in those cases in which I
am *merely* moving my body (rather than using my body to move
something else). If Hornsby seems to alienate us from our bodies by
claiming that our actions are internal events that cause our bodies to
move, Aristotle alienates us from our bodies by claiming that some
of our actions are external to our bodies.

One way to bring out the Aristotelian version of this problem is
to consider what Aristotle would have to say about the timing of an
action. I have already argued that it is an advantage of his view that
he can deny that my raising my arm is an event that precedes my
arm's going up. However, he too is committed to implausible conclusions about the timing of certain actions. Suppose, for instance,
that Fred puts a slow-acting poison in Bill's drink. If Bill dies as a result, then Fred has killed Bill. On Aristotle's view, Fred's action of
killing Bill and Bill's dying are one and the same process, a process
that ends in Bill's being dead. The worry here is that Bill's death
might occur some time after we would intuitively want to say that
Fred has stopped doing anything. Indeed, Fred himself might die in

---

[28] Of course, Hornsby is not committed to the view that Jane moves her body *in just the
same way as* she moves a glass of water. Haddock's objection is to the claim that, just as
moving a glass of water is causing the glass to move, so also moving one's body is causing
one's body to move.

the meantime. Can Fred really be killing Bill after Fred himself has ceased to exist?[29]

Finally, Aristotle's account faces a further difficulty that is, I think, unique to it.[30] This difficulty stems from his view that the action of changing something is the causing of the end state of the change: raising one's arm is causing one's arm to be up; walking to the pier is causing oneself to be at the pier. This raises an obvious question. There are, surely, different types of action that result in one's arm being up, and also different types of action that result in one's being at the pier. How is Aristotle to distinguish between these? How, for instance, is he to distinguish between walking to the pier and swimming to the pier? Each of these actions would, after all, be an incomplete fulfilment of the potential for being at the pier.

It is interesting that Aristotle himself never considers this problem. Perhaps the reason is that, in his discussion of animal movement, he tends to think of different types of movement as being appropriate to different animals. For instance, he begins *The Movement of Animals* with the remark that 'some animals move by flying, some by swimming, some by walking, some in other comparable ways' (698a5–7). He may be assuming that, in the type of animal that walks, the incomplete fulfilment of an active potential for being at *P* will be an act of walking to *P*, whereas in an animal that swims, the incomplete fulfilment of such a potential will be an act of swimming. The thought would be that the manner in which an animal incompletely fulfilled this potential would depend upon the animal's bodily make-up (e.g. whether it had feet or fins).

Of course, this by itself is not a full solution to the problem. After all, some animals (humans, for instance) are capable of swimming and of walking. Perhaps, though, we can get some hint of a solution from the idea that *swimming to P* and *walking to P* are different *ways* of incompletely fulfilling one and the same potential. Aristotle

---

[29] This problem with Aristotle's view is pointed out by Charles (1984, pp. 79–81) and by Heinaman (1985). Davidson also discusses a problem about the timing of an action. He identifies Fred's killing Bill with Fred's administering the poison. His problem, then, is to explain how Fred's action of killing Bill can be over before Bill is dead. See Davidson (1971, pp. 57–9; 1969, pp. 177–8; and 1985, pp. 299–300).

[30] At least, none of the modern accounts *I have considered here* face this problem. Davidson (1967, pp. 110–11) argues that Anthony Kenny's account is vulnerable to this objection, but Kenny's account itself clearly owes much to his reading of Aristotle. (For Kenny's account see his discussion of performances in Kenny, 1963, ch. 8).

could say that walking to P is incompletely fulfilling (in a walking manner) the potential to be at P, whereas swimming to P is incompletely fulfilling (in a swimming manner) the potential to be at P, and so on.

VI

The Relevance of Aristotle's Account: His Questions and Ours. I have suggested that there are certain ways in which the account I have extracted from Aristotle is superior to those found in modern philosophy, but I have also drawn attention to problems that would need to be resolved in any defence of this account. In this final section, I shall discuss an objection to the whole project of comparing Aristotle, in this way, to modern philosophers of action. It might be claimed that the kind of comparison I have been drawing is based on a false assumption: the assumption that Aristotle's discussion of agency is designed to answer the very questions that are posed in modern philosophy of action, by philosophers such as Davidson and Hornsby. If it is a mistake to think that Aristotle's questions are the same as ours, can his account nevertheless be relevant to these modern discussions?

One important difference between Aristotle and Davidson is in the scope of their accounts. Aristotle's account has a scope that is, in one respect, narrower and in another broader, than Davidsonian accounts of action. The scope of Aristotle's account is narrower because it is concerned only with actions of changing (or moving) something. Although Davidson (1971, p. 49) says that all actions are 'bodily movements', he makes it clear that he means his account to apply to actions that are not, in any ordinary sense, movements. The term 'movement' must, he says, be interpreted generously enough to include such actions as 'standing fast'. Aristotle would not count standing fast as a movement or change. And it is not just an accident that his account is only about actions of changing, or moving, something. The arguments I have presented in its defence depend crucially on this fact. This, for instance, is what allows Aristotle to claim that an action is a causing of an end state of a change (and hence to escape the objection that on his view, causing an event would be the same event as the event caused).

As I said above, there is also a way in which Aristotle's account has a *broader* scope than Davidson's. When Davidson asks what makes it the case that my arm's going up is an instance of my raising my arm, he is asking what makes this event an *intentional* action. But the *Physics* III.3 account of agency is not, primarily, an account of intentional action. For this account applies also to the actions of inanimate things. The fire's action of heating the stone is the incomplete fulfilment of the fire's potential for the stone to be hot, and this action of the fire's is one and the same change as the stone's becoming hot.

However, these differences of scope do not show that Aristotle's account is irrelevant to the questions with which Davidson is concerned. Instead, they pose an interesting challenge to certain modern ways of answering these questions. Is it right, for instance, to suppose (with most modern philosophers) that there must be one account of action that applies both to the action of changing something and to actions, such as standing fast, that do not involve changing or moving anything? It might be considered a merit of Aristotle's discussion that he does not lump together changes and other kinds of activity under the general heading 'events'. Once it is recognized, though, that there are significant differences between changes and other kinds of activity, it becomes less obvious there must be some single account that is an account both of what it is to change something and of what it is to engage in an activity.

As for Aristotle's assumption that there can be a single account of what it is to change something, an account that applies both to human and to inanimate action, I want to suggest that this assumption captures an important insight that is missed by Davidsonian accounts. Davidson asks what makes it the case that my arm's going up is (in certain cases) an instance of my raising my arm. On Aristotle's view, human agency and inanimate agency have something important in common: they are both exercises of a certain kind of causal power. For Aristotle, we cannot say what makes a certain event an intentional action, unless we can say first what makes it an action. On this view, giving a general account of agency is a necessary precursor to explaining what it is to be an intentional action.[31]

---

[31] Cf. Alvarez and Hyman (1998, pp. 243–5).

I shall turn now to one final way in which Aristotle differs significantly from all the modern philosophers of action I have discussed. This difference arises not from the scope of Aristotle's account, but rather from his conception of change. The *question* 'What makes my arm's going up a case of my raising my arm?' cannot mean quite the same for Aristotle as it does for modern philosophers. When modern philosophers ask this question, they assume that the event of my arm's going up is an event that could have occurred even though there was no action of arm-raising: my arm could have just happened to go up, without me or anyone else raising it. For instance, someone's arm might go up against her will because she has anarchic hand syndrome. The question, then, is how to distinguish cases like this from cases in which her arm goes up because she raises it. Davidson's answer is that when someone's arm goes up because she suffers from anarchic hand syndrome, the event of her arm's going up is not caused, in the appropriate way, by her beliefs and desires. Hornsby's answer is that the sufferer from anarchic hand syndrome, when her arm rises because of this condition, is not exercising her capacity to raise her arm at will. On Hornsby's view (2004b, §5, p. 179), one must be exercising such a capacity if one is to count as intentionally raising one's arm.

Aristotle does not face quite the same question. The reason is that his conception of the event of *my arm's going up* is different from that presupposed in these modern accounts. On Aristotle's view, a change is the incomplete fulfilment of a thing's potential to be in some end state. For something to count as a change, then, it must already exhibit a kind of directedness: it must be a *going towards* some end. This account of change is sometimes criticized on the grounds that there are certain things that we would, intuitively, want to count as changes that are not, in this way, directed towards an end. One example of such a change might be the movement of a stone that rolls out of the way when it is accidentally knocked by a walker.[32] Another might be the arm movements to which a sufferer of anarchic hand syndrome is subject. A movement of this kind is not the fulfilment of a potential anything has to be in some particular end state. If it is right that such accidental movements do not

---

[32] This is Waterlow's example (1982, p. 127). For a discussion of this and other criticisms of Aristotle's account see Coope (forthcoming).

qualify as Aristotelian changes, then this has an interesting consequence for his views about action. On Aristotle's view, there is not
one type of event, *my arm's going up*, which could occur because I
raise my arm, but could equally occur because I suffer from anarchic hand syndrome. The event which occurs when I raise my arm is
of quite a different kind from the event that would occur if my arm
moved about because I suffered from this condition. The one event
is a change and hence a progression towards some end; the other is
not. According to Aristotle, if my arm's rising is a change, it must
have *some* agent (though the agent could be someone other than
me, and it could, even, be something inanimate).[33] On the other
hand, if it is *not* a change, then it is not even a candidate for being
identical with an action of the sort I have discussed in this paper: an
action of changing something.[34]

Because of this, if Aristotle were asked 'What makes my arm's going up a case of my raising my arm?', he could not understand this
question in the way that it is generally understood in modern philosophy of action. On his view, when my arm's rising is a change, it is
an event that *simply in virtue of being a change* has a kind of directedness towards an end: it is the incomplete fulfilment of a potential
of my arm to be up. Thus, in asking what makes this event an action, one is not asking what gives it this end-directedness (since this
end-directedness is presupposed by its being a change at all).

Again, this feature of Aristotle's account raises important questions for modern philosophers. It challenges us to ask whether there
really is one and the same type of event, arm-rising, which occurs
both when I raise my arm and also when my arm moves upwards
without my (or anyone else) raising it (perhaps because of a condition like anarchic hand syndrome). Even if one is not convinced that

---

[33] Aristotle makes it clear that he thinks a change must have an agent in *Physics*
III.3.202b26–28, when he redefines change in terms of agency and patiency.

[34] Elsewhere, Hornsby (1997, pp. 102–10) puts forward a 'disjunctive conception of bodily
movements' that has something in common with the view that I am attributing to Aristotle.
She suggests that 'the concept of bodily movements subsumes events of significantly different kinds: there is no unitary category to which both the effects of actions and mere B-move-
ments [bodily movements that are not the effects of actions] both belong' (p. 104). Of
course, as we have already seen, Aristotle holds (unlike Hornsby) that my action of moving
my body is itself a bodily movement (not something that causes a bodily movement). His
view is that there is no unitary category to which those bodily movements that are actions
(ie those which are exercises of the power to bring something about) and those that are not
both belong. They are not even 'movements' in the same sense.

Aristotle's definition of change succeeds in capturing the notion of change in general, there remains a question whether this account (or something like it) applies to certain changes: changes that are the exercise of an agent's power to bring something about. More generally, once we recognize the central role Aristotle's account of change plays in his philosophy of action, we are faced again with a question about the modern notion of an event: does the general notion of an event obscure distinctions that are needed for a satisfactory account of agency?

Though Aristotle's own concerns are often different from ours, this is not a reason to suppose that his account has no bearing on the questions asked by modern philosophers of action. What I have tried to show in this paper is that these very differences suggest interesting alternatives to the ways in which modern philosophers tend to approach such questions. It would be a much larger project to assess whether any of these alternative approaches should, in fact, be adopted. My aim here has simply been to argue that such a project is worth pursuing.[35]

REFERENCES

Alvarez, M. and J. Hyman 1998: 'Agents and their Actions', *Philosophy*, 73, pp. 219–45.

Bach, K. 1980: 'Actions Are Not Events', *Mind*, 89, pp. 114–20.

Charles, D. 1984: *Aristotle's Philosophy of Action* (London: Duckworth).

Coope, U. 2004: 'Aristotle's Account of Agency in *Physics* III.3', *Proceedings of the Boston Area Colloquium in Ancient Philosophy*.

——forthcoming: 'Change and its Relation to Potentiality and Actuality', in G. Anagnostopoulos (ed.), *Blackwell Companion to Aristotle* (Oxford: Blackwell).

Cooper, J. M. 1997: *Plato: Complete Works* (Indianapolis: Hackett).

Davidson, D. 1963: 'Actions, Reasons and Causes', in Davidson (2001).

——1967: 'The Logical Form of Action Sentences', in Davidson (2001).

——1969: 'The Individuation of Events', in Davidson (2001).

——1971: 'Agency', in Davidson (2001).

——1985: 'Adverbs of Action', Appendix A in Davidson (2001).

——2001: *Essays on Actions and Events* (Oxford: Clarendon Press).

---

[35] This paper was written during research leave supported by the AHRC. I would like to thank John Hyman for comments on a draft.

Frankfurt, H. 1988: 'The Problem of Action', in *The Importance of What We Care About* (Cambridge: Cambridge University Press).

Haddock, A. 2005: 'At One With Our Actions, But At Two With Our Bodies: Hornsby's Account of Action', *Philosophical Explorations*, 8 (2), pp. 157–72.

Heinaman R. 1985: 'Aristotle on Housebuilding', *History of Philosophy Quarterly*, 2, pp. 145–62.

——1994: 'Is Aristotle's Definition of Change Circular?', *Apeiron*.

Hornsby, J. 1980: *Actions* (London: Routledge & Kegan Paul).

——1997: *Simple Mindedness* (Cambridge, MA: Harvard University Press).

——2004a: 'Agency and Actions', in H. Steward and J. Hyman (eds.), *Agency and Action* (Cambridge: Cambridge University Press), pp. 1–23.

——2004b: 'Alienated Agents', in M. De Caro and D. Macarthur (eds.), *Naturalism in Question* (Cambridge, MA: Harvard University Press), pp. 173–87.

Hussey, E. 1983: *Aristotle's Physics. Books III and IV* (Oxford: Clarendon Press).

Kenny, A. J. P 1963: *Action, Emotion and Will* (London: Routledge & Kegan Paul).

Kosman, L. A. 1969: 'Aristotle's Definition of Motion', *Phronesis*, 14, pp. 40–62.

Kostman, J. 1987: 'Aristotle's Definition of Change', *History of Philosophy Quarterly*.

Makin, S. 1991: 'An Ancient Principle about Causation', *Proceedings of the Aristotelian Society*.

Sedley, D. 1998: 'Platonic Causes', *Phronesis*, 43 (2), pp. 114–32.

von Wright, G. H. 1963: *Norm and Action* (London: Routledge & Kegan Paul).

Waterlow, S. 1982: *Nature, Change and Agency in Aristotle's Physics* (Oxford: Clarendon Press).

ARISTOTLE ON ACTION
URSULA COOPE AND CHRISTOPHER SHIELDS

II—CHRISTOPHER SHIELDS

THE PECULIAR MOTION OF ARISTOTELIAN SOULS

Aristotle has qualms about the movement of the soul. He contends directly, indeed, that 'it is impossible that motion should belong to the soul'
(*DA* 406a2). This is surprising in both large and small ways. Still, when
we appreciate the explanatory framework set by his hylomorphic analysis
of change, we can see why Aristotle should think of the soul's motion as
involving a kind of category mistake-not the putative Rylean mistake, but
rather the mistake of treating a change as itself capable of changing.

I

Introduction. Aristotle contends that 'it is impossible that motion
should belong to the soul' (*DA* 406a2). This is surprising in both
large and small ways. For he believes that Socrates has a soul, and
he also believes that Socrates sometimes moves around the agora
while he talks. So, one might expect him therefore also to believe
that Socrates' soul moves right along with him as he walks and
talks. Surely, in any event, he cannot leave it behind as he rises to
stroll. Of course, one might think it already unfortunate, or at best
rather quaint, that Aristotle should speak of Socrates having a soul
at all. Souls are, one may suppose, ghostly stuffs, somehow inexpli-
cably linked to the more familiar material stuff of the body in some
yet to be specified quasi-spatial way.[1] Looked from this perspective,
one might regard Aristotle as right, though ludicrously antiquated,
to implicate himself in a discussion of problems pertaining to the
soul's motion. It is, after all, not even a little clear what it might
mean to suggest that an immaterial substance has the ability to
move through space.

These sorts of reservations are, however, alien to Aristotle's point
of view: he nowhere conceives of the soul as a sort of Cartesian immaterial substance, and he has no interest in appealing to the soul as

---

[1] On quasi-spatial properties, see Shoemaker (1984).

a primary vehicle for securing *post mortem* existence. Rather, he thinks that all living things are ensouled, where his notion of being ensouled (*empsuchon*) is more closely related to an untroubling conception of being *animate* than it is to any kind of Cartesianism. On Aristotle's approach, plants and animals no less than human beings are ensouled (*DA* 423a20–6, 412a13; cf. *Gen. An.* 736b13; *Part. An.* 681a12)); being ensouled is simply being alive. In consequence, so far at least, there is no more reason to deny that Socrates is ensouled than there is to say that Socrates is a hylomorphic compound of form and matter, that his body is his matter and his soul is his form (*DA* 412a20–1), and that Socrates would cease to exist if his soul were lost (*DA* 413a3–5). In these ways, then, Aristotle's commitment to the existence of the soul is as deep as his commitment to hylomorphism, and in his metaphysical scheme that is very deep indeed.

For this reason, in fact, Aristotle's qualms about the motion of the soul should strike us as more surprising still. For he analyses perception, thought, and desire in the terms provided by his hylomorphic theory of change, and that theory of change is expressly couched in terms of motion and alteration (*DA* 409b15–17, 411a24–30, 418a3–6, 429a23, 429b29–430a2, 433b16–17). So, in these smaller ways too we should expect the soul to undergo motion: if Socrates' seeing red is an instance of change, and seeing is a psychic event, then since change is a kind of motion, Socrates' soul should be said to move in each time it perceives. Yet this, Aristotle announces, is impossible.

It is noteworthy that Aristotle's is not merely the factive contention that motion does not pertain to the soul; rather, he stakes out the stronger modal contention that that it is altogether *impossible* that the soul should move. It is tempting, in view of this sort of stridency, to hypothesize that Aristotle regards the suggestion that the soul moves as involving what is today called a *category mistake*. The suggestion along these lines would be that in his view the soul is simply not the sort of thing which *could* move, that it belongs to a category of being for which motion is simply unthinkable, where any claim that it could move would be on par, for example, with the suggestion that squares snore or that a rubbish bin has a factorial greater than 120. I will argue that this temptation, when suitably understood, is to be indulged: Aristotle believes that the soul is sim-

ply not the sort of thing which can move. The interest in his contention lies precisely in the character of the category mistake in
question. Interestingly, unlike some contemporary figures who make
loud allegations concerning the category mistakes of others without
having the benefit of a category theory of their own at their disposal,[2] Aristotle can and does proceed with an articulated theory of categories to which he may legitimately appeal in this context. Thus,
while he does not allege that anyone who maintains that the soul
moves is guilty of a category mistake, this seems to be the impetus
behind his remark; moreover, he has the category theory needed to
secure this sort of complaint.

By explicating his conception of the soul's inability to move, we
position ourselves to appreciate some features of his ontology of
soul which are otherwise easily overlooked. We also, to the degree
that we are sympathetic to his basic hylomorphic framework, come
to a deeper understanding of its treatment of those features of psychic motion which continue to cause qualms even today. In the end,
I will suggest, Aristotle's concerns about the motion of the soul
highlight a defect in his hylomorphic treatment of perception and
thought. I conclude not that this defect is irremediable, but rather
that the resources of Aristotle's own hylomorphism provide no
ready remedy. Consequently, any advance within his broad metaphysical framework will need to determine ways to augment his
analysis of change.

II

The Context of Aristotle's Contention. Aristotle's contention that
the soul is incapable of motion occurs towards the beginning of *De
Anima* i.3, a primarily endoxic chapter. That is, the chapter occurs
early in the treatise, in a section in which Aristotle is surveying the
views of the soul handed down by his predecessors in an effort to re-
cover what is of value in them while setting aside what is untenable,
in preparation for offering his own positive characterization later in
De Anima ii.[3] He has already in the previous chapter, *De Anima* i.2,

---

[2] So Ryle (1949).

[3] Aristotle makes his most overt methodological remark in this respect at *DA* 403b20–24.

taken note of two commonalities in the views of his predecessors: all had differentiated the ensouled from the unensouled in terms motion (*kinêsis*) and perception (*aisthêsis*) (*DA* 403b25–27). Subsequently, he adds a third trait, incorporeality (*asômaton*) to these two (*DA* 405b11–12). The later addition comes from the summary near the end of the same chapter, where he strengthens his earlier report in another way as well. Initially Aristotle says only that his predecessors had differentiated the ensouled, or animate (*empsuchon*) from the unensouled, or inanimate (*apsuchon*) by means of motion and perception. In the summary, he appeals to these same two traits in addition to incorporeality by way of reporting that his predecessors had all *defined* (*horizontai*) the soul (*psuchê*) itself in terms of them (*DA* 405b20).

Aristotle's stronger characterization commits his predecessors to advancing defining features of the soul, and so has them assessing its intrinsic nature, rather than merely adverting to criteria in terms of which the living might be differentiated from the non-living. This is significant in so far as one might well be willing to agree that living beings tend to move themselves about without ascribing their ability to do so more narrowly to their souls. Still, given the comparatively broad notion of the soul with which he is working, it would be reasonable enough for Aristotle to slide from reporting his predecessors as differentiating the living from the non-living in terms of certain traits to his characterizing them as defining the soul—the principle in virtue of which living beings qualify as living—in terms of those same traits. That allowed, matters become less innocent when we reflect upon a simple point of Aristotle's Greek: when he speaks of the soul's *moving* (*kinein*) as defining its nature, foremost in his mind is not the thought that the soul is capable of *being in motion*, that it moves in an intransitive sense of the verb, but rather that it *initiates motion*, that it causes motion, or moves things about, in, that is, the transitive sense of the verb. To say that the soul moves in this sense is to say, more fully, that the soul is responsible for bringing about motion, that it is the ultimate initiator of motion in living beings; accordingly, to ascribe to his predecessors this claim, Aristotle needs to show that they treat the soul as the primary causal agent responsible for bringing about the motion we undeniably observe in living beings.

One may dispute whether the doxographical evidence adduced by Aristotle in *De Anima* i.2–3 warrants his making this stronger claim about his predecessors.[4] For our purposes, however, we may leave that issue unassayed. For in thinking about Aristotle's criticisms of his predecessors, and of the genesis of those criticisms, we may simply allow that his characterizations are apt or then acknowledge, if they are not, that his own views about the motion of the soul do not in fact address the views of his predecessors. What is of moment in the present inquiry concerns *why* Aristotle should think, whether or not his predecessors in fact ran afoul of his contentions, that it is impossible that motion should belong to the soul.

It is, however, paramount to appreciate that his contentions about the motion of the soul do emerge in an endoxic context, where we might normally be inclined to regard Aristotle as speaking not *in propria persona*, or, if he is, not to be offering his considered judgments. So, normally, one might be cautious about ascribing a view mooted directly to Aristotle. That allowed, in the context of *De Anima* i.3, Aristotle does sound as if he is offering his own view of the matter. What he says, more fully, is:

> One ought first to inquire into motion. For it is presumably not merely false to say that the essence of the soul is as supposed by those who say that the soul moves itself, or is able to move itself; it is, rather, impossible that motion belong to the soul. First, it has already been stated that it is not necessary that what initiates motion is also itself in motion. Moreover, everything in motion is so in either of two ways: in virtue of another or in virtue of itself. By 'in virtue of another' we mean whatever is moved by being in something in motion, as for instance sailors are. For they are not moved in the same way as the ship is: the one is moved in virtue of itself and the other by being in what is in motion. This is clear with regard to their parts. For the proper motion of the feet is walking, as it is of humans as well. But this does not belong to the sailors when on board. Hence, given that being moved is spoken of in two ways, we are now investigating whether the soul is moved, and shares in motion, in virtue of itself. (*DA* 405b31–406a11)

Aristotle is keen to make two points in this passage, the first concerning the necessary conditions of initiating motion as he understands them, and the second concerning a distinction between two

---

[4] See Cherniss (1971) for a full exploration of this question.

ways of being moved, 'in virtue of another' (*kath' heteron*) and 'in virtue of oneself' (*kath' hauto*). The first point seeks to remove an argument in favour of the view that the soul moves and the second paves the way for a discussion of the merits of the view in its own right.

Aristotle's first contention in this passage serves as a reminder of his considered opinion that it is not a necessary condition of initiating motion that the initiator be itself in motion. Throughout *De Anima* i.2, Aristotle repeatedly assails the views of his predecessors on the grounds that they make the soul move because they accept the view that it initiates the motion of the body. Because they suppose that only what is in motion can initiate motion—that what moves in the intransitive sense can move in the transitive sense—they conclude on that basis that the soul too must be in motion (*DA* 408b28–30). To take only the first of Aristotle's several targets, Democritus, as Aristotle represents him, is motivated to make the soul out of round, fiery atoms because such atoms move most easily and are in fact incessantly darting about, like the small motes visible in shafts of light (*DA* 403b31–404a16). It is thus precisely their easy mobility which qualifies them for the soul's undisputed role as mover, in the transitive sense.

The argument upon which Aristotle's predecessors implicitly rely, then, is straightforward: (i) the soul initiates motion; (ii) only what is in motion can initiate motion; hence (iii) the soul is in motion. Aristotle defuses this argument by denying (ii). As he represents them, in fact, Aristotle's predecessors simply assume (ii) without reflecting upon it. This premiss is, however, according to Aristotle, simply false (*Phys.* 192a16–18, 256b23–31, 258b7–10; *Gen. et Corr.* 336b27–29; *Part. An.* 687a15–17; *Meta.* 1072a25–26). We need not worry about the source of Aristotle's confidence on this point, though it will prove salient that his star instance of a non-moving initiator of movement is an end or goal, something good which serves as an object of desire or love.

The second point in this passage proves more ambitious. If his first concern is to remove a plank from an argument offered on behalf of the soul's motion, his second is to begin the process of showing that, however motivated, the view is false: the soul cannot be in motion. He sets the stage by drawing a distinction between two ways of being moved: something may be moved in virtue of itself (*kath' hauto*) or in virtue of something else (*kath' heteron*). Although the initial gloss on this distinction is clear enough, it proves to be a complex matter to specify precisely how Aristotle understands it. It is also consequential for our understanding of the motion of the soul, since Aristotle will ultimately restrict his strictures about the soul's motion to its *kath' hauto* motion: he will in the end concede that the soul can be moved in virtue of something other than itself, even while denying that it is so much as possible for it to be moved in virtue of itself.

III

Aristotle's Framework of Motion. Aristotle's initial gloss on this distinction in *De Anima* i.3 seems reasonably straightforward: 'By "in virtue of another" I mean whatever is moved by being in something in motion, as for instance sailors are' (*DA* 406a5–6). As he explains, sailors 'are not moved in the same way as the ship is: the one is moved in virtue of itself and the other by being in what is in motion' (*DA* 406a6–7). In terms of this illustration, being moved *kath' heteron* is simply being moved by being a passenger on something moved in its own right: as the wind fills the ship's sails, the ship is moved across the waters and the sailors are moved right along with it. Minimally, if we want to say that the sailors are moved by the wind, we will have to posit as a mediating mover the ship: they are moved because, and only because, the ship is moved.

We can see directly, however, that this simple illustration cannot be the whole of the matter: for, plainly, a sailor *could* be moved in his own right, even if he is at present being moved in virtue of another, by standing upon the deck of a moving ship. Consequently, the distinction as given cannot suffice for Aristotle's ultimate purposes regarding the motion of the soul. As we have seen, he aims to show not that the soul *does* not move in its own right (the factive claim), but rather that it *cannot* move in its own right (the stronger modal claim). Thus, if by drawing the *kath' hauto-kath' heteron* distinction Aristotle intends to find space for the soul's being moved *kath' heteron* even while it cannot move *kath' hauto*, he will have fallen short of his stated goal. He will need somehow to refine or augment the distinction as drawn.

In fact, in another context Aristotle does provide the wanted augmentation; and it is safe to assume that in the current passage he is implicitly relying upon his more nuanced treatment. In the *Physics*, using a different though related distinction, between what is moved in its own right (*kath' hauto*) and what is moved coincidentally (*kata sumbebêkos*), he observes that among the class of entities moved coincidentally some, like the sailors we have just encountered, *can* be moved in their own rights, while others never are, because they cannot be:

> Some things are *actually* moved in their own rights, while others are moved co-incidentally. Among things moved co-incidentally, some *can* be moved in their own right, like the parts of the body or a nail in a ship, but others, like whiteness and knowledge, are always moved co-incidentally. These have changed in place because that in which they are present change. (*Phys.* 211a17–23; cf. 196b23–9, 198a6–9, 226a19, 254b7–14)

Again adverting to the illustration of a ship, Aristotle allows that a nail in a ship is moved along with the whole ship, coincidentally, while his contrast implies that the entire ship, as in *De Anima*, is moved in its own right.

There are, however, two additional bits of information derivable from his treatment in the *Physics*. First, and less consequentially, he allows that the physical parts of something are moved coincidentally when the whole is moved in itself. This is clear from both illustrations, nails in a ship and the parts of the body. Second, and more importantly, in the *Physics* he illustrates a class of entities which cannot be moved in their own right but are always moved coincidentally: whiteness (*leutkotês*) and knowledge (*epistêmê*). We know immediately from the contrast class that these are—reasonably enough—not to be regarded as parts of the body. Less immediately clear is why they cannot be moved in their own rights. Aristotle does not say in the current context. One may conjecture on the basis of the illustrations that Aristotle is presuming that whiteness and knowledge are simply not the sorts of thing which might be moved in their own rights. Something white, or someone who knows, might be well be moved in its own right: a white and scholarly sailor might be moved in his own right or coincidentally, depending upon whether he happens to be aboard a ship. Indeed, as far as Aristotle's examples thus far allow, he might be simultaneously moved in both ways, when he is aboard a ship which is moved *kath' hauto*, in which case he is moved *kata sumbebêkos*, even while he is walking along the deck under his own power, in which case he is moved *kath' hauto*. By contrast, the whiteness he instantiates, like the knowledge he possesses, is unlike any given bodily part: a part, though moved *kata sumbebêkos* might also be moved *kath' hauto*. If his whiteness and knowledge are moved with him at all, they are moved coincidentally. Thus, if the last scholarly sailor leaves the ship, the remaining sailors may lament his departure by noting that he took his knowledge with him, but they would only be thinking of knowledge as leaving the ship along with the sailor whose knowledge it is.

Now, this suspicion is fair enough. After all, it does seem strained to speak of *whiteness* or *knowledge* as moving about, or as capable of being moved in their own rights—on a par, perhaps, with thinking that the whole universe might be moved to the left a few centimeters, or, more locally, that the aspirations of the middle class could be painted purple.

That much is, however, merely a conjecture. Aristotle does not in the present context undertake to explicate the specific unsuitability of whiteness and knowledge as candidates for motion *kath' hauta*. Fortunately, however, he does provide an abstract characterization elsewhere in which his view of the matter emerges with reasonable clarity. That characterization occurs at the at the beginning of *Physics* v:

> Everything which changes (*to metaballon pan*) changes either (i) co-incidentally (*kata sumbebêkos*), as for instance when we say that the musical thing walks, because a musical thing co-incided with this thing and this thing walked; (ii) that which changes by belonging to what is said to change *simpliciter*, for instance what is said with respect to parts, as when the body is made healthy since the eye or chest is made healthy and these are parts of the body; (iii) and then there is what is changed neither co-incidentally nor in virtue of something else belonging to it, but is moved primarily by being itself moved. And this is capable of motion in its own right (*kath' hauto*). (*Phys.* 224a21–29)

After making this distinction, Aristotle observes that the three ways of being changed have their corresponding initiators: (i) those which initiate motion coincidentally; (ii) those which do so by being part of what initiates motion; and (iii) that which initiates motion primarily and in its own right, like a doctor doctoring, or a hand striking (*Phys.* 224a30–34).

Finally, in an observation evidently cutting across these coordinate distinctions, Aristotle observes the following factors involved in all motion. First, there is that which initiates motion in its own right; second, there is what is moved; and finally, there is the framework within which its motion occurs (*Phys.* 224a34–35). Importantly, the framework of motion itself involves some subdimensions: time and a continuum from which and along which the motion transpires, since, Aristotle contends, 'every motion is from something and into something' (*Phys.* 224b1).

Aristotle's requirement regarding the continuum of motion sets the context for his concerns about the motion of the soul. He illustrates this requirement simply enough: a piece of wood changes when it alters *from* being cold *to* being warm. Significantly, upon making this simple observation, Aristotle almost immediately adverts to some features of his category theory presupposed by his theory of motion and then raises a difficulty: 'It is therefore clear that the motion is in the wood and not in the form (*eidos*): for the form, the place, and the quantity neither initiate motion nor are in motion' (*Phys.* 224b4–6). The point is not that quantities, for example, cannot change. It is rather that motion is *category-relative*. When a piece of wood becomes warm, as Aristotle understands it, its change is either, for example, *qualitative* or *quantitative*—that is, a change transpires exclusively in one category or another, so that if it is, for instance, in the category of quantity, it is not also in the category of quality. Nothing changes, properly speaking *from* being cool *to* being large, even if a soufflé expands as it cooks. Rather, one change is along the continuum of cool-hot and the other along a distinct continuum of small-large.

In this connection, however, Aristotle says something surprising. When wood changes from cold to hot, he says, the change is not in the *form*, but in the wood. This may seem odd, since, after all, it precisely along a formal dimension, from cold to hot, that a qualitative change seems to be taking place. If a man changes from pale to dark while sitting in the sun, then it seems that the accidental form, *being coloured*, is precisely the thing changing. Aristotle observes:

The forms (*eidê*) and affections (*pathê*) and the place—that into which things being moved are moved—are immovable (*akinêta*), as for instance, knowledge (*epistêmê*) and heat (*thermotês*). Yet someone might raise an objection: if affections (*pathê*) are motions (*kinêseis*), and whiteness (*leukotês*) is an affection, there will be a change (*metabolê*) to a motion (*kinêsis*). (*Phys.* 224b11–15)

Aristotle's response is brief: 'Rather, it is not the whiteness (*leukotês*) which is the change, but the whitening (*leukansis*)' (*Phys.* 224b15–16).

As Ross notes,[5] Aristotle is presumably understanding forms to be substantial forms in this passage, and affections to be accidents. The objection is thus generated by the thought that we think of something's being affected as an alteration: when a child falls and scrapes her knee, her scraping her knee involves her being affected adversely. Yet *being scraped* surely involves a kind of change or motion. So, if an affection is a change or motion, then since whiteness is an affection, it must be a motion. In turn, if an affection is already a kind of process, then when *it* changes, motion itself will undergo change. That will be in violation of Aristotle's otherwise reasonable categorial restriction: changes do not change, but subjects change in some category or other, perhaps quantity or quality.

Taken narrowly, Aristotle's response is plain. The objection holds: since (i) affections are motions, and (ii) whiteness is an affection, it follows (iii) that whiteness is a motion. Aristotle denies (ii) by insisting that properly speaking, whiteness is not the relevant affection, which is, rather, *whitening*. So, the second premiss is false and the objection founded upon an unsound argument.

Still, one may press: why is whiteness not an affection (*pathos*)? It certainly seems to be a *pathos*, in Aristotle's standard terminology. When pressed in this way, the less obvious texture of Aristotle's response begins to emerge. If whiteness is a *pathos*, then it is not the sort of *pathos* which qualifies as a motion. So, either, in fact (i) is true and (ii) false, or (ii) is true and (i) false. The significance of this way of understanding Aristotle's response is that it highlights that *pathos* may be taken in two ways: as a kind of *process* of being affected, or as a *result* of a process leading to it. It is in this way, to illustrate, that we may speak of a perception as either an occurrent

---

[5] See Ross (1936, p. 614).

process ('Her perception varies with the lighting conditions') or as a result of such a process ('Probably we have different perceptions of his expression, because we had different vantage points as he walked by'). In general, then, it is only when a *pathos* is a process that it is a motion; but then *whiteness* could never be a *pathos* of this sort, since it is not a process. Rather, whitening is. Hence, we do not find ourselves in a situation where we have a motion undergoing a change; it also follows that it is not the form which is changing. Although a change may be characterized in terms of a migration from one contrary to another, it is not the qualitative form that is the subject of the migration, but rather the enformed entity which is changing, in respect of its qualitative form.

With this much framework in place, we are prepared to see in a general way why Aristotle has such scruples about the soul's motion: the soul, he maintains, is the form of the body. Since motion pertains not to the form, but to the enformed entity, we should not say that motion is in the soul; or, rather, we should say only that coincidental motion belongs to the soul, but that, as a form, the soul can never be moved in its own right. In this respect, souls are hardly exceptional.

That said, Aristotle's treatment of the issue in *De Anima* invites confusion, in two separate arguments. We will consider each in turn, the first pertaining to the soul as a whole, and the other centered on a question about perception.

IV

A First Argument from De Anima *i Reconsidered: Displacement.* Aristotle's first argument addresses the question of whether the soul might move in its own right (*kath' hauto*). Unfortunately, at least initially, this argument seems to prove too much, if it proves anything at all. In *De Anima* i.3, Aristotle argues as follows:

> There being four types of motion—locomotion, alteration, decay, and growth—the soul would move in respect of one, or some, or all of these. If it is moved non-coincidentally, then motion would belong to it by nature; but if so, so too would place, for all of the motions mentioned are in place. Further, if it is the case that the essence of the soul is to move itself, being moved will not belong to it coincidentally, as it

does to white or to three cubits long. For these things too are moved, but coincidentally, since that to which they belong, the body, is what is moved. For this reason, neither does place belong to them; but it will belong to the soul, if indeed it partakes of motion by nature.

Further, if it is moved by nature, then it would be moved by force; and if it were moved by force, then also by nature. The situation is the same with respect to rest. For something rests by nature in the state into which it is moved by nature; and similarly, something rests by force in the state into which it is moved by force. But it will not be easy to provide an account of how these sorts of forced motions and rests are to belong to the soul—not even for those willing to fabricate one.

Further, if it is moved upward, it will be fire, but if downward, earth; for these are the motions belonging to these bodies. And the same argument obtains concerning those in between.

Further, since it is evident that it moves the body, it is reasonable that it impart those motions in terms of which it is itself moved. If so, it will also be true to say, conversely, that the motion in terms of which the body is moved, the soul has as well. The body, however, is moved by locomotion, with the result that the soul would change in place,[6] with either the whole soul altering or with respect to its parts. If this is possible, then it would also be possible for the soul to enter back into the body once it has left it. And upon this would follow the resurrection of the dead among animals.

The soul could be moved coincidentally, by another, for an animal could be knocked off course by force. It is not necessary for that which is moved by itself, in its essence, to be moved by another, except and unless it is moved coincidentally, just as it is not necessary for that which is good in virtue of itself to be good for the sake of something else, or for what is good because of itself to be good because of something other.

One should say that the soul is most of all moved by sensible objects, if indeed it is moved. Moreover, if in fact the soul moves itself, it would itself be moved. So, if every motion is a dislodging of what is moved in so far as it is moved, the soul too would be dislodged from its essence, if, that is, it does not move itself coincidentally, but motion belongs to its essence in virtue of itself. (405a12–b15)

Aristotle recounts a series of concerns about the motion of the soul in this passage. Several of them are a bit obscure; but none seems as immediately vexing as the last.

---

[6] Reading *kata topon* for *kata to soma* with Bonitz at 406b2.

©2007 THE ARISTOTELIAN SOCIETY
Proceedings of the Aristotelian Society Supplementary Volume LXXXI

It might be expanded in a number of different ways, though the most immediate way will be as follows:

(1) If the soul is moved, then it is moved either coincidentally (*kata sumbebêkos*) or in its own right (*kath' hauto*).
(2) The soul is moved.
(3) So, the soul is moved either coincidentally (*kata sumbebêkos*) or in its own right (*kath' hauto*).
(4) Everything moved in its own right (*kath' hauto*) is a dislodging (*existasthai*; 406b13) of what it is moved, in so far as it is moved.
(5) So, if it is moved (*kath' hauto*), then the soul will be dislodged from its own being (*ousia*; 406b13).
(6) The soul, when moved, is not dislodged from its own being.
(7) So, the soul is not moved in its own right (*kath' hauto*).
(8) So, the soul is moved coincidentally (*kata sumbebêkos*).

This argument has the result Aristotle seeks, but it does seem to rely on a premiss which is too strong.

The difficult premiss is (5). As stated, it does not follow from what has preceded it, at least not without a bridge principle of some sort. Moreover, as we have already intimated, it seems to prove much too much, if it proves anything at all: we already know that many things are moved *kath' hauta*, and so we know many things may be moved without being dislodged from their essence—if, as it has seemed, that entails their being destroyed.[7] Our first question concerns, then, what 'dislodging' or, perhaps, 'displacement' is meant to imply. Aristotle does not use the language of dislodging often in connection with motion,[8] though when he does it seems to have a fairly unobjectionable meaning, once we have appreciated the general framework of Aristotle's analysis of change, as provided. Every change is conducted along a framework involving contraries. So, when something changes in the category of quality, it will move from one contrary along a continuum to another. If it is to change within this category at all, then, it will be displaced, or dislodged,

[7] This is the meaning Philoponus understandably associated with Aristotle's claim (*In DA* 113, 14).
[8] He uses the word only four times in the *Physics* (216a28, 221b3, 222b15, 261a2); only the last of these instances involves a point directly about change.

from its original position: if x moves from being F to not being F, then x may be said to be dislodged or displaced from its being F; indeed, if this could not be said, then x could not be regarded as changing in the category of quality. As Aristotle observes in the *Physics*, this principle obtains, though only in a relaxed sort of way, even as regards location: intrinsically specified, what is moved in location is not displaced from its being, but only extrinsically is it displaced from its being *in this location* (*Phys.* 261a20–24). One can observe the intrinsic displacement in quantity or quality when Socrates becomes tanned or grows fat. When he moves about the agora, however, nothing intrinsic to him need be made to cease to be.

Now, so much helps to explain why, if the soul is moved *kath' hauto*, it will need to be dislodged in one way or another. What remains unclear, however, is precisely why this should be objectionable. If 'being' (*ousia*) in (5) is taken predicatively, then it will be true that the soul will suffer dislodging at each time it changes; but in that, it will not differ from any other perfectly pedestrian change. On the other hand, if 'being' (*ousia*) is take existentially, in the manner of Philoponus (*In DA* 113, 14), then it is unclear why the soul should be made to lose its being simply because it changes: the theory of change does not seem to warrant any such inference. More to the point, if every change *kath' hauto* were sufficient for x's being dislodged from its being, where 'being' (*ousia*) is taken existentially, then every change would result in the destruction of what is changed. Taking that all together, then, (5) either gives little cause for alarm, and does not warrant (6), or it does warrant (6) and gives great cause for alarm, since it will require that all change yields destruction—a result Aristotle was rightly at pains to deny to Parmenides and others among his predecessors.

If Aristotle is not simply to be mistaken in either of these two ways, then we may expect that neither of these straightforward interpretations of (6) obtains. In fact, neither does. Rather, if we focus on the general framework for change as it has been adumbrated, we see a distinct, less obvious but more likely interpretation coming to the fore. Aristotle's point is the categorially driven observation that the soul, as form, *is* the qualitative character undergoing the change, whether conceived substantially or accidentally. As we have seen, he holds, 'It is therefore clear that the motion is in the wood and not in the form (*eidos*): for the form, the place, and the quantity neither initiate motion nor are in motion' (*Phys.* 224b4–6). If the soul were also to be a subject of motion, then we would have the result that Aristotle had wanted to avoid, namely that a change would (*metabolê*) itself be subject to motion (*kinêsis*) (*Phys.* 224b11–15). This, Aristotle avers, is impossible, akin to a time changing in time, by speeding up or slowing down. Time is rather a quantity of motion, and not itself the sort of being capable of undergoing qualitative change. Or, to take a simpler example, the quantity of a pile of bricks does not itself grow larger when the bricks are added to the pile. Rather, the pile of bricks grows larger and thus dislodges its old quantity in favour of a contrary along a continuum of smaller–larger. To treat the soul as capable of change would thus be to fail to appreciate that it is already a qualifier.

If interpreted this way, (6) proves to be moored not to any direct incoherence regarding the soul's ability to move, but rather to the difficulties attendant, as Aristotle sees them, upon treating anything which is a terminus of change as itself capable of changing. A terminus is a departure point or a destination. It is the sort of thing, thinks Aristotle, which is left or sought as an end, but not the sort of being which leaves or seeks. So, (6) is just the categorially enmeshed judgment that souls, as forms, belong to the wrong category of being to move in their own right (*kath' hauto*). It is in this connection noteworthy that Aristotle deploys the same illustration in both the *Physics* and *De Anima* when explaining his meaning: knowledge (*epistêmê*). Knowledge is a terminus state of someone who is learning, someone who is leaving behind ignorance, as a terminus from which the change has begun. Knowldge does not change when someone approaches it, any more than a location changes when someone leaves or approaches it. Aristotle's contention is that to suppose otherwise involves one in a category mistake given rise by ignoring the requirements for any adequate account of change.

Of course, anyone wishing to say that souls are moved by their association with things moved in their own right is perfectly entitled to do so. It will not be dislodged from anything by such a motion, since no motion will be intrinsic to it. In this sense, then, Socrates' soul does move as he moves around the agora, namely, by virtue of another (*kath' heteron*) and by coinciding with what moves in its own right.

V

A Second Argument from De Anima *Reconsidered: Perception and Other Mental States.* Aristotle's treatment of the motion of the soul thus far may seem somehow to skirt a main issue still confronting him. It may be granted that the soul, as *form*, provides a continuum along which change takes place, so that it does not itself move in its own right as changes accrue. Rather, for example, Socrates is the subject of changing from pale to dark, where this is to be analysed as his pale formal features being dislodged and replaced by a contrary formal feature, the quality *being darkly complected.* That granted, it will also be observed that this sort of response works exclusively by its fastidiously refraining from treating the soul as *subject* of the change in question. Indeed, that is the core of Aristotle's contention: the soul is not the proper subject of such states. This is, after all, part of what it means to say that the soul is moved only with reference to another (*kath' heteron*) or only by coinciding (*kata sumbebêkos*) with something else, a body, a magnitude moved in its own right (*kath' hauto*).

It will rightly be protested, however, that it seems strained, or worse, for Aristotle then to offer perception as a *defining* feature of the soul to his predecessors (*DA* 403b25–27, 405b11–12), only to say that the soul may be said to perceive only by its relation to something else, the body, which primarily perceives. For he himself agrees with his predecessors that one type of soul is essentially perceptual. More directly, since perceptions are motions, and since the subject of perception is the soul, the soul must be subject to motion—and not merely coincidentally.

It turns out that Aristotle is sympathetic with this sort of worry. He indicates that it would be reasonable for someone to object as follows to his appealing to a distinction between coincidental motion and motion in its own right when he treats of the soul's motion:

> Someone might more reasonably raise a difficulty concerning how the soul is in motion, by focusing on these sorts of considerations: we say that soul is pained and pleased, is confident and afraid, and further that it is angry and also that it perceives and thinks. But all of these seem to be motions. On this basis, one might think that the soul is in motion; but this is not necessary. For let it be the case that being pained or pleased or thinking are motions, and that each of these

counts as being moved, and that the movement is effected by the soul—for example that being angry or afraid is the heart's being moved in such and such a way, while thinking is presumably this or some other part's being moved, and this comes about in some cases in virtue of something's being in motion in space and in other cases in virtue of alteration. (Questions regarding what sorts of motions and how they occur require another discussion.) Yet saying that the soul is angry would be like saying that the soul weaves or builds. For it is perhaps better to say not that the soul pities or learns or thinks, but that the human being does these things with the soul. This is not in so far as there is motion in the soul, but in so far as motion sometimes reaches as far as the soul, and sometimes proceeds from it. Thus, perception is from these objects and reaches as far as the soul, whereas recollection proceeds from the soul ranging over the motions or traces in the sense organs. (*DA* 408a34–b18)

In introducing this concern as he does, Aristotle seems sensitive to the fact that the difficulty it poses has not yet been addressed. This, at any rate, seems to be the purport of his suggestion that a still more reasonable objections is yet to be raised (*eulogôteron d' aporê-seien*; 408a34).

Once again the objection seems easy to state in its directness:

(1) The soul perceives, pities, thinks (and so on).
(2) Each episode of perception, pitying, thinking (and so on) is an instance of motion in its own right.
(3) If (1) and (2), then the soul moves in its own right.
(4) Hence, the soul moves in its own right.

Since he rejects (4), by maintaining that 'it is impossible that motion should belong to the soul' (*DA* 406a2), where this is expressly qualified to mean that it impossible for motion to belong in its own right (*DA* 405b31–406a11), Aristotle must also reject one or more of (1)–(3). Which?

Most commentators have understood him to reject (1), since he asserts immediately in responding to this objection that 'it is perhaps better to say not that the soul pities or learns or thinks, but that the human being does these things with the soul' (*DA* 408b13–15)—where Aristotle's Greek permits a more emphatic rendering as well. Thus, for example, Hicks fairly translates: 'Doubtless it would be better not to say …'.[9] This seems an easy resolution, and it has lead some commentators to regard this stretch of *De Anima* as a featuring a 'celebrated Rylean passage'.[10] In regarding it as Rylean, such commentators presumably mean to imply that Aristotle has appreciated, well in advance of Ryle, that the soul is not a substance, but rather a capacity of the body, and that although we may speak of our minds or souls as subjects of mental states, it would be more hygienic to forbear these misleading ways of proceeding, leading, as they do, to Cartesian presuppositions even among those who reject Cartesian dualism.

This is at best a partial resolution, first because Aristotle *does* treat the soul as a subject—in his terms a *hupokeimenon*[11]—and second because it fails to address the actual concern Aristotle is voicing in this passage. We may set aside the first point, in the present context, because it does not address our concerns about psychic motion and change, except to say, as is clear, that Aristotle does *not* say that the soul is a capacity of the body, but insists that it is a substance, an *ousia* (*DA* 421a19–10, *Meta.* 1037a5). It is thus hard to appreciate how he might be thought to be anticipating Ryle, who found precisely this view anathema. In any case, in this passage Aristotle is plainly concerned with issues pertaining to the motion of the soul, and it is not clear how any such response addresses his concern. That is, even if we think that he denies (1), the question remains as to *how* these alterations are to be understood with respect to the soul. The thought may be that he simply intends to rely upon what he has already said regarding the case of locomotion: the soul in these cases moves coincidentally, but never in its own right. It is the human being (the *anthrôpos*; *DA* 408b14–15) who suffers these motions, even if his doing so is possible only because he is ensouled. (He does these things *with* his soul, or *because* of his soul, or *in virtue of* his soul: *tê(i) psuchê(i)*; *DA* 408b15).

This speculation takes us part of the way, but only part of the way. First, it does not address Aristotle's thought that one may more reasonably raise again a difficulty regarding the soul in terms of perception (*eulogôteron d' aporêseien*; 408a34). The implied contrast seems to require that this objection is still to be considered, despite

---

[9] Hicks (1907, p. 33).

[10] Barnes (1971–2, p. 104).

[11] I discuss this aspect of the passage in Shields (1988). For a critical discussion of my treatment, see Granger (1995), together with a further development in Shields (1995).

his already having distinguished between movement in its own right and coincidental movement. More importantly, the inescapable fact is that Aristotle does speak of the soul as subject to various mental states. For example, he opens *De Anima* iii.4 by saying, in unequivocal terms: 'Concerning the part of the soul by which the soul both knows and understands: it is necessary to consider, whether it is separable or is not separable in magnitude but only in account, what its *differentia* is and how thinking ever comes about' (*DA* 429a10–14). And then again, a bit further on, he refers to 'that part of the soul called reason—and by *reason* I mean that by which the soul thinks and conceives' (*DA* 429a22–24). To adopt the expedient that he is speaking loosely in this context is already to have determined that he rejects (1); but this has yet to be determined.

It is difficult to make any such determination if we restrict ourselves to the context within which Aristotle raises his qualms about the soul's non-standard motion. For immediately after the 'celebrated Rylean passage', Aristotle forthrightly acknowledges a problem about reason (*nous*):

> Reasoning and loving or hating are not affections of reason, but rather of that which has reason, in so far as it has it. As a consequence, when this is destroyed, one neither remembers nor loves. For these did not belong to reason alone, but to the common thing, which has perished. But reason is presumably something more divine and unaffected. (*DA* 408b25–29)

The exceptional character of reason is explicated later in *De Anima* iii.4, where Aristotle insists that it is organless (*DA* 429a24–27) and that it is in no way affected by the objects of cognition.

There is a tendency, in the face of the difficulties given rise to by his suggestion, quietly to ignore his contentions regarding reason, and to overlook them as some of the more empirically embarrassing aspects of Aristotle's philosophy of mind. This is unfortunate, since it is in this connection that the difficulties Aristotle faces with respect to all psychic motion come into their sharpest relief. For it is in this context that he most clearly acknowledges a difficulty about the motion of the soul, and it is one which is indifferent to the question of whether or not reason has an organ. Indeed, it is not a problem restricted to cognitive alterations at all. In *De Anima* ii.5, when considering the sorts of changes to which a student is subject when learning, Aristotle observes:

> Nor is being affected unqualified. Rather, in one way it is a kind of de-
> struction by an opposite, and in another way it is rather a preservation
> of what is in potentiality by what is in actuality, and of what is like
> something in the way potentiality is like something in relation to actu-
> ality. For whenever the one who has knowledge comes to contemplate,
> he is either not altered, since this is a progression into the same state
> and into actuality, or his is a different kind of alteration. For this rea-
> son, it is inappropriate to say that one who reasons is altered whenev-
> er he reasons … [T]he one who, after being in potentiality, learns and
> receives knowledge from one who is in actuality, and a teacher, either
> should not be said to be affected or there are two types of alteration,[12]
> one a change towards conditions of privation and the other towards
> positive states and a thing's nature. (*DA* 417b1–16)

What occurs, in certain sorts of transitions, contends Aristotle, is a
progression involving no destruction or displacement at all.

As Aristotle forthrightly acknowledges, this kind of progression
proves difficult to capture within the terms provided by his canonical theory of change. In the case of the reasoning, when moving
from a state of dispositional knowledge to active and occurrent con-
templation, there is no destruction at all. It follows, then, that there
is no displacement, but only a form of realization. It further follows,
in cases where one moves from a first actuality (actually knowing)
to a second actuality (actually contemplating), that the framework
of change which is the backbone of Aristotle's analysis of perceiving
and thinking, no longer applies. We are thus left with what seems an
unsatisfactory overextension of a theory of change, a theory which,
however fruitful in its basic application, runs out of resources as
more complex phenomena come into its view. These phenomena include centrally, though not exclusively, the kinds of changes which
are the currency of our mental and perceptual lives.

It would, of course, be wrong to insist that Aristotle has contra-
dicted himself, on the grounds that he maintains both that change
requires displacement and that there are psychic changes which do
not require displacement. For, as we have seen, he is aware of a need
to develop and extend his account. What is lacking in *De Anima*,
however, is precisely the wanted development. In the current con-

---

[12] Del. *hôsper eirêtai* at 417b14.

text what is striking is this: given that Aristotle allows that there may be a kind of alteration not subject to the restrictions of his canonical account of change, it is open to him, in principle, to respond to our current dialectical argument not by denying (1), the premiss that the soul perceives, pities, thinks and so on. Rather, he seems at liberty to embrace the conclusion (4), and simply to allow that the soul moves in its own right (*kath' hauto*)—precisely when it perceives, pities and thinks. This is all the more so, given that he plainly is wont to speak as if (1) were false, even well into his own positive treatment of the soul. His final treatment of the motion of the soul is thus peculiar, and in some ways inexplicable. He locates a problem flowing from his own well-worked out framework of change, denies then that the framework covers the context of the problem, namely perception and thinking, and yet remains wed to the contention with which we began, viz. that 'it is impossible that motion should belong to the soul' (*DA* 406a2).

VI

Conclusion. Aristotle has qualms about the movement of the soul. Given his broadly hylomorphic analysis of change, it is right that he should do so. We see, when we appreciate the explanatory framework set by that analysis, that he does not want to think of *forms* as changing, but rather of enformed entities as changing by trading one form for another. In this exchange, the form acquired displaces the form lost. To this meager extent, and no further, it is right to think of Aristotle as maintaining that ascribing motion to the soul threatens a kind of category mistake—not the putative Rylean mistake, but rather the mistake of treating a change as itself capable of changing.

Even so, when Aristotle develops the more nuanced aspects of his account of perception and thought, the framework imposed by his hylomorphic account of change finds no easy application. That Aristotle should find his explanatory framework overtaxed in the domain of the psychic is perhaps only to be expected. Today, these many years of philosophy later, we still find ourselves challenged to provide a serviceable account of the mind's motions and causal powers. Often enough now, as then, we find ourselves employing an explanatory framework whose imposition proves a false economy, even to the extent where we discover ourselves denying the data of mental causation altogether. Aristotle has no such inclination, since he thinks that the soul moves the body and moreover that this *phainomenon* is not to be repudiated. Like us, however, he finds it difficult to say just how the soul manages to do its job.[13]

REFERENCES

Barnes, J. 1972: 'Aristotle's Concept of Mind', *Proceedings of the Aristotelian Society*, 72, pp. 101–10.
Cherniss, H. 1971: *Aristotle's Criticism of Presocratic Philosophy* (New York: Octagon Books).
Granger, H. 1995: 'Aristotle on the Subjecthood of Form', *Oxford Studies in Ancient Philosophy*, 13, pp. 135–60.
Hicks, R. D. 1907: *Aristotle: De Anima* (Cambridge: Cambridge University Press).
Menn, S. 2002: 'Aristotle's Definition of Soul and the Programme of the *De Anima*', *Oxford Studies in Ancient Philosophy*, 22, pp. 83–139.
Ross, W. D. 1936: *Aristotle: Physics* (Oxford: Oxford University Press).
Ryle, G. 1949: *The Concept of Mind* (London: Hutchinson).
Shoemaker, S. 1984: 'On An Argument for Dualism', in *Identity, Cause, and Mind* (Cambridge: Cambridge University Press), pp. 287–308.
Shields, C. 1988: 'Soul as Subject in Aristotle's *De Anima*', *Classical Quarterly*, 38, pp. 140–9.
——1995: 'The Subjecthood of Souls and Some Other Forms: A Response to Granger', *Oxford Studies in Ancient Philosophy*, 13, pp. 161–76.
Tweedale, M. 1990: 'Aristotle's Motionless Soul', *Dialogue*, 29, pp. 123–32.
Witt, C. 1992: 'Dialectic, Motion, and Perception: *De Anima*, Book 1', in M. C. Nussbaum and A. O. Rorty (eds.), *Essays on Aristotle's* De Anima (Oxford: Oxford University Press).

[13] I have benefited from conversations on the topic of this paper with Nathanael Stein and Thomas Hannaford. I am most grateful to them both for their insights and kindly assistance. I am especially grateful to Thomas Hanniford for first calling to my attention the significance—and peculiarity—of Aristotle's contention at *DA* i.3 that the soul's *kath' hauto* motion would result in a dislodging of its own ousia (406b13). My formulation of the argument in §IV of the present paper owes much to our numerous and productive discussions of this chapter.

HUMES OLD AND NEW
PETER MILLICAN AND HELEN BEEBEE

I—PETER MILLICAN

HUMES OLD AND NEW: FOUR FASHIONABLE FALSEHOODS, AND ONE UNFASHIONABLE TRUTH

Hume has traditionally been understood as an inductive sceptic with positivist tendencies, reducing causation to regular succession and anticipating the modern distinctions between analytic and synthetic, deduction and induction. The dominant fashion in recent Hume scholarship is to reject all this, replacing the 'Old Hume' with various New alternatives. Here I aim to counter four of these revisionist readings, presenting instead a broadly traditional interpretation but with important nuances, based especially on Hume's later works. He asked that we should treat these—notably the first *Enquiry*—as his authoritative philosophical statements, and with good reason.

I

Introduction. The contemporary student of Hume has every right to feel bewildered by the range of interpretations on offer. And this extraordinary variety is not confined to the murky depths of *Treatise* Book I—Hume's discussions of the external world, or of personal identity, or the concluding section—where almost every commentator seems to find a new reading. Even in the far more familiar topics of induction and causation, which generations of scholars took to be relatively well understood, several would-be revolutions have been initiated over the last couple of decades, and their pace has been increasing. Helen Beebee's excellent book *Hume on Causation* (London: Routledge, 2006) is only the latest of an impressive series of recent scholarly works, each presenting an interpretation that differs markedly from the classic Hume as portrayed for most of the twentieth century by introductory books and university courses: acknowledging deduction, sceptical about induction, reductionist about causation, and a paradigm soft determinist.

All these new debates are exciting, and have greatly enriched our understanding of Hume's philosophy in many ways. But nevertheless I take what is currently a minority view amongst the active par-

©2007 THE ARISTOTELIAN SOCIETY
Proceedings of the Aristotelian Society Supplementary Volume LXXXI

ticipants, namely, that the classic picture of Hume is broadly correct. This is not to say that the revolutionary interpretations are groundless. On induction, for example, there really is a problem about reconciling a sceptical interpretation of Hume's famous argument (in *Treatise* 1.3.6 and *Enquiry* IV) with the positive view of inductive science that he takes elsewhere. And it is no longer considered plausible for commentators simply to dismiss as crude inconsistency his repeated recommendation that we should rigorously base our factual beliefs on experience, like 'the wise man' who 'proportions his belief to the evidence' (*Enquiry* 10.4) when judging miracle stories.[1] Similarly on causation, a crude anti-realist reading is no longer convincing, and any comprehensive understanding of Hume's philosophy has to be able to explain how, after presenting his seemingly sceptical account of our idea of *cause*, he can so soon follow up by urging us to search systematically for hidden underlying causes of both physical and mental phenomena (e.g. *Enquiry* 8.13–15, cf. *Treatise* 1.3.12.5). I believe such an understanding to be achievable, and that the overall picture of Hume that emerges is philosophically far more powerful than either the straightforward scepticism of the traditional reading or the relatively anaemic naturalism of more recent rivals.

There will not be time now to discuss even the broader features of this position, let alone to consider it in any detail. I shall focus instead on a more limited negative task, of sketching and then attacking four major 'Humean heresies' that have been advanced in recent years, and explaining—fairly briefly—why I think each of them should be dismissed. None of them will be given any sort of comprehensive treatment, but I shall try to give a flavour of what I consider to be the most damning points against them, together with references to other publications where these criticisms can be followed up. My aim is provide a generally sceptical overview of the relevant contemporary Hume scholarship, and—by blowing away some recently acquired cobwebs—to reveal a cleaned up, but still eminently recognizable, Old Hume that so many of us know and love.

---

[1] Compare Antony Flew (1961, p. 171): 'The inconsistency [is] flagrant and embarrassing ... [and] has not escaped the notice or the assault of his critics [e.g. Broad and Taylor].'

II

The Good Old Hume. To situate the discussions that follow, I shall start with an outline of what I take to be the genuine main themes of Hume's mature treatment of induction and causation; in other words, a sketch of the Old Hume as I believe he ought to be understood. To many of the new 'heretics', this may seem like a crude positivist caricature of the real Hume, but I shall make no attempt to defend it in detail. Instead, I shall use it as a framework for locating the various heresies, and a base from which I can set out to attack them.

The main thrust of Hume's theoretical philosophy concerns the epistemology of induction and the metaphysics of causation, which are closely related. His primary target is the view of reason taken by philosophers such as Descartes, who claimed to be able to establish certain knowledge of the world through rational insight based (at least in part) on innate ideas, and Locke, who more modestly sought to achieve probable belief through rational insight based on ideas derived from experience.[2] Hume denies that we have any such capacity for rational insight into the world and its workings. Instead we must rely on fallible inductive generalization from experience, ultimately based on the brute assumption—for which no rational foundation can be given—that the laws of nature are uniform. Though this assumption itself is instinctive rather than reasoned, it can nevertheless provide a sufficient grounding for science if we follow it through sys-

---

[2] Two positions I reject but cannot consider fully here are those of Stephen Buckle (2001), who sees Hume's *Enquiry* as primarily an attack on Aristotelianism and Roman Catholicism, and Edward Craig (1987), who takes Hume's main target to be the Judaeo-Christian idea of man as made in the image of God. One obvious objection to Buckle is that Hume, at least by 1748, viewed 'The fame of ... ARISTOTLE [as] utterly decayed' (*Enquiry* 1.4). Buckle ignores this passage, and his response to the objection (pp. 53–6) is unconvincing. Nor, as I argue in my (2002b) and (2007a), is there any difficulty in reading the *Enquiry* as systematically aimed at early modern targets, contrary to Buckle (pp. 35–43). Craig's position is more plausible, because it incorporates an evident truth: that a major part of Hume's aim is to attack a view of rational insight which was thought by its early modern adherents to be in some sense angelic or godlike rather than based on animal instinct. Where I part company with him is in seeing this view itself as specifically tied to the Image of God doctrine, or that doctrine as specially pervasive. Many philosophers, since pre-Christian times, have understood our reason to be a distinctively human faculty of perceptual insight, and nothing in Hume's main arguments against this notion requires reference to Craig's Similarity Thesis. I also consider Craig mistaken in viewing Hume's arguments, and that concerning induction in particular, as in any way taking for granted a deductivist view of reason, which as he points out (pp. 77–8) would favour his case. If, as I believe (2002c, §2), it is Locke's perceptual view of *probable* reason that was Hume's main target here, then for the same reason this counts strongly on the other side.

tematically. This involves weighing up evidence in the light of experience, preferring those beliefs that are best inductively supported, rejecting claims that are contrary to our experience (such as religious miracle stories), and generally seeking reliable causal uniformities that underlie the inconstant superficial phenomena. By this means we can distinguish reasonable from unreasonable belief, the 'philosophy' of the 'wise' from the 'superstition' of the 'vulgar', without any reliance on Cartesian or Lockean insight into the workings of the world.

There are two main threads to Hume's 'chief argument' by which he reaches this overall position, and which is most thoroughly developed in the first *Enquiry*.[3] The first of these starts from 'Hume's Fork', his distinction between *relations of ideas* and *matters of fact*, which corresponds roughly to the distinction between analytic and synthetic propositions (as understood by the logical positivists, rather than by Kant or Frege). Closely related to this is another distinction, between two different types of reasoning: *demonstrative*, which we now call deduction (in the general informal sense of an argument whose premises guarantee the truth of its conclusion), and *reasoning concerning matter of fact* (*factual reasoning* for short), which we now call induction. Since no 'matter of fact, beyond the present testimony of our senses, or the records of our memory' (*Enquiry* 4.3) can be inferred deductively from what we observe, only induction can enable us to discover such matters of fact. Hume accordingly investigates the epistemological basis of induction, finding that it ultimately depends on an animal instinct, *custom*, which irresistibly leads us to expect that unobserved objects will resemble those we have observed. This principle of resemblance or uniformity (often called his Uniformity Principle, or UP) has no possible basis in reason, because it is not intuitively evident, cannot be established on the basis of what we perceive, cannot be inferred deductively from anything that we have experienced, and cannot be inferred inductively without begging the question. Thus our factual inference not only *is not*, but *could not be*, founded on reason. And so were we to rely on reason 'without the influence of custom, we should be

---

[3] The full subtitle of Hume's *Abstract* of the *Treatise* is 'Wherein The CHIEF ARGUMENT of that BOOK is farther ILLUSTRATED and EXPLAINED'. Of the thirty-five paragraphs in the *Abstract*, only three (28–30) are devoted to material that falls outside the scope of the summary that follows here. Apart from the sections on religion and the final Section XII, the *Enquiry* broadly follows the pattern of the *Abstract*; see Millican (2002b, §7) for an outline comparison of the two.

entirely ignorant of every matter of fact beyond what is immediately present to our memory and senses' (*Enquiry* 5.6).

The second main thread of Hume's 'chief argument' starts from the conceptual empiricism which he inherited from Locke. Expressed in Hume's terminology, this becomes his Copy Principle that all ideas are composed of—and derive their significance from—material copied from impressions of sensation or reflection. He applies this Principle to convict some terms (e.g. 'substance') of meaninglessness, through lack of any appropriate impression to generate the supposed idea.[4] In other cases, he searches for the impression-source of the idea to shed light on the corresponding term's meaning. The Copy Principle's most important application—which takes this second form—is to the idea of power, force, or necessary connexion, the key *consequential* component of the idea of causation.[5] This turns out to be derived not from anything that we perceive or understand about causal interactions in the world (e.g. collisions of billiard balls), but instead from our reflexive awareness of making inductive inferences under the influence of custom in response to observed constant conjunctions. Thus causal necessity—in so far as it is anything beyond the constant conjunctions that induce our predictions—is not so much 'read off' the world, as 'read into' it. Hume concludes his discussion of causation with two 'definitions of cause', one of which makes reference only to the *objective* factor of constant conjunction, while the other focuses instead on the *subjective* factor of the mind's tendency to infer accordingly. These definitions are intended to encapsulate all that we can legitimately mean by 'cause' or 'necessity'.

So far this picture is very familiar, even though, as I have acknowledged, some might describe it as a positivist caricature rather than the real Hume. But rather less well known is how he goes on to connect one more important topic to his 'chief argument', namely, free will and determinism. Having framed his two definitions of 'cause', he

---

[4] For Hume's discussions of the supposed simple idea of substance in the light of his Copy Principle, see especially *Treatise* 1.1.6 and 1.4.5.2–6, *Appendix* 11, *Abstract* 7 and 28, 'Of the Immortality of the Soul', paragraph 3 (*Essays*, p. 591), and *New Letters*, p. 20.

[5] My term 'consequential' is intended to capture what is in common to terms such as 'power', 'force', and 'necessary connexion', in that all of them involve one thing's being, in some sense, a consequence of another. Hume treats them all as virtually synonymous for the purposes of his argument, whcih suggests that his concern is with this simple common element, whose impression-source turns out to be a different kind of consequential relation: 'that inference of the understanding, which is the only connexion, that we have any comprehension of' (*Enquiry* 8.25). For more on this, see §2.2 of my (2007b).

uses the corresponding understanding of 'necessity' to argue against the libertarian claim that human actions lack the necessity that characterizes physical events. He accordingly endorses the 'doctrine of necessity', but as a *soft determinist*, pursuing a compatibilist 'reconciling project' (*Enquiry* 8.23) that interprets moral freedom in terms of intentional agency rather than libertarian contingency. Much of this has Hobbesian echoes, but though Hume is often taken to be a paradigm compatibilist,[6] his position is actually rather different from those in the mainstream compatibilist tradition passed from Hobbes down to twentieth-century positivists such as Schlick and Ayer.[7]

III

Four Fashionable 'Heresies' of Hume Interpretation. Non-specialists might be slightly surprised by the very approving attitude to inductive science that I have attributed to Hume (though mention of his discussion of miracles, and his emphatic contrast between science and superstition, might allay this). But in other respects, most of them would, I imagine, take the account that I have given above as more-or-less orthodox, and as describing—perhaps with some small refinements here or there—the standard Hume of so many introductory books and courses in epistemology and history of philosophy. Yet almost every fundamental aspect of it has been vigorously challenged in recent years, in a sequence of high-profile scholarly publications by numerous well-respected authors. Some of these have had to be confined here to brief footnotes, but the following are the four main 'Humean heresies' on which I shall focus:

Stove: Demonstration and Deduction. My account of Hume's important distinction between *demonstrative* and *factual* reasoning equates

---

[6] James Harris has recently challenged this soft determinist consensus, arguing that Hume 'does not subscribe to determinism of any kind, whether Hobbesian or merely nomological' (2005, p. 69, n.15; cf. 2003, p. 464). Harris's discussion is valuable but I believe this claim to be quite wrong, and in my (2008) pull together the relevant evidence from various sources, including letters, Hume's discussions of the Causal Maxim and the Rules by which to Judge of Causes and Effects, his accounts of scientific practice and the search for hidden causes, and also a range of other texts and philosophical considerations.

[7] For a very clear account of Hume's position and how it is commonly misunderstood, see Botterill (2002).

it more or less with the familiar distinction between *deduction* (in the informal sense) and *induction*. But numerous interpreters over the last few decades have disputed this, claiming that Hume's notion of demonstration is confined to *deductive reasoning from a priori (or even self-evident) premises*. Most influential here has been David Stove, whose *Probability and Hume's Inductive Scepticism* (1973) was widely considered for some time to be the most authoritative analysis of Hume on induction. Stove's arguments (pp. 35–6) against the equation of *demonstration* with *deduction* are still widely accepted, even by some (for example, David Owen and Helen Beebee) who nevertheless reject Stove's own account of Humean demonstration.

Garrett: Not Epistemology but Cognitive Science. Don Garrett's influential interpretation of Hume's famous argument concerning induction, proposed in his major book *Cognition and Commitment in Hume's Philosophy* (1997), takes it to be an exercise in cognitive science rather than epistemology. There are also some variations on this theme, developed by a range of scholars including Harold Noonan, David Owen and Helen Beebee, but what is common to all of them is the idea that Hume's argument is essentially *descriptive* rather than *normative*, and is intended to draw a conclusion about the *causation* of our inductive inferences (or of the resulting beliefs), rather than about their rationality. Thus the argument in itself is entirely non-sceptical, and its conclusion—that induction is not 'founded on reason'—should be read as merely denying that induction results from some psychological process of *reasoning* (i.e. stepwise argument or *ratiocination*). This leaves open the possibility that Hume may consider induction to be entirely rational, and indeed those who advocate this sort of interpretation are keen to emphasize that he does so.

Loeb: Hume the Externalist. Louis Loeb is strongly critical of Garrett's 'descriptivist' interpretation, but is motivated by somewhat similar considerations in viewing Hume's famous argument as non-sceptical. Loeb takes Hume to be an externalist, whose criterion of epistemic justification is based not so much on a belief's resulting from (internalist) reason, but rather, on its arising from a process that effectively contributes to the believer's cognitive *stability*. Loeb explored this approach in detail in his *Stability and Justification in Hume's Treatise* (2002), but other externalist interpretations have also been tried, replacing stability as a criterion with such things as irresistibility, proper functioning, adaptiveness, or reliability (Loeb, 2006, p. 334).

Wright: The Causal Realist 'New Hume'. John Wright's *The Sceptical Realism of David Hume* (1983) was the first major salvo in the most intense debate in recent Hume scholarship, with his claim that Hume is not a reductionist about causation, but is instead a believer in 'thick' (or 'upper-case') Causal powers that outrun his two 'definitions of cause'. Evidence adduced in favour of this claim includes Hume's comments on the apparent defectiveness of those definitions, his frequent references to hidden powers or causes, and his apparent assumption that a genuine impression of necessity must license a priori inference from cause to effect. The main evidence on the other side appeals to the texts of his discussions 'Of the Idea of Necessary Connexion' in *Treatise* 1.3.14 and *Enquiry* VII, and in particular, Hume's apparent use of the Copy Principle to circumscribe the limits of our ideas and hence the possible meaning of 'power' or 'necessity'. Those following Wright's 'New Hume' revolution,[8] such as Edward Craig, Galen Strawson, Stephen Buckle and Peter Kail, have sought to undermine this objection by insisting that Hume countenances 'relative ideas' (e.g. of 'the ultimate cause of any natural operation', *Enquiry* 4.12) which need not be impression-derived, and hence can extend beyond the limits of the Copy Principle.

That completes my catalogue of the four 'Humean heresies', all of which concern aspects of the central core of his philosophy on induction and causation. If the field were drawn more widely, it would be easy to add more would-be revolutionary readings, some equally surprising to traditionalists.[9] But for fecundity of novel in-

---

[8] The term 'New Hume' was originally due to Winkler (1991), but has since caught on more generally. Most of the main papers are to be found in *The New Hume Debate*, ed. Read and Richman, whose forthcoming second edition will also include a long paper of my own (2007b) in which I attempt a comprehensive refutation.

[9] It was particularly tempting to include here John Earman's gratuitously abusive account (2000) of the famous argument on miracles, which is a direct application of Hume's philosophy of induction. I discuss Earman's interpretation in my (2003), but its inadequacy can quickly be shown. A careful reading of *Enquiry* 10.5–8 makes very clear that Hume sees the unusualness of a reported event as *one factor amongst others* bearing on the credibility of testimony. Where the other factors are all maximally favourable (so we have a 'proof' of the

terpretation in the most familiar philosophical territory, the last dec-
ade or two of scholarship on Hume's 'chief argument' would, I
imagine, be hard to match.

IV

The Treatise, *the* Enquiry, *and Induction.* Besides these four recent
'Humean heresies', my subtitle alludes to 'one unfashionable truth',
which I shall not defend in much detail but is of considerable significance. Namely, that in interpreting and assessing the central core of
Hume's philosophy—his epistemology of induction and his metaphysics of causation—we must take the *Enquiry Concerning Human Understanding,* originally published in 1748 and revised
numerous times during his life, as our authoritative source. Again I
have argued extensively for this elsewhere,[10] and will here just
sketch my reasons. They start from the evidence of Hume's letters in
the wake of the publication of Books I and II of the *Treatise,* which
took place in January 1739. In these letters, starting barely four
months later, Hume already expresses serious dissatisfaction with
his work and regrets his haste in publishing; this message is then repeated through 1740 to 1745 and 1754, and even in his posthu-
mous 'My Own Life' written in 1776. At first, Hume looks forward
to making corrections in a second edition (*Letters,* i, 38), and indeed
he inserted some revisions into the appendix published with Book

---

testimony), but the event would be miraculous (so we also have a 'proof' of its falsehood),
we are to weigh these proofs against each other in the balance, and it is the result of this
comparison that yields the overall judgement as to whether the testimony should be believed. Earman's interpretation, by contrast, involves the prior calculation of two overall
judgements—namely the conditional probability (given the testimony) of the event, and of
its absence—which are then put in the balance against each other. But since these two conditional probabilities must sum to 1, this reduces the weighing operation to a complete
triviality: the first 'wins' simply if it exceeds 0.5, and a probability exceeding 0.5 is, by definition, precisely what is required to make the event credible. Trivial indeed, but the triviality is Earman's, not Hume's. In view of the regrettably insulting tone of Earman's book, I
wonder why a reading of my (1993)—which appears in his bibliography (but nowhere
else), explicitly anticipates his formula, and expresses serious reservations about its interpretative adequacy—did not inspire him with a little more of that 'degree of doubt, and
caution, and modesty, which ... ought for ever to accompany a just reasoner'
(*Enquiry* 12.24).

[10] See for example my (1995, pp. 93–4; 2002b, pp. 40–52; and especially 2006).

III in November 1740 (plus a frank admission of defeat in respect of personal identity). Later he loses all interest in a second edition, and by 1754 is confiding that the *Treatise* 'so much displeases me, that I have not Patience to review it' (*Letters*, i, 187). Hume's recasting of his philosophy instead took a different path, starting with the *Abstract* of the *Treatise*—probably composed late in 1739—in which his arguments get substantially reorganized and refocused. The *Abstract*'s subtitle declares its intended purpose of illustrating and explaining 'the chief argument' of the 1739 *Treatise* (see note 3 above). But since it closely anticipates the *Enquiry* both in approach and choice of material, we have good reason for taking the later work—which is of course far more substantial than the *Abstract*—as representing the main core of Hume's philosophy not only as he saw it after 1748, but even as early as 1739. Moreover Hume's attitude to the *Enquiry* after publication was in complete contrast with his attitude to the *Treatise*, as shown by his written recommendations to his friends, for example Gilbert Elliot in 1751:

> I believe the philosophical Essays [i.e. the *Enquiry* as originally titled] contain every thing of consequence relating to the Understanding, which you would meet with in the Treatise; & I give you my Advice against reading the latter. (*Letters*, i, 158)

Nearly twenty-five years later, suffering from terminal cancer and anxiously preparing his philosophical legacy for posterity, he wrote to his printer William Strahan with the 'Advertisement' that he insisted should be affixed to all future editions of the volume containing the *Enquiry*. This famously refers to the *Treatise* as a 'juvenile work', and ends with the request: 'Henceforth, the Author desires, that the following Pieces may alone be regarded as containing his philosophical sentiments and principles'.

No doubt Hume's complete dismissal of his own *Treatise* goes too far, but this does not warrant that we should ignore his request in the wholesale way exhibited by so much work on Hume over recent decades. For it is very clear that on a number of the most prominent topics in his philosophy—for example induction, free will, natural theology, and the overall orientation of his scepticism—the *Enquiry* is not only more superficially polished, but is also more fully developed, explicit and comprehensive. This point is entirely obvious in respect of free will, miracles, the Design Argument, and his mitigated scepticism, so I shall take as my illustration the case of induction.

It is, I suggest, surprising and even perverse that so many of those who wish to understand Hume's famous argument concerning induction study it primarily in the pages of the *Treatise*, where it is somewhat convoluted and condensed beyond the limits of clarity, as opposed to the *Enquiry*, where it is far more explicitly spelt out and more than twice as long. In practice, such interpreters commonly find themselves obliged to smuggle in passages from the *Enquiry* to plaster over stages that are unclear or omitted from the *Treatise*. For example, the distinction between relations of ideas and matters of fact is a frequent import from *Enquiry* 4.1–2, brought in as a clarifying refinement of the distinction in *Treatise* 1.3.1 between the 'seven different kinds of philosophical relation'.[11] But other passages are often imported that have no such parallel in the *Treatise*, and sometimes even structural aspects of the *Enquiry* argument may be superimposed onto what purports to be an analysis of *Treatise* 1.3.6. In Barry Stroud's well-known book *Hume*, for example, shortly after introducing the 'Uniformity Principle', consideration is given to the various ways in which this Principle could be supported:

> The uniformity principle cannot be established by observation alone, since it makes a claim about some things that are not, and have not been, observed. ... Therefore, any experiential justification for the uniformity principle must consist of a justified inference from what *has* been observed to the truth of that principle. (Stroud, 1977, pp. 54–5)

The trouble is that these stages of the argument are completely absent from the *Treatise* version. Instead, at *Treatise* 1.3.6.4, Hume's first statement of the Uniformity Principle is immediately followed by the sentence:

> In order therefore to clear up this matter, let us consider all the arguments, upon which such a proposition may be suppos'd to be founded; and as these must be deriv'd either from *knowledge* or *probability*, let us cast our eye on each of these degrees of evidence, and see whether they afford any just conclusion of this nature.

He then moves on to dismiss demonstrative and probable reasoning as possible sources of foundation for the Uniformity Principle, and

---

[11] For example, in Noonan (1999, pp. 92–6).

thus concludes his main argument.[12] Hence he is clearly taking for granted here that if the Principle is to be established, then this must be on the basis of either a demonstrative argument (yielding *knowledge*) or a probable argument. In the *Enquiry*, by contrast, he explicitly includes the stages that Stroud takes to be implicit:

> It is allowed on all hands, that there is no known connexion between the sensible qualities and the secret powers; and consequently, that the mind is not led to form such a conclusion concerning their constant and regular conjunction, by any thing which it knows of their nature. As to past *Experience*, it can be allowed to give *direct* and *certain* information of those precise objects only, and that precise period of time, which fell under its cognizance: But why this experience should be extended to future times, and to other objects, which, for aught we know, may be only in appearance similar; this is the main question on which I would insist. ... The connexion [from past to future] is not intuitive. There is required a medium, which may enable the mind to draw such an inference, if indeed it be drawn by reasoning and argument. (*Enquiry* 4.16)

Hume thus carefully rules out inference to the Uniformity Principle from anything that we can learn a priori through 'the sensible qualities' of bodies.[13] He also emphasizes the additional point that there is no intuitively evident link between past and future occurrences, so that we require some 'medium' or intermediate step—hence some demonstrative or probable reasoning—if we are to have a basis for extrapolating from one to the other (he then goes on to dismiss both types of reasoning in the familiar way). In short, where the *Treatise* rules out only demonstrative and probable argument as potential grounds for the Uniformity Principle, the *Enquiry* deals also with sensation and intuition.

All this impacts quite directly on the interpretation of Hume's famous argument, because one of the most popular recent heresies which I shall be discussing below, originally due to Don Garrett and then strongly promoted by Harold Noonan, holds that:

---

[12] The last of these passages, in which Hume presses the charge of circularity against any would-be inductive argument for the Principle, is immediately followed by a sentence beginning 'Shou'd any one think to elude this argument ...' (*Treatise* 1.3.6.8).

[13] For detailed analysis of the *Enquiry* argument, see my (1995) and especially (2002c). §§3.2 and 10.2 of the latter discuss the nature and role of the Uniformity Principle, while §4.1 explicates the relevant Humean notion of 'a priori'.

Hume should be interpreted ... as making a specific claim, within cognitive psychology, about the underlying causal mechanism that gives rise to inductive inferences: namely, that it is not itself dependent on any reasoning or inference. (Garrett, 2002, p. 333; cf. 1997, pp. 91–2)

Likewise David Owen, whose interpretation is in some respects followed by Helen Beebee, claims that Hume's fundamental concern is to rule out any possibility of *reasoning*—understood as ratiocination involving intermediate steps—that could underlie our inductive processes:

Hume ... is denying that [inductive] inferences can be explained as an activity of the faculty of reason conceived as functioning by the discovery of intermediate ideas ... (Owen, 1999, p. 132)

Both Garrett's analysis (1997, p. 82) and Owen's focus almost exclusively on the text of the *Treatise*, and both therefore ignore the wider scope of the *Enquiry* discussion, which as we have seen is not confined to argument by means of intermediate ideas. In the *Enquiry*, indeed, Hume does not even give overt priority to demonstrative and probable (i.e. 'moral') argument, since he moves on to consider them only after having ruled out sensation and intuition as potential sources of support for the Uniformity Principle. Consider now a passage from Hume's *Letter from a Gentleman to his friend in Edinburgh* (p. 22), composed in 1745 at exactly the time when he was working on the *Enquiry*:

It is common for Philosophers to distinguish the Kinds of Evidence into *intuitive*, *demonstrative*, *sensible*, and *moral*.

Is it coincidental that Hume's argument in *Enquiry* IV rules out exactly these four 'Kinds of Evidence' for the Uniformity Principle? I don't think so. But if he really does conceive his argument as ruling out *any kind of evidence* for the Principle, this puts a far more sceptical light on it than something like a mere denial that the Principle is 'dependent on ... reasoning ... conceived as functioning [through] intermediate ideas'. I would suggest, therefore, that the currently fashionable non-sceptical interpretations of Hume's argument derive much of their plausibility from their predominant reliance on the relatively cursory and crude version in the *Treatise*, and their neglect of the far more comprehensive, polished, and authoritative version in the *Enquiry*. Analysing the *Treatise* on induction—as on much else—may be more fun for Hume scholars, precisely because its confusing (and sometimes confused) unclarity allows so much more scope for inventive new interpretation. But the widespread focus on it as Hume's supposedly authoritative text, against his explicit and oft-repeated wishes, and in the teeth of such clear evidence of the *Enquiry*'s more systematic treatment of the issue, seems utterly indefensible.[14]

So much for my one unfashionable truth. Now let us move on to my four fashionable falsehoods.

V

What Does Hume Mean by 'Demonstrative'? Anyone who approaches Hume's texts having a basic familiarity with the standard distinctions of analytic philosophy is likely to be tempted to identify his notion of *demonstration* with what we now call *deduction*. Here of course I do not mean *formal* deduction; that would be most implausible given the informality of Hume's texts, and his contempt for the formal logic he knew. But his talk of 'demonstrative arguments' seems to map very easily onto our very familiar *informal* notion, of an argument whose premises guarantee the truth of its conclusion.[15] Yet a host of recent interpreters insist that any such identification would be mistaken,[16] and most of these take Hume's notion of a demonstrative argument to be confined to deductive arguments with a priori, and perhaps even self-evident, premises.

Two main pieces of evidence are usually given against the straightforward identification of Humean demonstration with de-

---

[14] This is not to deny value in investigating 'the view of the *Treatise*' on its own terms and independently of any later thoughts that Hume might have had. But if the aim of such an investigation is genuinely to establish Hume's own view in early 1739—rather than merely to use the *Treatise* text as a platform for imaginative 'rational reconstruction'—then it is obvious that some of the very best evidence to be had lies in Hume's published texts of 1740 and 1748, which treat many of the same topics as the *Treatise*, and sometimes do so far more clearly and unambiguously.

[15] Though it seems unlikely that Hume—with his dislike of the artificialities of formal logic—would have welcomed the somewhat paradoxical implications of the standard refinement of this informal notion, as an argument whose counterexample set is inconsistent. Hence I am unmoved by Owen's arguments that appeal to such considerations (1999, pp. 90–1).

[16] See, for example, Garrett (1997, p. 87), Owen (1999, p. 87), Buckle (2001, p. 166), and Beebee (2006, p. 20). For references to earlier scholars (Beauchamp and Rosenberg, Gaskin, Passmore, and Stove) see my (2002c, p. 113, n.36).

duction. First, the various passages in which he appears to say 'that there can be no demonstrative arguments for any conclusion concerning matter of fact' (Stove, 1973, p. 35). And secondly, his comments on the limited province of demonstration, most notably:

> It seems to me, that the only objects of the abstract sciences or of demonstration are quantity and number, and that all attempts to extend this more perfect species of knowledge beyond these bounds are mere sophistry and illusion. (*Enquiry* 12.27)

If Hume believes that demonstrative arguments can lead only to pure mathematical truths, and never to matters of fact, then doesn't that settle the question? Well, it would if he did believe these things, but in fact he doesn't believe either of them. To start with, his reason for limiting the scope of useful demonstration to the realm of mathematics has nothing to do with *apriority*, but is instead a matter of *precise composition* of ideas. The quotation above continues:

> As the component parts of quantity and number are entirely similar, their relations become intricate and involved [which enables us] to trace, by a variety of mediums, their equality or inequality, through their different appearances.

Non-mathematical ideas, by contrast, have no such identical component parts, so in attempting to reason demonstratively with them, 'we can never advance farther … than to observe this diversity'.

Notice, however, that in confining useful demonstrative argument to the realm of mathematics, Hume has not confined it only to *pure* mathematics. So the crucial test case has to be what he says about *applied* mathematics, in which the same precisely composed ideas are used, but within arguments whose premises and conclusions concern the contingent world. I have elsewhere (2002c, pp. 133–4) taken as illustration the example of conservation of momentum at *Enquiry* 4.13, where Hume makes a point of emphasizing the contingency of that physical law. But for variety I shall here turn instead to the *Treatise*:

> Mechanics are the art of regulating the motions of bodies *to some design'd end or purpose*; and the reason why we employ arithmetic in fixing the proportions of numbers, is only that we may discover the proportions of their influence and operation. A merchant is desirous of knowing the sum total of his accounts with any person: Why? but

that he may learn what sum will have the same *effects* in paying his debt, and going to market, as all the particular articles taken together. Abstract or demonstrative reasoning, therefore, never influences any of our actions, but only as it directs our judgment concerning causes and effects. (*Treatise* 2.3.3.2)

This looks pretty decisive: if demonstrative reasoning is applicable in this way to mechanics and accounting, then it's clearly not confined to the realm of a priori truths. Nor is it is possible to weasel out of this by claiming that applied mathematics is somehow purely hypothetical and therefore a priori after all. First, such a manoeuvre is psychologically implausible: the merchant does not think '*If* I owe her £60 plus £50 minus £20 *then* I owe her £90'.[17] But even if he did, in drawing the conclusion that he in fact owes £90 by *modus ponens*, he is still applying demonstrative reasoning to yield a contingent truth.[18]

All this is just as well for Hume, because if he were to insist that demonstrative reasoning can only have a priori premises and conclusions, then he would leave a massive lacuna in his logical taxonomy. He repeatedly insists that 'all reasonings may be divided into two kinds', namely *demonstrative* and *factual* (*Enquiry* 4.18, cf. *Treatise* 1.3.6.4, 2.3.3.2, 3.1.1.18), with the former proceeding on the basis of relations of ideas, and the latter on the basis of causal inference from experience. Moreover his argument concerning induction crucially depends on this claim, since he uses it to enumerate—with a view to elimination—'all the branches of hu-

---

[17] Besides which, if the line between categorical and hypothetical reasoning is blurred in this way, then it becomes impossible to sustain the view that Hume distinguishes between arguments on the basis of the modal status of their premises. An argument from one contingent premiss *P* to conclusion *Q* requires exactly the same logic as the corresponding argument with no contingent premiss and the conclusion *if P then Q*. Hume, I believe, would not distinguish between these, but those who hold that demonstrative reasoning is possible only from a priori premises clearly must do so.

[18] It seems deeply implausible to go to the extreme of denying that a simple application of *modus ponens* (if *P* then *Q*; *P*; therefore *Q*) or *modus tollens* (if *P* then *Q*; not-*Q*; therefore not-*P*) is demonstrative, purely on the grounds that *P* and *Q* themselves are contingent. Hume cannot consistently count such simple logical inference as 'reasoning concerning matter of fact' because it does not in any way depend on causation (cf. *Enquiry* 4.4), but it can hardly be ignored. Without it, Hume will be unable ever to draw a conclusion from any hypothetical piece of reasoning, even an application of *reductio ad absurdum*. For example, at *Treatise* 1.2.4.10 he talks of 'demonstrations from these very ideas to prove, that they are impossible'; but this sounds like a categorical rather than hypothetical conclusion. Note also the clear implication of this passage, that Hume doesn't in fact require the premises of a demonstration to be *possibly* true, let alone *self-evidently* or *a priori* true.

man knowledge' (*Enquiry* 4.17) that might be thought to furnish an argument for the Uniformity Principle. But if demonstration is restricted to deduction from a priori or self-evident premisses, then his supposedly exhaustive taxonomy is manifestly incomplete, overlooking entirely any deductive argument from contingent premisses.[19] This would be particularly egregious when his taxonomy is presented in the context of his discussion of inferences that may be drawn from a contingent premiss: 'such an object has always been attended with such an effect' (*Enquiry* 4.16). Hume has not lacked valiant defenders, going to great and elaborate lengths to save his system from disaster (e.g. Owen, 1999, pp. 87–112; Beebee, 2006, pp. 20–31), and one can learn much from their interesting discussions. But I believe their efforts to be entirely unnecessary: everything is much more straightforward if we simply identify 'demonstrative' with 'deductive', as generations of Hume's readers have been happy to do without a second thought.

That will do for the positive case, but how should we then respond to Stove's influential appeal to those familiar passages in which Hume appears to assert 'that there can be no demonstrative arguments for any conclusion concerning matter of fact'? Is he just flatly inconsistent? Well again, he might be if he were saying this, but in fact he never does. What he actually says is subtly different:

> To form a clear idea of any thing [is] a refutation of any pretended demonstration against it. (*Treatise* 1.3.6.5)

> [N]o matter of fact is capable of being demonstrated. (*Treatise* 3.1.1.18)

> [W]herever a demonstration takes place, the contrary ... implies a contradiction. (*Abstract* 11)

> What is possible can never be demonstrated to be false. (*Abstract* 14; cf. *Enquiry* 4.2)

> [The contrary of a matter of fact] can never be proved false by any demonstrative argument or abstract reasoning a priori. (*Enquiry* 4.18)

---

[19] Nor, as indicated in the previous note, can such deductions be classed as 'reasoning concerning matter of fact' on pain of even greater damage to Hume's system, since this would blow apart his fundamental claim that all factual inference is founded on causation and experience, on which he builds the core of his philosophy.

> [M]atter[s] of fact and existence are evidently incapable of demonstration. (*Enquiry* 12.28)

To focus on this difference, note that even in our everyday speech, we would draw a clear distinction between 'demonstrating Q' *tout court* and 'demonstrating Q *from* P'. And a similar point applies to what I claim to be our modern equivalent, 'deductive proof'. If I provide a valid argument from P to Q, then I can legitimately claim to have deductively proved Q *from* P. But if my premiss P itself is controversial or uncertain, then it would be grossly misleading of me to claim on this basis to have deductively proved Q *tout court*. Applying this lesson to the Humean quotations above, there is no difficulty whatever for my interpretation in Hume's denying that a matter of fact can be demonstrated *tout court*, or its contrary 'proved false by any demonstrative argument ... a priori'. Neither of these denials implies any such bar on demonstrating one matter of fact *from another*. Nor, I believe, is there any significant problem in dealing with Hume's claim that 'the contrary [of a demonstration] implies a contradiction'. If the demonstration in question is a proof of Q *from* P, then its 'contrary' is not simply the negation of Q, but rather the conjunction of P with that negation. And again this conforms with our everyday understanding: if I claim that P necessarily implies Q, and you contradict me, then you are clearly asserting that (P and not Q) is a possibility.

To sum up, then, Hume's notion of demonstration is best read in the most straightforward manner, as broadly equivalent to deduction (in the familiar informal sense). A successful demonstration is therefore a deductively valid argument, either from some hypothetical premiss(es) to a conclusion, or for a conclusion *tout court* (in which case any premisses must themselves be already certain). When Hume says that some proposition 'cannot be demonstrated', he invariably means the latter, as indeed would be expected from our own standard usage. All of Hume's relevant texts can, I believe, be straightforwardly understood in this way, and—unless this claim can be refuted—I would conclude that the far more complex interpretations proposed by Owen and Beebee are entirely unwarranted.

VI

Hume's Epistemology of Induction. I have written at considerable length on Hume's argument concerning induction, and it would be impossible here to rehearse all the objections that can be brought against the now fashionable claim that his argument is primarily descriptive rather than normative.[20] Instead, I shall repeat a simple challenge to those who take this view: to account for the *logic* of that argument in terms consistent with their interpretation. This requires a clear statement of the argument's premises and conclusion, an elucidation of the main concepts that play a significant role within it (such as the 'founded on' relation and the Uniformity Principle), and finally—most crucially—an explication of the argument's structure which demonstrates how its logical sequence is appropriate for getting from the premises to the conclusion.

All this might seem obvious and unproblematic, but in fact working out such an account within a non-normative, descriptive interpretation is far from straightforward, and this challenge (which I first delivered six years ago in the presence of Don Garrett and David Owen) is so far unanswered. To illustrate the difficulties, I shall focus mainly on Owen's interpretation,[21] according to which—as we saw earlier—the conclusion to Hume's argument can be glossed as follows:

> Hume ... is denying that [inductive] inferences can be explained as an activity of the faculty of reason conceived as functioning by the discovery of intermediate ideas ... (Owen, 1999, p. 132)

Hume's own stated conclusion is that factual inference is not 'founded on reason', so if Owen's interpretation is to work, 'X is founded on reason' must mean something like 'X is explicable in terms of ratiocination involving intermediate steps'. But consider now Hume's argument for this conclusion, which in broad outline,

---

[20] My 1995 paper gives detailed criticism of the old 'deductivist' (e.g. Stove) and 'anti-deductivist' (e.g. Beauchamp) interpretations, whereas (2002c) focuses more on Garrett and Owen, incorporating criticisms sketched originally in my PhD thesis of 1996 and presented at greater length in my (1998). Various of these later criticisms are collated, supplemented, and summarized very effectively by Loeb (2006, pp. 324–30). The challenge mentioned below is first presented at the end of my (2001), and then repeated in (2002c, §10.3).

[21] For more detailed criticism of a similar kind focusing on Garrett's interpretation, see my (1998; 2002c, pp. 157–60).

and on detailed textual grounds, I take to have the logical structure shown below:[22]

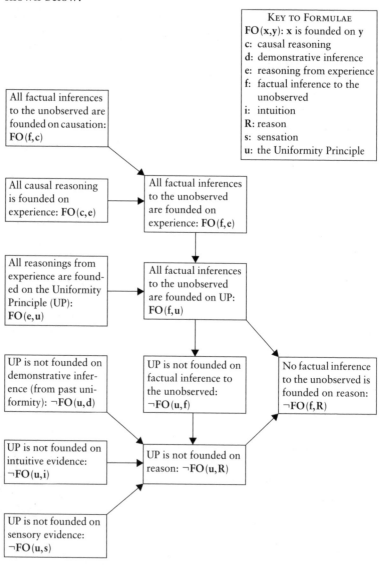

KEY TO FORMULAE
FO(x,y): x is founded on y
c: causal reasoning
d: demonstrative inference
e: reasoning from experience
f: factual inference to the
    unobserved
i: intuition
R: reason
s: sensation
u: the Uniformity Principle

All factual inferences to the unobserved are founded on causation: FO(f,c)

All causal reasoning is founded on experience: FO(c,e)

All factual inferences to the unobserved are founded on experience: FO(f,e)

All reasonings from experience are founded on the Uniformity Principle (UP): FO(e,u)

All factual inferences to the unobserved are founded on UP: FO(f,u)

UP is not founded on demonstrative inference (from past uniformity): ¬FO(u,d)

UP is not founded on factual inference to the unobserved: ¬FO(u,f)

No factual inference to the unobserved is founded on reason: ¬FO(f,R)

UP is not founded on intuitive evidence: ¬FO(u,i)

UP is not founded on reason: ¬FO(u,R)

UP is not founded on sensory evidence: ¬FO(u,s)

---

[22] See my (2002c, pp. 146–7) or pp. 170–3 for a more detailed analysis which is built up between pp. 120–39.

Suppose (though this is far from obvious) that Owen is able to explain all of this argument up to the final stage, and let us put to one side the query hinted at earlier, of why on his account Hume should show any interest in whether or not the Uniformity Principle can be founded on sensory or intuitive evidence (neither of which essentially involves intermediate ideas). The remaining problem is then to justify the concluding step:

> All factual inferences to the unobserved are founded on UP.
> UP is not founded on reason.
>
> ---
>
> ∴ No factual inference to the unobserved is founded on reason.

On Owen's account, recall, 'founded on reason' means roughly 'explicable in terms of ratiocination involving intermediate steps', and hence 'founded on the Uniformity Principle' presumably means something like 'explicable in terms of the Uniformity Principle'. But the mystery here is why Hume should then see this step as valid. Compare, for example, the following two short arguments:

> David's only surviving parent is Katherine.
> Katherine has no surviving ancestors.
>
> ---
>
> ∴ David has no surviving ancestors.

This is plainly invalid, because Katherine herself—if alive—furnishes David with a surviving ancestor, even though she has none herself.[23]

> Factual inference F is explicable in terms of UP.
> UP is not explicable in terms of ratiocination involving intermediate steps.
>
> ---
>
> ∴ Factual inference F is not explicable in terms of ratiocination involving intermediate steps.

---

[23] The argument is also invalid for another reason, since David's dead father could yet have surviving ancestors. This too provides some analogy to the argument that follows, if factual inference F is explained by UP together with some other proposition P which is itself explicable in terms of ratiocination. Here, however, I shall ignore this further difficulty for the Owen/Garrett/Noonan account.

If a factual inference F is founded on UP, then UP presumably plays some role in explaining F. Suppose that role is precisely to serve as an intermediate step by which F functions (so we might call UP a 'parent' proposition for F's conclusion). Clearly this is not in any way ruled out by the premiss that UP itself has no such intermediate-involving explanation (i.e. no 'parent' proposition of its own). On Owen's account, therefore, this argument is as invalid as the previous one, and it is left completely obscure why Hume should take for granted that a lack of *inferential* foundation for UP itself should then be 'inherited' by conclusions that are themselves *inferred* on the basis of UP.

Exactly the same sort of inheritance difficulty arises on the account of Garrett and Noonan, who interpret 'X is founded on reason' as (roughly) 'X is caused by argument'. For the fact—if it be one—that a belief in UP is not caused by argument cannot prevent UP from itself featuring in an argument that causes some *further* belief. UP could be a whimsy, an innate prejudice, a God-given instinctive belief, or whatever: none of this would a priori prevent it from playing a role in argument for *other* propositions. So the entire structure of Hume's argument is rendered inexplicable on this interpretation: we have been given no apparent reason why the foundation of the Uniformity Principle itself should be thought to have any direct relevance to the question supposedly at issue (i.e. whether individual factual inferences are 'caused by argument'). The only recourse seems to be to appeal to very un-Humean rationalist prejudices, such as those expressed by Noonan, who recognizes the problem and attempts to address it:

> We could not be caused to engage in the practice of inductive inference by our acceptance of an argument, a premiss of which was the Uniformity Principle, unless we also had available an argument *for* the Uniformity Principle (for we could not believe in the Uniformity Principle, antecedently to acquiring a disposition to engage in inductive inference, except on the basis of argument). (Noonan, 1999, pp. 119–20)

But where has Hume given any rationale whatever for saying that 'we could not believe in the Uniformity Principle ... except on the basis of argument'? Surely one of the main points of his philosophy is precisely that we *do*, and *have to*, take that Principle for granted all the time, even though it has no independent foundation! The same objection can be made against Owen, and—with a caveat to be discussed in §VII below—against Beebee:

> [S]ince [the Uniformity Principle] is neither intuited nor sensed, then if it is available to us at all, it must be known demonstratively or believed as a result of probable reasoning. (Owen, 1999, p. 129)

> We cannot know *a priori* ... that unobserved instances resemble observed instances ... Nor can we come to *believe* [this] Uniformity Principle without employing causal reasoning. (Beebee, 2006, p. 44)

Such interpretations are thus forced to turn Hume into a twofold rationalist about the human mind. First, he thinks that we can only come to have belief in the Uniformity Principle on some (at least quasi-) rational basis: it cannot just be the causal result of a brute instinct, a whimsy, or whatever. Secondly, he can supposedly tell a priori that this must be the case: in framing his discussion of induction, he is apparently purporting to have a priori knowledge of the mind's causal processes!

This entire problem disappears if '*X* is founded on *Y*' is interpreted *normatively* rather than just causally, as involving *the derivation of rational authority* (an interpretation I justify at length in my 2001 and 2002c, §10.1). For it seems clear that a proposition can pass on rational authority to its 'inheritors' only if it has such authority itself. The final stage of Hume's argument then becomes the plainly valid:

> Factual inferences to the unobserved derive whatever authority they possess from UP.
> UP has no authority derived from reason.
> _____
> ∴ No factual inference to the unobserved has authority derived from reason.

But any such normative interpretation will make the negative conclusion of the argument, at least to some extent, sceptical.[24] To sum

---

[24] Beebee (2006) is non-committal regarding the nature of Hume's conclusion, but she instances Owen's and Garrett's interpretations as illustrating 'that Hume's remarks about our not being "determin'd by reason" to infer from causes to effects are perfectly consistent with the claim that he is no inductive sceptic' (p. 40). If my argument here is successful, however, their interpretations fail to provide any such illustration.

up, proponents of the recently fashionable non-sceptical readings of Hume's famous argument have apparently tended to assume that its logic can survive transposition from a normative to a descriptive key. But it is far from clear that this is the case, and the challenge remains.

VII

Humean Externalism? Very recently yet another novel interpretation of Hume on induction has been proposed by Louis Loeb, sharing some interesting features with Helen Beebee's discussion. Loeb endorses the criticisms I have made of what he calls the 'descriptivist' readings of Hume, but he is anxious also to avoid any sceptical interpretation, given the manifest and widespread evidence that Hume is committed to inductive science. Loeb finds a surprising middle way between these two extremes, by suggesting that Hume is a non-sceptical *externalist*, who takes for granted from the start that induction is epistemically justified, and indeed sees that as part of what is to be explained:

> Does recognition of the epistemic character of [*Treatise* 1.3.6] saddle us with the skeptical interpretation ... after all? It would, if Hume thought that a belief is justified only if it is supported or supportable by good argument. Roughly speaking, this is an *internalist* assumption. ... In light of the massive evidence that Hume is not a skeptic about induction, he must reject this internalist way of thinking. (Loeb, 2006, p. 333)

> The linchpin in my interpretation is ... [that Hume] incorporates this positive epistemic status into his description of the subject matter under investigation. ... [T]he assumption that inductive inference is justified *is* part and parcel of the *phenomenon under investigation* ... (Loeb, 2006, pp. 330–1)

Helen Beebee hints at a somewhat similar approach, though without stressing any externalist implications:

> Hume's argumentative method in his discussion of the Uniformity Principle *presupposes* that causal reasoning is 'just' reasoning. After all, why should we think that the Uniformity Principle depends on the relation between causes and effects, as Hume claims? Because that relation is

'the only one, on which we can found a *just* inference from one object to another' ... if he did not think that causal reasoning is 'just' inference ... he would not be in a position to claim that the Uniformity Principle depends on causal reasoning, since there are many other possible sources of the principle (see Millican 2002[c]: 157–8). ... Presumably Hume ignores [these] other possible sources ... because they *manifestly* do not provide a 'just' way of inferring effects from causes. ... The upshot of all this is that Hume is not *solely* concerned with the genetic question [of the causal basis of our inductive beliefs]. ... But it does not follow that he is interested in whether or not causal reasoning can be justified. On the contrary: it is his *assumption* that causal reasoning is just reasoning that explains this omission. (Beebee, 2006, pp. 55–6)

This is an ingenious way of attempting to square the circle, by introducing normative constraints into a discussion whose upshot is nevertheless seen as descriptive. If we can take for granted from the start that the causal explanation of inductive inference must render it epistemically justified, then this will indeed restrict the range of acceptable explanations to those that satisfy normative requirements, and thus evade the objections of §VI above which devastate a purely 'descriptivist' approach.[25]

But there is, I suggest, an elephant in the room, namely, the clearly negative thrust of Hume's argument, which delivers no such epistemically satisfying explanation, and indeed appears to rule out the very possibility. Having identified the Uniformity Principle as the essential prerequisite for any rational foundation of factual inference, Hume then explicitly and systematically eliminates any possible rational foundation for the Uniformity Principle itself,[26] and he goes on to draw the natural conclusion, that factual inference lacks any

---

[25] Perhaps there is space—at least on Beebee's account—for taking Hume to be merely seeking a causal explanation that does not *conflict* with its being epistemically justified. Then the idea would be that normative constraints enter into his famous argument because explanation in terms of a Uniformity Principle that is founded on whimsy or innate prejudice (etc.) would be ruled out. However this seems rather implausible: *if* Hume can accept that induction is somehow justified, in a way that does not depend *at all* on rational considerations, then why should the involvement of *faulty* rational considerations undermine this? The point is particularly clear if we consider the possibility that the Uniformity Principle might be a natural belief providentially implanted by God. It is hard to envisage a conception of justification which would, on the one hand, rule out reliance on any such natural belief as incompatible with justification, but on the other hand, accept that induction is nevertheless justified in some way that doesn't depend on our use of reason. An externalist could not do the former, and an internalist could not do the latter.

[26] Again, this is particularly clear in the *Enquiry* version of the argument: see §IV above.

foundation in reason. Nothing here suggests that he is taking for granted that factual inference is justified; quite the reverse. And at least in the *Enquiry*, he entitles his section 'Sceptical Doubts Concerning the Operations of the Understanding', and later refers back to his argument as containing '*philosophical* objections' that give 'the sceptic ... ample matter of triumph' (*Enquiry* 12.22). Even Hume's ultimate appeal to custom—the 'Sceptical Solution' to his 'Sceptical Doubts'—seems an unlikely candidate as an explanation intended to deliver epistemic justification:

> [N]othing leads us to this inference but custom or a certain instinct of our nature; which it is indeed difficult to resist, but which, like other instincts, may be fallacious and deceitful. (*Enquiry* 12.23)

Hume is clearly aware that custom's having served us well in the past gives no guarantee whatever for the future. So even if he is tempted towards externalist considerations in pondering custom's *past* success (e.g. in delivering apparent truth, reliability or stability to our beliefs), he cannot extrapolate these into the future and commend custom on that basis, unless he is *already* under the spell of inductive convictions. He is, of course, under this spell: he does, in fact, firmly believe that the future will resemble the past, that the same causal laws will continue to operate, and that custom will continue to be reliable. But if the future externalist sanction of custom depends entirely on the truth of this inductive belief, then what benefit does that hypothetical sanction bring? The epistemic problem that Hume seems to be addressing is why we should be justified in believing anything about the *future*, in advance of knowing how well custom will serve us. If this is his agenda, then any appeal to custom's externalist virtues 'must be evidently going in a circle, and taking that for granted, which is the very point in question' (*Enquiry* 4.19).

All this suggests that externalism is ill-suited to providing what Hume—on these interpretations—is supposed to be looking for: an account of induction that explains why it is epistemically justified. There seems to be something peculiarly problematic about appealing to externalism to justify induction (as opposed to perception, say, or even specific inductive beliefs), since any inference to induction's *enduring* reliability, truth, stability, or whatever, presupposes *exactly* the point in question. Some have suggested that the problem might be tractable by using second-order inductive arguments to justify first-order induction from an externalist perspective (see Lipton, 2000). But given how uncompromisingly Hume dismisses as circular the *Enquiry* 4.21 argument from past regularity of powers to future powers, I find the attribution of any such viewpoint to him deeply implausible. It is also, I would suggest, quite unnecessary.

As we have seen, Loeb attributes externalism to Hume on the ground that it is the only way of resolving what would otherwise be a contradiction, between the sceptical internalism of his famous argument, and his positive attitude to inductive science. But this is not the only option left, nor is it the best. Far simpler is to allow Hume to build *directly* on his basic inductive belief that the world is uniform, the same belief that an externalist Hume *must* appeal to anyway to get his account off the ground. If Hume is right to say that we cannot help having this belief, then even if his sceptical argument succeeds in denying it any rational foundation, the plain fact is that we are stuck with it. Well, if we are stuck with it, then let us at least reason consistently on that basis, for consistency is clearly a rational virtue. 'But why should there be any virtue in being consistent with a totally unjustified belief?' That response misses the point by ignoring our genuine doxastic immersion: if we really *believe* that the world is uniform, then in seeking consistency with that belief, we are motivated by consistency with what we take to be *true*. That, at any rate, is surely a paradigm internalist epistemic virtue.

In short, there is available to Hume a straightforward way of reconciling his sceptical argument with inductive science, without compromising the scepticism, and without having to take on board any interpretatively implausible (and surely anachronistic) externalism. Now is not the time to explore this further, but I believe it can provide the basis for a persuasive account of Hume's epistemology and philosophy of science, especially as portrayed in his *Enquiry Concerning Human Understanding*.[27]

---

[27] For much more on this, see Millican (2002b; 2002c, §§11–12; 2007a). My new edition of the *Enquiry*, Hume (2007), is informed by this perspective, and has the aim of explicating the work as a thoroughly coherent and self-contained presentation of Hume's core philosophy, responding to the historical context explained in the edition's Introduction.

VIII

The New Hume, Liberty, and Necessity. The contentious and sometimes heated 'New Hume' debate over Hume's metaphysics of causation is far too big to take on comprehensively here, but in my
survey of prominent 'Humean heresies' it could hardly be overlooked. Having recently written a substantial discussion of the debate as a whole—coming down strongly on the 'Old Hume' side—I
shall make do with referring readers to that for most of the issues
(2007b), and focus here on just one: the vital, but generally ignored,
connections with Hume's treatment of 'liberty and necessity', or as
we call it today, 'free will and determinism'.

   This crucial finale of Hume's 'chief argument' is presented first in
two sections of Book II of the *Treatise*, is given no fewer than four
paragraphs in the *Abstract*, and constitutes the principal subject-
matter of the longest section of the *Enquiry*.[28] Moreover it involves
the only clear and repeated application of Hume's two 'definitions
of cause', which are amongst the most famous passages in his entire
corpus. In the *Enquiry*, this link is explicitly highlighted by the posi-
tioning and naming of the relevant sections, with the two definitions
occurring in the penultimate paragraph of Section VII, 'Of the Idea
of Necessary Connexion', and their application being explained in
the first six paragraphs of Section VIII, 'Of Liberty and Necessity'.
Yet most students of Hume's philosophy are taught about his views
on causation without any mention of this crucial argument, and it is
commonly omitted completely from books on his philosophy. Most
surprising of all, it has even been generally overlooked in the literature of the recent New Hume debate, even though the main topic of
that debate is precisely the interpretation of Hume's views on causation and necessity![29] Such is the impact of what I consider to be the
lopsided enduring focus on the text and topics of *Treatise* Book I to
the exclusion of Hume's more mature philosophical works, in clear
violation—as we saw in §IV above—of his explicit and settled
wishes.

---

[28] At least as measured by body text, though Section X is longer if the note on Jansenist miracles is included. Both of these sections are significantly longer than any other, together
making up over 30% of the *Enquiry* text.
[29] In Read and Richman's collection *The New Hume Debate*, for example, not one of the
authors mentions the role of the two definitions in Hume's argument on liberty and necessity, and only Winkler (1991, pp. 73–4) even refers to their occurrence there.

Hume's key argument concerning liberty and necessity is very explicit, straightforward, and logical, and it is consistent in all three presentations, though its main stages appear at various places and sometimes differently ordered:[30]

    (1) A cause may be defined in one of two ways:

       either 'an object, followed by another, and where all the objects, similar to the first, are followed by objects similar to the second'

       or   'an object followed by another, and whose appearance always conveys the thought to that other' (*Enquiry* 7.29; cf. *Treatise* 1.3.14.31, *Abstract* 32).

    (2) '*Necessity* may be defined two ways, conformably to the two definitions of *cause*, of which it makes an essential part. It consists

       either in the constant conjunction of like objects

       or   in the inference of the understanding from one object to another' (*Enquiry* 8.27; cf. *Treatise* 2.3.1.4, *Treatise* 2.3.2.4, *Abstract* 32, *Enquiry* 8.5).

    (3) 'These two circumstances form the whole of that necessity, which we ascribe to matter. Beyond the constant *conjunction* of similar objects, and the consequent *inference* from one to the other, we have no notion of any necessity, or connexion' (*Enquiry* 8.5; cf. *Treatise* 1.4.14.33, *Enquiry* 8.21–2).

    (4) 'If it appear, therefore, that all mankind have ever allowed … that these two circumstances take place in the voluntary actions of men, and in the operations of the mind; it must follow, that all mankind have ever agreed in the doctrine of necessity' [i.e. the doctrine that determinism applies to human actions and the mind's operations, just as it does to material things] (*Enquiry* 8.6; cf. *Treatise* 2.3.1.3).

---

[30] In particular, the argument occurs twice both in the *Treatise* and the *Enquiry*, first to make the case as presented here, and then relatively briefly (*Treatise* 2.3.2.4, *Enquiry* 8.27) with a different emphasis, to remove an objection based on its supposed pernicious consequences. In this second occurrence, Hume's concern is to show that the necessity he ascribes to the mind is 'innocent', neither conflicting with 'orthodoxy' nor undermining morality. So here he stresses the apparent relative mildness of his notion of necessity, rather than the central point of his argument that this notion of necessity is the only one available.

(5) '[I]t appears, not only that the conjunction between motives and voluntary actions is as regular and uniform, as that between the cause and effect in any part of nature; but also that this regular conjunction has been universally acknowledged among mankind' (*Enquiry* 8.16; cf. *Treatise* 2.3.1.16, *Treatise* 2.3.2.4, *Abstract* 32, *Enquiry* 8.27).

(6) '[T]his experienced uniformity in human actions, is a source, whence we draw *inferences* concerning them ... this experimental inference and reasoning concerning the actions of others enters so much into human life, that no man, while awake, is ever a moment without employing it' (*Enquiry* 8.16–17; cf. *Treatise* 2.3.1.17, *Treatise* 2.3.2.4, *Abstract* 33, *Enquiry* 8.18–20, *Enquiry* 8.27).

(7) 'It may ... perhaps, be pretended, that the mind can perceive, in the operations of matter, some farther connexion between the cause and effect; and a connexion that has not place in the voluntary actions of intelligent beings' (*Enquiry* 8.21; cf. *Enquiry* 8.27, *Treatise* 2.3.2.4, *Abstract* 34).

(8) But the mind cannot even frame an idea of any such farther connexion: 'a constant conjunction of objects, and subsequent inference of the mind from one to another ... form, in reality, the whole of that necessity which we conceive in matter', and 'there is no idea of any other necessity or connexion in the actions of body' (*Enquiry* 8.22 and 8.27; cf. *Treatise* 2.3.2.4, *Abstract* 34).

These last four stages are elegantly summarized in the *Abstract* (34):

> [T]he most zealous advocates for free-will must allow this union and inference with regard to human actions. They will only deny, that this makes the whole of necessity. But then they must shew, that we have an idea of something else in the actions of matter; which, according to the foregoing reasoning, is impossible.

Note that here Hume is explicitly appealing to the limits of coherent thought, as revealed by his search for the impression of necessary connexion, and summarized at stage (3):

Beyond the constant *conjunction* of similar objects, and the consequent *inference* from one to the other, we have no notion of any necessity, or connexion.

Thus his libertarian opponent, in supposing that 'the actions of matter' involve some objective necessity that outruns the Humean definitions, is trying to think the unthinkable.

This simple argument, is—it seems to me—a torpedo into the
core of the New Humeans' position, for Hume is here denying exactly what they assert, namely, that we can coherently ascribe to
things some kind of 'upper-case' Causation or 'thick' necessity that
goes beyond his two definitions. If we could indeed do this, then the
libertarian would be able to ascribe that thick necessity to matter
but not to minds, and thus undermine Hume's claim of equivalence
between the necessity of the two domains, which is the entire point
of his argument. Nor can there be any serious doubt about his intentions here: the argument occurs in the *Treatise*, the *Abstract* and
the *Enquiry*, and it is the principal application of his two definitions
in all three of these works. Those definitions are clearly intended
precisely for this role, and it is a role that requires them to be interpreted *semantically* rather than merely *epistemologically*: as con-
straining what we are able to *mean* or coherently refer to. Thus we
can completely invert the typical New Humean claim, that we
should 'view Hume's talk about "meaning" as meaning "acquaintance with", as opposed to "thinkable content"' (Kail, 2001, p. 39).
To the contrary: when Hume tells us that he plans to give 'a precise
definition of cause and effect' to 'fix their meaning' (*Treatise*
1.3.14.30), he is preparing the ground for one of his most important
arguments, which turns crucially on the use of his definitions to circumscribe the limits of our thinkable content.[31]

---

[31] In the *Treatise* there is another important argument that rarely gets into the standard text-
books, in the long section 'Of the Immateriality of the Soul'. This is an attack on those who
claim that thinking matter is impossible (usually with a theological agenda, cf. my 2007a, §6),
and again appeals to Hume's analysis of causation. Having argued 'that all objects, which are
found to be constantly conjoin'd, are upon that account alone to be regarded as causes and
effects', he draws the corollary 'that for aught we can determine by the mere ideas, any thing
may be the cause or effect of any thing' (1.4.5.32). This then clears the way for concluding
that 'as the constant conjunction of objects constitutes the very essence of cause and effect,
matter and motion may often be regarded as the causes of thought' (1.4.5.33). Here Hume's
underlying project is much the same as in his discussion of liberty and necessity: to bring the
mental realm within the reach of causal explanation and thus open the way for systematic
inductive moral science, in opposition to aprioristic metaphysics or superstition.

IX

Conclusion: Hume and Inductive Science. I started by declaring my allegiance to an 'Old Hume' who is sceptical about induction, re-ductionist about causation, soft determinist about free will, and who acknowledges (more or less) the same fundamental logical dis-tinctions that would have been familiar to a twentieth-century posi-tivist: between analytic and synthetic propositions (i.e. relations of ideas and matters of fact), and between deduction and induction (i.e. demonstrative and factual reasoning). But despite all this agree-ment with interpretative tradition, it is probably clear by now that my picture of Hume's philosophy is in other respects very different from the classic sceptical caricature. Here the most crucial need is to get a balanced view of Hume's 'scepticism' about induction. On the one hand, I have insisted—against Garrett, Owen, Noonan and Beebee—that Hume's famous argument on the matter is *genuinely* sceptical, and I have rejected Loeb's suggestion that he is an exter-nalist. But it would be quite wrong to conclude from this that, as Loeb would imply, the only logical space remaining is that of the traditional undiscrimating sceptic for whom (in Stroud's delightful phrase) 'as far as the competition for degrees of reasonableness is concerned, all possible beliefs about the unobserved are tied for last place' (1977, p. 54). Indeed it is this false dichotomy—the assump-tion that Hume's attitude to induction must either be totally scepti-cal, or totally non-sceptical—that lies behind so many distorted interpretations of his philosophy.

The key to Hume's attitude is to focus clearly on what his scepti-cal argument is attacking, and I have argued at length elsewhere (2002c) that his primary target is Locke's view of probable reason-ing as founded on rational *perception*. Hume obliterates this target, by proving that our inductive inferences must all take for granted something that cannot be rationally perceived, namely, that the past is a guide to the future (or more precisely, that the behaviour of things we have observed is *positively evidentially relevant* to the be-haviour of things we have not observed). So far, Hume's argument is indeed purely sceptical, but he does not rest there. Because his result is so fundamental, impacting on all our beliefs that outrun the nar-row reach of our senses and memory, he has no option but to move beyond it, and nor do we. Here a reasoned pragmatic argument can be given, on the basis that accepting some beliefs is better than rejecting all. But in practice any such strategic deliberation is unnecessary, because a far more pressing pragmatic factor comes into play. The instinctive mechanism of *custom*, though not in any way supplying the rational perception that Locke had taken for granted as a requirement for rational belief, steps into the breach and leaves us psychologically unable to refrain from forming beliefs about the unobserved.

Having identified custom as the 'sceptical solution' to his 'sceptical doubts', Hume's procedure is to follow through its demands systematically. If we cannot help making judgements and forming beliefs on the basis of conformity with our past experience, then we can at least be discriminating in applying this standard.[32] We can also dismiss aprioristic metaphysics, since only experience can receive custom's endorsement. The best illustration of Hume's application of this technique is to the case of miracles, which is yet another very important section of his philosophy that is all too frequently neglected in discussions of his epistemology, partly because it had the misfortune to be removed from *Treatise* Book I when Hume 'castrated' that work shortly before publication.[33] What Hume first does in this case is to emphasize that testimony lacks any a priori warrant, its strength being derived from the inductive force of custom. Thus the religionist's own belief in a miracle is itself implicitly founded on custom, in so far as experience tells in favour of the credibility of the reporting witnesses. Against this, Hume now sets the countervailing inductive evidence of nature's lawlike uniformity, together with a range of observations that highlight the relative empirical unreliability of testimony (especially when religiously inspired). Whether all this can succeed as a way of vindicating empirical science over superstition can, of course, be debated. But I think it is very clear that Hume himself was committed to something like this strategy, which is sufficient to refute that pervasive false dichotomy which has for so long bedevilled his interpreters. The key to understanding Hume is to appreciate that he is *both* deeply sceptical about induction (in a sense), *and* totally committed to inductive science.

---

[32] As I have sketched in response to Loeb in §VII above, such a prescription can perfectly well be supported by appeal to rational considerations that are conventionally internalist.

[33] See *New Letters*, p. 2 and Millican (2002b, p. 34).

A somewhat similar conclusion can be drawn about his view of causation, though the case for this must be made elsewhere (cf. my 2007b). On the one hand, Hume is deeply sceptical about what causation is usually taken to be, and he denies even the meaningfulness of anything that purports to go beyond functional relations of regular succession and our corresponding tendency to make customary inferences.[34] On the other hand, and as in the case of induction, this negative result makes room for a positive thesis, that causation— *genuine causation*—is to be understood in accordance with his two definitions, and that we should apply it accordingly. Hence his unequivocal recommendation 'that all objects, which are found to be constantly conjoin'd, are upon that account alone to be regarded as causes and effects' (1.4.5.32). This is central to much of his mature philosophy, for as we saw in §VIII above, it is the basis for his insistence that deterministic causal laws are as applicable to the moral world as to the natural, and thus paves the way for his advocacy of inductive moral science.

Hume's philosophy involves a delicate balance between science and scepticism, which play complementary roles in his overall project: on the one hand to promote systematic inductive investigation of man and nature, and on the other hand, to undermine any would-be alternative way of understanding the world, whether through aprioristic metaphysics or religious doctrine. These themes—both positive and negative—dominate most of his philosophical writings, from the *Essays* whose publication began in 1741, through the first *Enquiry* in 1748, the *Four Dissertations* and especially the *Natural History of Religion* of 1757, and ultimately the *Dialogues Concerning Natural Religion* which Hume prepared for publication on his deathbed. They are also pervasive in the *Treatise*, though not so emphasized or clearly developed, presumably because in that 'juvenile work' Hume had yet to clarify the main focus of his thought. 'Carry'd away by the Heat of Youth & Invention' (*Letters*, i, 158), he could not resist packing his work with fascinating but confusing lines of thought on other topics, including his du-

---

[34] The phrase 'functional relations of regular succession' is intended to take into account Hume's full recognition that scientific causal laws tend to be framed in terms of complex mathematical relationships involving quantitative forces (e.g. *Enquiry* 4.13, 7.25 n.16, 7.29 n.17), rather than just the simple 'constant conjunctions' on which he tends to focus in his discussions. For more on this, see my (2002c, §9.2) and especially (2007b, §3.2).

biously aprioristic discussions of space and time, and those
famously obscure arguments on the external world and personal
identity that continue to challenge his commentators. The latter are
dramatic and conveniently focused on familiar 'topics' of the history
of philosophy curriculum, but they play relatively little role in his
overall philosophical orientation or his mature thought. If we wish
to understand the central thrust of Hume's epistemology and metaphysics correctly, I suggest, then it is instead to the later works, and
especially the first *Enquiry*, that we must turn.[35]

REFERENCES

Beebee, H. 2006: *Hume on Causation* (London: Routledge).
Botterill, G. 2002: 'Hume on Liberty and Necessity', in Millican (2002a,
    pp. 277–300).
Buckle, S. 2001: *Hume's Enlightenment Tract: The Unity and Purpose of An
    Enquiry Concerning Human Understanding* (Oxford: Clarendon Press).
Craig, E. 1987: *The Mind of God and the Works of Man* (Oxford: Claren-
    don Press).
Earman, J. 2000: *Hume's Abject Failure: The Argument against Miracles*
    (Oxford and New York: Oxford University Press).
Flew, A. 1961: *Hume's Philosophy of Belief* (London: Routledge & Kegan
    Paul).
Garrett, D. 1997: *Cognition and Commitment in Hume's Philosophy* (Ox-
    ford and New York: Oxford University Press).
——2002: 'The Meaning of Hume's Conclusion Concerning "Inductive"
    Inferences', in Millican (2002a, pp. 332–4).
Harris, J. A. 2003: 'Hume's Reconciling Project and "The Common Dis-
    tinction betwixt *Moral* and *Physical* Necessity"', *British Journal for the
    History of Philosophy*, 11, pp. 451–71.
——2005: *Of Liberty and Necessity: The Free Will Debate in Eighteenth-
    Century British Philosophy* (Oxford: Clarendon Press).
Hume, D. 1739–40: *A Treatise of Human Nature,* ed. D. F. Norton and
    M. J. Norton (Oxford and New York: Oxford University Press, 2000).
    (References given to book, part, section and paragraph numbers, or to
    paragraph number of the *Appendix*.)

---

[35] For discussions on the topics of this paper over the years, I am especially grateful to Mar-
tin Bell, Simon Blackburn, Lorne Falkenstein, Don Garrett, Jani Hakkarainen, James Harris, Peter Kail, Peter Lipton, Louis Loeb, David Owen, Paul Russell, Ken Winkler and John
Wright.

——1740: *Abstract* of the *Treatise*, ed. P. Millican, in Millican (2002a, pp. 399–411). (References given to paragraph numbers.)

——1741–77: *Essays, Moral, Political, and Literary*, ed. E. F. Miller (Indianapolis: Liberty Classics, 2nd edn., 1987). (References indicated by '*Essays*'.)

——1745: *A Letter from a Gentleman to his Friend in Edinburgh*, ed. E. C. Mossner and J. V. Price (Edinburgh: Edinburgh University Press, 1967).

——1748: *An Enquiry Concerning Human Understanding*, ed. T. L. Beauchamp (Oxford and New York: Oxford University Press, 1999). (References given to section and paragraph numbers.)

——1777: 'My Own Life', ed. P. Millican, in Millican (2002a, pp. 393–8).

——1932: *The Letters of David Hume*, ed. J. Y. T. Greig (Oxford: Clarendon Press). (References indicated by '*Letters*'.)

——1978: *New Letters of David Hume*, ed. R. Klibansky and J. V. Price (Oxford: Clarendon Press). (References indicated by '*New Letters*'.)

——2007: *An Enquiry Concerning Human Understanding* [1777 edition], ed. P. Millican (Oxford: Oxford University Press).

Kail, P. 2001: 'Projection and Necessity in Hume', *European Journal of Philosophy*, 9, pp. 24–54.

Lipton, P. 2000: 'Tracking Truth Records', *Proceedings of the Aristotelian Society Supplementary Volume* 74, pp. 179–205.

Loeb, L. 2002: *Stability and Justification in Hume's Treatise* (New York: Oxford University Press).

——2006: 'Psychology, Epistemology, and Skepticism in Hume's Argument about Induction', *Synthese*, 152, pp. 321–38.

Millican, P. 1993: '"Hume's Theorem" Concerning Miracles', *Philosophical Quarterly*, 43, pp. 489–95.

——1995: 'Hume's Argument Concerning Induction: Structure and Interpretation', in S. Tweyman (ed.), *David Hume: Critical Assessments*, Volume 2, (London: Routledge), pp. 91–144; reprinted in Owen (2000, pp. 165–218).

——1998: 'Hume on Reason and Induction: Epistemology or Cognitive Science?', *Hume Studies*, 24, pp.141–59.

——2001: 'The Logic of Hume's Sceptical Doubts'. Presented to the Hume Conference, Victoria, British Columbia, and available from <http://www.davidhume.org>.

——2002a (ed.): *Reading Hume on Human Understanding: Essays on the First Enquiry* (Oxford: Clarendon Press). (See 2002b, 2002c and 2002d below.)

——2002b: 'The Context, Aims, and Structure of Hume's First *Enquiry*'; chapter 1 of 2002a, pp. 27–65.

——2002c: 'Hume's Sceptical Doubts Concerning Induction'; chapter 4 of 2002a, pp. 107–73.

——2002d: 'Critical Survey of the Literature on Hume and the First *Enquiry*', in 2002a, pp. 413–74.
——2003: 'Hume, Miracles, and Probabilities: Meeting Earman's Challenge'. Presented to the Hume Conference, Las Vegas, and available from <http://www. davidhume.org>.
——2006: 'Hume's "Compleat Answer to Dr Reid"'. Presented to the Hume Conference, Koblenz, and available from <http://www.davidhume.org>.
——2007a: 'Introduction' to Hume (2007, pp. ix–lvi).
——2007b: 'Against the New Hume', forthcoming in R. Read and K. A. Richman (eds.), *The New Hume Debate*, 2nd edn. (London: Routledge).
——2008: 'Hume's Determinism', forthcoming in *Canadian Journal of Philosophy*.
Noonan, H. 1999: *Hume on Knowledge* (London: Routledge).
Owen, D. 1999: *Hume's Reason* (New York: Oxford University Press).
——2000 (ed): *Hume: General Philosophy* (Aldershot: Ashgate).
Read, R. and K. A. Richman (eds.) 2000: *The New Hume Debate*, 1st edn. (London: Routledge).
Stove, D. 1973: *Probability and Hume's Inductive Scepticism* (Oxford: Clarendon Press).
Strawson, G. 1989: *The Secret Connexion: Causation, Realism, and David Hume* (Oxford: Clarendon Press).
Stroud, B. 1977: *Hume* (London: Routledge & Kegan Paul).
Winkler, K. P. 1991: 'The New Hume', *Philosophical Review*, 100, pp. 541–79; reprinted in Owen (2000, pp. 347–85) and in Read and Richman (2000, pp. 52–74).
Wright, J. P. 1983: *The Sceptical Realism of David Hume* (Manchester: Manchester University Press).

Neo-Fregeanism and Quantifier Variance
Theodore Sider and Katherine Hawley

I—Theodore Sider

Neo-Fregeanism and Quantifier Variance

Neo-Fregeans say that a definition by abstraction (e.g. 'the direction of line 1 = the direction of line 2 iff lines 1 and 2 are parallel') 'reconceptualizes' its subject matter (talk of parallelism among lines is reconceptualized as talk about new entities, directions). What does that mean? Suppose Neo-Fregeans accepted 'quantifier variance': there are many equally good things one can mean by quantifiers. Reconceptualization could then mean: selecting a meaning for the quantifiers under which the definition comes out true.

Neo-Fregeanism is an intriguing but elusive philosophy of mathematical existence. At crucial points, it goes cryptic and metaphorical. I want to put forward an interpretation of neo-Fregeanism—perhaps not one that actual neo-Fregeans will embrace—that makes sense of much of what they say. Neo-Fregeans should embrace *quantifier variance*.[1]

I

Neo-Fregeanism. The neo-Fregeanism of Bob Hale and Crispin Wright is an attempt to resuscitate Frege's logicism about arithmetic. Its goal is to combine two ideas. First: platonism about arithmetic. There really do exist numbers; numbers are mind-independent. Second: logicism. Arithmetic derives from logic plus definitions. Thus, arithmetic knowledge rests on logical knowledge, even though its object is a realm of mind-independent abstract entities.

1.1. Frege on Arithmetic. Let us review Frege's attempt to derive arithmetic from logic plus definitions. 'Arithmetic' here means second-order Peano arithmetic. 'Logic' means (impredicative) second-

---

[1] I recommend quantifier variance to neo-Fregeans about non-mathematical ontology as well (e.g. Schiffer, 2003). The term 'quantifier variance' is from Hirsch (2002b).

order logic.[2] The 'definition' is what is now known as *Hume's Principle*:

Hume's Principle: $\forall F \forall G \ (\#x{:}Fx = \#x{:}Gx \leftrightarrow \text{Eq}(F,G))$

'The number of Fs = the number of Gs iff F and G are equinumerous.'

'$\#x{:}\phi$' is to be read as 'the number of ϕs'. (Grammatically, '#' combines with a variable and an open sentence to yield a term.) '$\text{Eq}(F,G)$' (read 'F and G are equinumerous') abbreviates the following formula:

$$\exists R \, [\forall x \forall y \forall z \forall w ([Rxy \wedge Rzw] \rightarrow [x = z \leftrightarrow y = w]) \wedge \\ \forall x (Fx \rightarrow \exists y [Gy \wedge Rxy]) \wedge \forall y (Gy \rightarrow \exists x [Fx \wedge Rxy])]$$

'There exists a one-to-one correspondence between the Fs and the Gs.'

Now, Frege himself did not regard Hume's Principle as a *definition* of the expression 'the number of'. Taken as a definition of the left-hand side of its biconditional, Hume's Principle would define only sentences of the form 'the number of ϕs = the number of ψs'. It would be inapplicable to sentences of other forms, such as 'The number of ϕs = Julius Caesar'. Any 'definition' of number that doesn't settle whether Julius Caesar is a number is no definition at all. Instead, Frege defined numbers as the extensions of certain concepts (these extensions were in essence sets). Given his background theory of extensions, Frege was able to derive Hume's Principle as a theorem, and went on to derive the axioms of second-order Peano arithmetic.

1.2. *From Fregeanism to Neo-Fregeanism.* Infamously, Frege's underlying theory of extensions was subject to Russell's paradox. Unable to repair the inconsistency in his system that Russell pointed out to him, Frege eventually came to regard his logicism as a failure. It

---

[2] See Boolos (1985) on the relationship between Frege's original logical system and contemporary systems.

was only noticed much later that Frege's derivation of arithmetic relied on the inconsistent theory of extensions at only one place: in the
derivation of Hume's Principle.[3] After that point, the extensions
were no longer needed; the derivation of arithmetic subsequently relied only on Hume's Principle. That raised the possibility that Hume's Principle itself, unlike Frege's theory of extensions, is *not*
inconsistent. This was indeed shown to be the case.[4]

This mathematical result—that Peano arithmetic (under appropriate definitions) follows in second-order logic from Hume's Principle, which is consistent—is remarkable indeed, but on its face is no
vindication of logicism. Since Hume's Principle implies the truth of
arithmetic, it implies the existence of infinitely many things. How
can something that implies the existence of even one thing, let alone
infinitely many, be a definition?

What the neo-Fregeans claim is that, despite its existential implications, Hume's Principle is nothing more than a definition of
number, and therefore can be known to be true a priori.[5] Thus, in a
sense, objects may be introduced by definition.[6]

Hume's Principle isn't an *explicit* definition of number, since as
noted above, it doesn't apply to all linguistic contexts containing
'the number of'. Nevertheless, neo-Fregeans say, it is an *implicit* definition: it defines the expression 'the number of' by stipulating how
that expression is to perform in *some* linguistic contexts. Think of
the act of laying down the definition as the delivery of instructions
to the semantic gods: 'Let my expression "the number of" be so understood as to obey Hume's principle.'

But of course, this just invites the question of whether there *is* any
way to understand 'the number of' so that Hume's Principle comes
out true.[7] If there do exist infinitely many objects, then perhaps

---

[3] The point was first made in passing by Charles Parsons (1965), and was later independently made by Crispin Wright (1983), who emphasized its philosophical significance.

[4] Hume's principle has been proved to be consistent with second-order logic, relative to the
consistency of systems that everyone believes to be consistent (Hazen, 1985; Burgess, 1984).

[5] The leading defenders are Crispin Wright and Bob Hale. See Wright (1983), Hale (1987),
Hale and Wright (2001).

[6] It is this aspect of neo-Fregeanism that has most perplexed commentators (see, for
instance, Field, 1984), and it is this aspect on which I will focus. I will set aside the 'Julius
Caesar problem', but see Rosen (1993) for some promising ideas.

[7] It also invites the question of whether there is more than one way; this, in essence, is the
Caesar problem.

there is a way,[8] but if there are not, one wants to say, there may simply be no way of interpreting 'the number of' so that Hume's Principle comes out true. In that case, the semantic gods will respond to our instructions with a blank look, as they would (assuming atheism) if we stipulated that 'God' is to denote the omnipotent being who created the world (Field, 1984).

It is in response to this worry that neo-Fregeanism becomes fascinatingly and maddeningly obscure. I will discuss two lines of thought: 'the priority of syntax' and 'reconceptualization'.

1.3. *The Priority of Syntax.* Neo-Fregeans want to reassure us that there is indeed a way of taking 'the number of' so that Hume's Principle comes out true. What if they just stipulated that '$\#x{:}Fx = \#x{:}Gx$' is to *abbreviate* 'Eq(F, G)'? Hume's Principle would then certainly come out true; it would abbreviate the logical truth '$\forall F \forall G$ (Eq(F, G) $\leftrightarrow$ Eq(F, G))'.

But you can't both stipulate that a complex string of symbols is to abbreviate something, and also treat the string's parts as semantically significant constituents. (If you coin a new name for me, 'AsonofaBush', you can't infer from the resulting truth of 'Ted is AsonofaBush' that I am related by birth to the esteemed president of the United States.) Neo-Fregeans certainly do assume that 'x', '$=$', 'F', and 'G' are semantically significant constituents of '$\#x{:}Fx = \#x{:}Gx$'; the derivation of Peano arithmetic from Hume's Principle depends on it. So they can't just say that '$\#x{:}Fx = \#x{:}Gx$' abbreviates 'Eq(F, G)'.

But real live neo-Fregeans say something that is almost this. Their position depends on the legitimacy of making *both* of the following stipulations:

(1) '$\#$' is to be understood so that it obeys Hume's Principle.

(2) $\ulcorner\#x{:}\phi\urcorner$ thus understood is to have the logical form it appears to have (e.g., existential generalization on the entire expression $\ulcorner\#x{:}\phi\urcorner$ is valid; e.g., the constituent expressions of ϕ are semantically significant, so that, for instance, variables in ϕ may be bound to external quantifiers).

---

[8] Though even here the way may not be straightforward. Hume's Principle implies the existence of an entity that is the number of absolutely all objects; the numbers of which it speaks cannot, therefore, be the cardinals of standard ZF set theory. See Boolos (1997).

They defend the propriety of jointly making these stipulations by saying that there is nothing more to having a certain logical form beyond having an appropriate syntactic distribution throughout the language. If an expression can occur grammatically in the sorts of places that a singular term can occur, then it *is* a singular term. Wright calls this view the 'priority of syntactic over ontological categories'; here is a representative quotation:

> According to [the thesis of the priority of syntactic over ontological categories], the question whether a particular expression is a candidate to refer to an object is entirely a matter of the sort of syntactic role which it plays in whole sentences. If it plays that sort of role, then the truth of appropriate sentences in which it so features will be sufficient to confer on it an objectual reference; and questions concerning the character of its reference should then be addressed by philosophical reflection on the truth conditions of sentences of the appropriate kind. If, therefore, certain expressions in a branch of our language function syntactically as singular terms, and descriptive and identity contexts containing them are true by ordinary criteria, there is no room for any ulterior failure of 'fit' between those contexts and the structure of the states of affairs which make them true. So there can be no philosophical science of ontology, no well-founded attempt to see past our categories of expression and glimpse the way in which the world is truly furnished. (Wright, 1983, pp. 51–2)

Thus, we can stipulate that the truth condition of '$\#x{:}Fx = \#x{:}Gx$' is simply $Eq(F,G)$ without forfeiting the status of '$\#x{:}Fx$' as a genuine singular term.[9] It is a genuine singular term because it occurs grammatically in the places where genuine singular terms can occur.

There is a complex literature on what a purely syntactic criterion for being a 'genuine singular term' might be. But the notion of a singular term is relevant to the current debate only because the neo-Fregean wants to employ the usual quantificational laws to sentences containing $\ulcorner\#x{:}\phi\urcorner$. So instead of fighting over what it means to be a genuine singular term, I suggest simply *stipulating* that '$\#$' is to create terms with semantically significant constituents to which the usual quantificational laws apply. The debate can then focus on the real issue: whether the joint stipulation of (1) and (2) is coherent.

---

[9] Focus on the category of singular terms is a bit misplaced, for in addition to '$\#x{:}Fx$' being a singular term, its parts must also be semantically significant.

This stipulation costs the neo-Fregean nothing and exposes the dispute over syntactic priority as distracting noise.

1.4. *Reconceptualization.* What guarantee is there that (1) and (2) may be jointly stipulated? Here we reach the crux of the issue. Wright says, in effect, that the state of affairs of *F* being equinumerous to *G* can be 'reconceptualized' as a state of affairs involving the existence of numbers. Or better: the totality of states of affairs about equinumerosity can be reconceptualized as states of affairs involving the existence of a domain of numbers. Wright makes the point with a different example, that of reconceptualizing states of affairs about parallel lines as states of affairs involving the existence of directions:

> Consider again the abstraction for directions:
>
> Da = Db if and only if a//b.
>
> The dilemma was that we either regard the left-hand side simply as a definitional transcription of the right, and thereby forfeit the possibility of taking its syntax at face value, of treating it as a genuine identity statement linking genuine singular terms in existentially generalizable position; or we take the principle as a substantial claim, to the effect that certain abstract objects—directions—are associated with lines in the way it describes, in which case we have no right simply to lay the principle down as a definition. But the key to Frege's view is that the dilemma is a false one—it is the thought, roughly, that we have the option, by laying down the Direction abstraction, of *reconceptualizing*, as it were, the type of state of affairs which is described on the right. That type of state of affairs is initially given to us as the obtaining of a certain equivalence relation—parallelism—among lines; but we have the option, by stipulating that the abstraction is to hold, of so reconceiving such states of affairs that they come to constitute the identity of a new kind of thing, directions, of which, by this very stipulation, we introduce the concept. The concept of direction is thus so introduced that that two lines are parallel *constitutes* the identity of their direction. It is in no sense a further substantial claim that their directions exist and are identical under the described circumstances. But nor is it the case that, by stipulating that the principle is to hold, we thereby forfeit the right to a face-value construal of its left-hand side, and thereby to the type of existential generalization which a face-value construal would license. When the abstraction principle is read in the way which Frege proposes, its effect is so to fix the concept of

direction that there is absolutely no gap between the existence of directions and the instantiation of properties and relations among lines.

It is important to be clear that it would be a misrepresentation of this idea to view it as involving the notion that abstract objects are creations of the human mind, *brought into being* by a kind of stipulation. What is formed—created—by such an abstraction is rather a *concept*: the effect is merely to fix the truth-conditions of identity statements concerning a new kind of thing, and it is quite another question whether those truth-conditions are ever realized. If we accept the concept-formation involved in the Fregean abstraction of Direction, the effect is not to define directions into existence but to coordinate the question of the existence of directions with that of the existence of lines; and the latter can remain, for all that is implicit in an acceptance of the abstraction, as objective and mind-independent a matter as you want. (Wright, 1997, pp. 277–8 in Hale and Wright, 2001)

If this idea of reconceptualization makes sense, then the question of whether 'the number of' forms 'genuine singular terms' is irrelevant, for the neo-Fregean can say that states of affairs concerning equinumerosity may be reconceptualized so as to admit of characterization using 'singular terms' in a sense stipulated to obey the usual quantificational laws. But this notion of reconceptualization is notoriously obscure. What exactly does it amount to?

My proposal: quantifier variance. There are many equally good things one can mean by the quantifiers. If on one 'there are numbers' comes out false, there is another on which 'there are numbers' comes out true. The facts are the same either way; it's just that the facts have no unique description using quantificational language. Compare the sense in which facts about measurable quantities have no unique description, given the arbitrariness of the choice of a unit of measure. We could use the expression 'one metre' so that 'this bar is one metre long' comes out true, or we could use 'one metre' so that it comes out false. Neither linguistic choice is better than the other. Similarly for quantificational language. 'Reconceptualization' means selecting a meaning for the quantifiers on which Hume's Principle comes out true.

II

Quantifier Variance

2.1. *Neo-Carnapianism*. Quantifier variance is the position of Rudolf Carnap's (1950) contemporary soulmates, who want to deflate philosophical debates over ontology.[10]

Consider, for example, the debate over the ontology of composite material objects. When are given material objects part of some further composite object? Some say: *always*. There exist scattered objects. Some say: *never*. No composite material objects exist. Some say *sometimes*. If objects are appropriately glued together (or whatever) then there exists a further material object that they compose, otherwise not.[11]

The neo-Carnapians recoil from all this in horror. Their guiding thought is that nothing is really at issue in this so-called debate, beyond how to talk. Now, the folks I have in mind reject Carnap's positivism (hence the 'neo'). In place of Carnap's linguistic frameworks, they have different languages. The languages correspond to different decisions about what quantificational expressions are to mean. In the different languages, quantificational sentences like 'there exist tables' express different propositions. In one language, 'there are tables' is true; in another, 'there are no tables' is true. Which proposition is expressed by a given sentence is of course a matter of convention; but the truth of the proposition itself can be as mind-independent and evidence-transcendent a matter as you like.[12]

The view is intended to be ontologically deflationary because:

(i) For each competing theory about the ontology of composite material objects, quantificational expressions can be interpreted so that the theory comes out true.

---

[10] I have in mind primarily Eli Hirsch (2002a; 2002b; 2005; forthcoming); see also Hilary Putnam (1987a; 1987b).

[11] The issue was thus framed by van Inwagen (1987; 1990).

[12] Neo-Carnapianism had better not collapse into the banal claim that since all language is conventional, any sentence, construed as a bare string of symbols, can be interpreted truly. The neo-Carnapian's languages are not supposed to be utterly semantically *alien* (compare the discussion of conventionality in Sider, MS). In each case, 'there exists' is to count as 'a kind of quantifier', one might say. But it can't be 'a kind of quantifier' in the most straightforward sense; see §2.2. The various interpretations of 'there exists' must count as being similar to one another, but in what way? Hirsch's suggestion (2002b, p. 53) is that they must share an appropriate inferential role.

(ii) None of these interpretations is any 'better' than the others.

Now, as I see it, in order to secure (ii), the quantifier variantist must hold that none of the interpretations is a more *natural* interpretation than the others; none 'carves logical reality at its joints' better than the others; no one is most 'basic' or 'fundamental'.[13] For if one distinguished interpretation were more natural than the others, then the ontological debate could continue undeflated: as a debate about what exists in the distinguished sense. So as a first pass, I formulate quantifier variance—as applied to the debate over composite material objects—as follows:[14]

> *Neo-Carnapian quantifier variance*: There is a class, C, containing *equally* and *maximally* natural candidate meanings for quantifier expressions, in that: (i) no member of C is more natural than any other member of C, and (ii) no candidate meaning for quantifier expressions that is not in C is as natural as any member of C. Each position in the debate over the ontology of composite material objects comes out true under some member of C.

2.2. *How Not to Refine Quantifier Variance.* What *are* these candidate quantifier meanings? The most straightforward characterization does not work. The most straightforward characterization is that the candidates result from choosing different domains for the quantifiers. To say this, we ourselves would need to quantify over all the objects in all the domains—we would be saying that *there is* a domain containing *all* of the objects over which the quantifiers of L range, for various languages L. But the language we're speaking might be one of the languages in question, and not the 'biggest' one.

Might the quantifier variantist stick to the straightforward characterization by (i) saying that the quantifiers in each of the 'smaller' languages are restrictions on the quantifiers in a single, biggest language; and (ii) admitting that the doctrine of quantifier variance can

---

[13] The notion of naturalness I have in mind is a generalization of Lewis's (1983, pp. 59–69; 1984, pp. 59–69; 1986, pp. 59–69); see Sider (2007) and my forthcoming book for an extended discussion of its application to metaontology and other questions of metametaphysics.

[14] I would cash out 'candidate meaning' in terms of inferential role; see note 12.

only be stated in this biggest language?[15] No: this would undermine
the quantifier variantist's egalitarianism. When one restricts a quantifier, one simply *ignores* some of the things to which one is committed. When pressed on whether the ignored things exist, one *ought* to
undo the restriction and admit that the things exist after all. In a
conversation with a biologist who is pointing out the existence of
microbes, air, and the like, it would be *wrong*—conversationally
and epistemically—to dig in one's heels and insist that there is absolutely nothing in the refrigerator. Indeed, there is something epistemically *superior* about the context in which one agrees that there
are some things in the refrigerator. But the quantifier variantist does
not want to say that, if one is speaking a language that eschews scattered objects, one ought to admit under pressure that the scattered
objects exist after all, or that the epistemic position of the user of
the more inclusive quantifier is superior. That would be taking sides
on the first-order debate.

Further, recall that the quantifier variantist thinks that the meanings corresponding to the various positions on the ontology of composite objects are all equally and maximally natural. But surely if Q^-
results from restricting a maximally natural quantifier meaning, Q,
then Q^- is *less* natural than Q.

So: the quantifier variantist cannot characterize the various quantifier meanings as corresponding to different domains. How, then,
can those meanings be characterized?

2.3. *Meanings and Contexts.*[16] On behalf of quantifier variantists, I
will take an 'algebraic' approach to quantifier meanings. Rather
than trying to specify what these meanings *are* intrinsically, I will
specify only what they are supposed to *do*. I will introduce a space
of quantifier meanings endowed with enough structure to do the
work that quantifier variantists want done.

Quantifier variantists might fill in this structure in different ways.
Some might, for instance, construe a quantifier meaning as a way of
translating quantified sentences into some chosen language. Others
might construe quantifier meanings as possible-worlds truth conditions of quantified sentences. Others might take quantifier meanings

---

[15] One objection I will not press is that there may be no biggest language.

[16] Those impatient with the following details may skip ahead to section 2.6 with little loss.

to be *sui generis* entities. Still others might be fictionalist about talk of meanings.[17] The algebraic approach gives merely the minimal structural commitments of quantifier variantism.

What are the quantifier meanings supposed to do? First, the notion of naturalness (carving at the joints) must apply to them. Second, they are to (help) determine truth values for quantified sentences. Third, it must make sense to speak of more or less 'expansive' quantifier meanings, where this is not merely a matter of varying domain restrictions.

So, let us speak of entities called *meanings*. Think of a 'meaning' as being a meaning for a whole language, though our primary focus is the quantifiers. In addition, to account for contextual variation of quantifier domains, let us speak of further entities called *contexts*. To the meanings and contexts let us apply the following undefined predicates:

meaning *m* is *at least as natural as* meaning *m'*.
context *c belongs to* meaning *m*.
model *M depicts* meaning-context pair $\langle m,c \rangle$.

The first predicate is used to measure how well meanings carve nature at the joints. The second predicate is needed to attach the contexts to the meanings ('contexts' are supposed to be contexts of utterance for quantified sentences given a certain meaning for the quantifiers.) Call a meaning-context pair $\langle m,c \rangle$, where *c* belongs to *m*, a *quantifier*; the idea of the third predicate is that the 'world according to a quantifier'—what the domain of existing objects 'looks like' from the perspective of that quantifier—can be depicted by a model. Given section 2.2, we cannot think of these models as *intended* models—models whose domains are the intended domains of quantification, under the quantifier meanings. That would turn each of the candidate quantifier meanings into restrictions of the quantifier used to formulate quantifier variantism. 'Models' here are *not* intended models; they're just models in the sense of model theory, in which the domains are allowed to contain any old objects.[18]

---

[17] See Turner (2008) for an interesting further approach.
[18] When *M* depicts *q*, which language *M* interprets depends on which sentences *q* interprets. I will assume that all the sentences to be considered have the usual syntactic categories: quantifiers, variables, predicates, etc. When we get to arithmetic (below), some of the sentences will be second-order.

It is natural to make the following assumptions about the meanings, contexts, and primitive predicates we have applied to them:

- Each context belongs to exactly one meaning.
- No model depicts anything other than a quantifier.
- Each quantifier is depicted by some model.
- The same sentences are true in any two models that depict the same quantifier.

Further, we can define a notion of truth for a sentence relative to a given meaning (in a given context):

> *Definition of truth*: Sentence ϕ is $true^c_m$ iff ϕ is true in some model that depicts $\langle m,c \rangle$.

We have seen how to use our meanings, contexts, and primitive predicates to do two of the three things that quantifier meanings are supposed to do: speak of naturalness of meanings, and of sentences being true relative to meanings. I show how to do the third thing—speak of more or less expansive quantifier meanings—in the next section.

The algebraic approach quantifies over meanings, sentences, and sets. But quantifier variantism might apply even to quantification over these entities. Does this threaten the approach?

I don't think so. Consider a few characters. An *opponent of quantifier variantism who accepts abstracta* can clearly adopt the approach. A *proponent of quantifier variantism* can also adopt the approach while speaking one of her languages that allows quantification over abstracta. Admitting that a 'large' language must be used to state quantifier variance is not an embarrassment, for it does not imply that the quantifier of the large language carves nature at its joints any better than do the quantifiers of smaller languages.[19] A *nominalist opponent of quantifier variance* is the character who is most likely to encounter trouble. But surely *some* way (fictionalist or otherwise) can be found to make talk of abstract entities nominalistically acceptable—and if not, the inability to formulate quantifier variance would be the least of the nominalist's worries.

---

[19] See also the end of §2.7.

2.4. *Expansion and Restriction.* Everyone agrees that one can 'shrink' the domain of quantification: by quantifier *restriction*.[20] The distinctive claim of quantifier variantism, on the other hand, is that quantifiers can be in some sense *expanded*; and as we saw in section 2.2, this expansion is not the mere removal of restrictions. We must characterize this distinctive claim within the algebraic approach. The rough idea is: mere restriction changes the context but retains the same meaning, whereas the distinctive kind of expansion changes the meaning as well as the context.

More precisely, consider the following definition:

> *Definition of supermodel*: Model M is a (proper) *supermodel* of model M' iff (i) the domain of M' is a (proper) subset of the domain of M, (ii) names interpreted by both M' and M have the same denotations in each case, and (iii) if a predicate or function symbol is interpreted by both M' and M, then its extension in M' is a subset of its extension in M.

> *Definition of expansion*: Quantifier q (properly) *expands* quantifier q' iff some model that depicts q is a (proper) supermodel of some model that depicts q'.

Suppose, then, that $\langle m, c \rangle$ properly expands $\langle m', c' \rangle$. This is unexciting if $m = m'$; this is the case where the quantifiers in m', c' are mere restrictions of those in m, c. But it is exciting if $m \neq m'$, for then m, c is not the result of dropping restrictions on the quantifiers in m', c'. We have instead the distinctive kind of expansion. The following definitions are therefore appropriate:

> *Definition of restriction*: $\langle m', c' \rangle$ is a (proper) *restriction* of $\langle m, c \rangle$ iff $m = m'$ and $\langle m, c \rangle$ (properly) expands $\langle m', c' \rangle$.

> *Definition of unrestricted*: A quantifier is *unrestricted* iff there exists no proper restriction of it.

2.5. *The Form of Quantifier Variance Theses.* Various theses of quantifier variance may be formulated in terms of this apparatus.

---

[20] Never mind whether to classify this as semantic or pragmatic.

For any quantifier, q, everyone believes in the mundane kind of quantifier variance that results from quantifier restriction:

Closure under restrictions: If some supermodel of M depicts q, then there exists a restriction of q that M depicts.

The quantifier variantist wants to go further. Let $\mathcal{M}$ be a set of models. Think of the models in $\mathcal{M}$ as 'quantifier worlds'—models that describe what the world would be like given various quantifier meanings. Let E be a set of meanings, and let $Q(E)$ be the set of quantifiers 'based on' E (i.e., $\{\langle m,c \rangle | c$ belongs to m and $m \in E\}$); the members of $Q(E)$ will be the multiple candidate quantifier meanings in which the quantifier variantist believes. Claims of quantifier variance are then plentitude theses for $Q(E)$; any such claim will say roughly that each quantifier world in $\mathcal{M}$ depicts some quantifier in $Q(E)$.

This idea needs to be made precise along two dimensions. First, an appropriate *range* of quantifier worlds—i.e. what goes into $\mathcal{M}$ —must be specified. That is the task of the next section. Second, the *form* of the correspondence between quantifier worlds and quantifiers must be specified. Let us turn to this second task.

The weakest form is simply this:

Weak $\mathcal{M}/E$-quantifier variance: Every member of $\mathcal{M}$ depicts some member of $Q(E)$.

But that is too weak, since it is consistent with all the quantifiers in $Q(E)$ being restrictions on a single maximal quantifier. Say that model M *outruns* meaning m iff for no c does M depict $\langle m,c \rangle$; here are some stronger forms:[21]

Moderate $\mathcal{M}/E$-quantifier variance: Weak $\mathcal{M}/E$-quantifier variance + some member of $\mathcal{M}$ outruns some member of E.

Strong $\mathcal{M}/E$-quantifier variance: Weak $\mathcal{M}/E$-quantifier variance + every $M \in \mathcal{M}$ outruns some member of E (provided M is a proper supermodel of some member of $\mathcal{M}$).

---

[21] Thanks to Joshua Brown for the moderate formulation.

> *Unrestricted M/E-quantifier variance*: Every member of M depicts some unrestricted member of $Q(E)$.

Moderate quantifier variance adds the claim that at least one quantifier world is 'beyond the reach' of at least one meaning—the meaning cannot be unrestricted to generate the world. Strong quantifier variance goes further by claiming that *each* quantifier world is beyond the reach of some meaning (except when the world is a 'minimal' member of M). Unrestricted quantifier variance goes the furthest: it says that each quantifier world depicts some unrestricted quantifier. Life would be simpler if we could focus solely on unrestricted quantifier variance, but I want to leave open the possibility that some meanings do not have contexts in which the quantifiers are absolutely unrestricted.

2.6. The Extent of Quantifier Variance. Section 2.5 provided various forms of quantifier variance. These may be given content in various ways.

Each form of quantifier variance assumes given a class M of 'quantifier-worlds' for which corresponding quantifier meanings are alleged to exist. Here is one fairly strong constraint that one might want to put on M.[22]

> *Upward closure*: Any supermodel of a member of M is itself a member of M.

(Weaker versions would require only closure under certain sorts of supermodels.)

The quantifier variantist may well *not* want to impose the following inverse constraint on the set, E, of meanings:

> *Downward E-closure*: If M is a supermodel of M' and M depicts some member of $Q(E)$, then M' outruns some member of E.

Downward closure says that we can choose arbitrarily 'small' quantifiers—and not just by restriction. That is, if we're speaking one

---

[22] If one does impose this constraint then M can no longer be a set. It could instead be a proper class (or talk of it could be understood in terms of plural quantification).

language, whose quantifier is depicted by some model, and we
choose a submodel of that model, then there is some other language
we can speak in which, no matter how far we unrestrict the quantifiers, we will not reach the chosen submodel. Why might our quantifier variantist not accept downward closure? Perhaps some
sentences are *atomic*, in that no meaning treats them as false except
because of quantifier restriction. 'There exist electrons' might be an
example. The relevant notion of an atom is this:

> *Definition of E-atom*: Sentence ϕ is *E-atomic* iff for every
> $m \in E$, there exists a c such that (i) ϕ is true$_m^c$, and (ii) for any c',
> if ϕ is not true$_m^{c'}$ then $\langle m', c' \rangle$ is a restriction of $\langle m, c \rangle$.

Supermodels are allowed to 'expand' non-logical expressions in
two ways: they can interpret new non-logical expressions that are
not interpreted by the submodel, and they can expand the extensions of non-logical expressions that are interpreted by the submodel. Either of these degrees of freedom could be constrained, by
allowing only non-logical expressions in certain chosen sets (K and
L below) to be thus expanded:

> *Definition of $\langle K, L \rangle$-supermodel*: M is a (proper) $\langle K, L \rangle$-super-
> model of M' iff (i) M is a (proper) supermodel of M', (ii) any
> non-logical expressions that are *newly* interpreted (i.e. inter-
> preted by M but not M') are in K, and (iii) any non-logical ex-
> pressions that are *altered* (i.e. have different extensions in M
> and M') are in L.

There result, then, corresponding notions of $\langle K, L \rangle$-restriction, various forms of $\langle K, L \rangle$-quantifier variance, and so on.

For instance, one might allow expansions of quantifiers to be accompanied by the introduction of new non-logical expressions for
the features of 'the newly introduced entities', while requiring that
old non-logical expressions have, as it were, exactly the same extensions that they originally had. The neo-Fregean, for instance, must
add a new non-logical expression—'#'—but need not change old
non-logical expressions. Neo-Fregeans, therefore, might restrict their
quantifier variance claims to $\langle \{'\#'\}, \varnothing \rangle$. Neo-Carnapians, on the
other hand, want the extension of 'part of' (and many other predi-

cates) to expand when the domain is expanded, but may not need new non-logical expressions. Neo-Carnapian quantifier variance claims may therefore have the form $\langle \varnothing, \{$'part of', 'material object', ...$\} \rangle$.

We now have the means to formulate quantifier variance theses. As an example, one might state a form of neo-Carnapian quantifier variance thus:

> *Neo-Carnapian quantifier variance restated*: There is a non-empty class of models, $\mathcal{M}$, and a class of meanings, E, such that:
> (1) $\mathcal{M}$ obeys upward $\langle \varnothing, \{$'part of', 'material object', ...$\} \rangle$-closure.
> (2) Every member of E is as natural as every other, and no meaning not in E is as natural as any meaning in E.
> (3) Strong $\mathcal{M}/E$-$\langle \varnothing, \{$'part of', 'material object', ...$\} \rangle$-quantifier variance is true.

2.7. *What Else Must Vary?* Suppose we vary what the quantifiers mean. The quantifier variantist should, I think, say that we then also vary the meaning of every other expression distinctive of predicate logic: names, predicates, function symbols.[23] Indeed, the meanings of these *categories*, construed as semantic categories, must vary.

This can be approached first by examining the following argument against quantifier variantism. Consider two putative languages in which the quantifiers mean different things. Surely, if these languages exist, one could introduce a third language containing symbols $\exists_1$ and $\exists_2$ for the quantifier-meanings of the first two languages. But if $\exists_1$ and $\exists_2$ obey the usual inference rules then they will be provably equivalent. (For example, suppose $\exists_1 x \phi(x)$. By $\exists_1$-elimination, $\phi(a)$. By $\exists_2$-introduction, $\exists_2 x \phi(x)$.)[24]

---

[23] Plausibility argument: pretend that giving meaning to a language is just a matter of describing its intended model. Models are described using quantifiers in the metalanguage. One uses metalanguage quantifiers to specify a domain, which fixes the meaning of the object-language's quantifiers; and one uses metalanguage quantifiers to give the meanings of object-language constants and predicates (a constant means an object in the domain; a predicate means a set of tuples from the domain). So if one then changes the meanings of the metalanguage quantifiers, different meanings for all the object-language's expressions would ensue.

[24] Compare Harris (1982), Hart (1982), Williamson (1988).

The defender of quantifier variance ought to reply that one cannot introduce a language with both $\exists_1$ and $\exists_2$ but with a common stock of names, predicates, and function symbols. For the notions of name, predicate, function symbol, and quantifier are all connected. If '$\exists_1$' is a quantifier in one sense—a quantifier$_1$—then it is only names$_1$, predicates$_1$, and function symbols$_1$ that connect to it in the usual ways. And expressions that inferentially connect to quantifiers$_2$ are not names$_1$, etc.; they are names$_2$, etc.[25]

A second route to the same conclusion emerges from reflection on a recent challenge to quantifier variantism presented by Matti Eklund (forthcoming) and John Hawthorne (2006). Quantifier variantism allows the following scenario involving two characters, Big and Small. Big speaks a language (Biglish) in which '$\exists x\,\mathrm{Table}(x)$' is true, and introduces a name, 'a', for a table. Small, on the other hand, speaks a 'smaller' language, in which one cannot quantify over tables. But Small is a quantifier variantist, and thinks that he does not genuinely disagree with Big. So even though Small does not himself accept the sentence 'Table(a)', he thinks that it is true in Biglish. But this commits Small to rejecting familiar Tarskian ideas about semantics. According to Tarskian semantics, for any language, L, a subject–predicate sentence is true-in-L iff the denotation-in-L of its subject term is a member of the extension-in-L of its predicate. If Small accepts this biconditional, then in order to admit the truth of 'Table(a)' in Biglish, Small himself would have to admit that there exists something that 'a' denotes-in-Biglish. (The quantifier 'the' in the biconditional is Small's, notice.) But there seems to be no such object—speaking *Small's* language, that is, one cannot say that such an object exists. So runs the Eklund-Hawthorne argument.

The quantifier variantist should reply as before: names and quantifiers are connected. Small should deny that Big's expression 'a' is a name (i.e. deny that it is a name$_{Small}$.)[26]

This reply is, I think, *correct*, but it doesn't fully answer Eklund

---

[25] A purely syntactic, inferentially inert, notion of grammatical category would classify names$_1$ and names$_2$ together, but would not rescue the argument.

An alternative route to blocking the argument, due to Jason Turner (2008), deserves mention. Turner claims that $\exists_1$ and $\exists_2$ obey only free-logical introduction and elimination rules. The move from $\phi(a)$ to $\exists_2 x\,\phi(x)$ would then be invalid because $\exists_2$-introduction would require the additional premiss $\exists_2 x\; x=a$.

[26] Compare Hirsch (2002b, p. 57).

and Hawthorne. For even if Small is right to deny that Biglish contains names or subject–predicate sentences, it would be hard for Small to deny that Big's use of language is in *some* sense compositional. And so, shouldn't Small say something systematic about how Big's sentences get their truth conditions?

Yes; but Small need not stick to the book in doing so. *Anyone* can agree that *some* extreme cases call for novel semantic ideas in order to make sense of alien but compositional linguistic behavior. From Small's point of view, the case of Big calls for a (slight) departure from the Tarskian paradigm: Big's sentence $\lceil Fa \rceil$ is true, Small might say, iff there are some referents (plural) of the 'subject' term a that are in the 'extension' (in a plural sense) of the 'predicate' F. The resulting theory might be complex and ugly. But if a full semantics is difficult (or even impossible) to give using Small's language, that wouldn't undermine quantifier variance. Granted, it would be an asymmetry between Small and Big, for there is no corresponding disadvantage to speaking Biglish. But quantifier variantists can admit that bigger is better for certain purposes; all they are committed to saying is that neither language adheres better to nature's joints. (French may be the language of love, but is no better for it ontologically speaking.)

III

The Epistemic Goal of Neo-Fregeanism. My reading of neo-Fregeanism appeals to quantifier variance. In essence: the neo-Fregean's claim that states of affairs can be 'reconceptualized' as involving quantification over abstracta is a metaphor for the claim that (i) there is a meaning for the quantifiers on which one can quantify over abstracta, and (ii) this meaning is not a 'second-class' citizen: it is just as natural as quantifier-meanings on which one cannot so quantify. In order to evaluate whether this view is an adequate reading *of neo-Fregeanism*, we must ask what neo-Fregeans want out of their theory, epistemically speaking.

Suppose you begin life as a platonist. You are convinced that there are many abstract entities, including numbers. In that case, you should be happy to accept Hume's principle.[27] Where there are

---

[27] Setting aside the issues of note 8.

finitely many *F*s, you would take 'the number of *F*s' to pick out the appropriate one of these abstract entities that you antecedently accept. Indeed, if you heard a neo-Fregean saying that Hume's Principle is a 'definition', you might simply take that as information about which of the functional correlations between pluralities and objects that you antecedently believe in, is to be associated with 'the number of'.

Neo-Fregeans want more than that. Their definition is supposed to have an epistemic payoff. You are not supposed to need an antecedent commitment to abstracta in order to accept Hume's Principle and subsequently derive arithmetic. The neo-Fregean program is supposed to erase doubts about abstracta. But how?

In the remainder of this section I want to do a few things. Ultimately I want to suggest that the potential epistemic payoff of neo-Fregeanism is more modest than what is usually supposed. I want thereby to dispel the false impression that neo-Fregeanism provides a way to avoid substantive metaphysical questions about mathematical existence. And I hope to clarify questions about the status of the logical knowledge that neo-Fregeans must presuppose.

3.1. *No Detour Around Substantive Metaphysics.* Platonists seem to face an epistemic problem. If mathematics is about a realm of mind-independent abstract entities, then how do we know about these entities? Models of other sorts of knowledge—perceptual, testimonial, historical, and scientific knowledge, for example—do not seem to apply to mathematics.

A powerful motivation for neo-Fregeanism is that it promises to solve this epistemic problem. The problem, one might think, is created by the traditional approach to ontology (the 'philosophical science of ontology' that Wright (1983, p. 52) deplores).

In fact this motivation is illusory. In effect, what neo-Fregeans are trying to do is argue for an underlying metaontology[28] (theory of the nature of ontology) that guarantees the success of their stipulation of Hume's Principle. They hope thereby to dispel doubts about mathematics. But in order to dispel all doubts, it is not enough that the underlying metaontology be *true*. It must itself be epistemically secure. And models of perceptual knowledge, testimonial knowl-

---

[28] The term is from van Inwagen (1998).

edge, and the like are of no more help in understanding how we could know the truth of neo-Fregean metaontology—a substantive bit of metaphysics—than they are in understanding how we could have mathematical knowledge.

Consider, for instance, the quantifier variance interpretation of neo-Fregeanism. If an appropriate quantifier variance hypothesis is true (section five), then the stipulation of Hume's Principle is bound to succeed. But quantifier variance itself is a substantive metaphysical hypothesis. An alternative hypothesis is that there is a single most natural quantificational meaning—a distinguished quantifier. Call this view *ontological realism*. Never mind whether it is true; what is important is that neo-Fregeanism, on the quantifier variance interpretation, is committed to its falsity. The rejection of ontological realism in favor of quantifier variance is, if anything, less epistemically secure than the mathematical knowledge it is supposed to ground.

The point is not limited to the quantifier variance interpretation. On any interpretation, neo-Fregeanism will be committed to the falsity of rival metaontological positions. Far from providing a detour around substantive fundamental metaphysics, neo-Fregeanism is itself a piece of substantive fundamental metaphysics.

3.2. *A Modest Goal.* None of this counts against neo-Fregeanism. On the contrary, it should be liberating. Once the goal of dispelling all arithmetic doubt by avoiding substantive metaphysics is off the table, neo-Fregeans can set themselves a more attainable goal: improving our epistemic position.

Neo-Fregeans need a metaontological hypothesis that guarantees the success of the stipulation of Hume's Principle. On the quantifier variance interpretation, as well as on another interpretation I will discuss, the needed metaontological hypothesis has independent plausibility. Thus, showing that the hypothesis guarantees the success of the stipulation could be argued to improve our epistemic position. For one route to epistemic improvement—perhaps the best route when it comes to the most fundamental matters—is to embed less certain beliefs within an attractive, explanatory, and general theory. Showing that mathematical knowledge can be thus embedded would not dispel all doubts about mathematics, but that was never in the cards anyway. Improving our epistemic position is a modest but attainable goal.

3.3. *Logical Knowledge*. Second-order logic is needed to derive the Peano axioms from Hume's Principle. So neo-Fregeans need an account of second-order logical knowledge to complete their mathematical epistemology. I want to comment briefly on two questions that are generally considered relevant here. First, is second-order logic really logic? Second, is second-order logic really set theory?

My comment about the first question is really just an opinionated remark. If we had an account of our knowledge of *first*-order logic, then it might matter whether second-order logic is logic (for it might affect whether our account of first-order logical knowledge would carry over to second-order logic.) But we don't, so it doesn't.[29]

Second question: is second-order logic just set theory in disguise, as Quine (1970) thought? If it is, then neo-Fregeanism provides no more secure an epistemic foundation for arithmetic than that provided by the more usual reduction of arithmetic to set theory plus definitions. Neo-Fregeans are thus committed to 'innocent' second-order quantification.[30] But is such quantification possible?

As many have pointed out, the fact that the standard model theory for second-order logic is set-theoretic is neither here nor there, for the standard model theory for first-order logic is also set-theoretic, and no one thinks that first-order reasoning is implicitly set-theoretic.

Also neither here nor there is the following. Suppose platonism about set theory is true, and imagine the semantic gods looking down upon an innocent who uses second-order quantifiers and variables. The semantic gods might well interpret the innocent as quantifying over sets. In the same way, the semantic gods might interpret a pre-Einsteinian innocent as meaning by 'simultaneous' simultaneity-in-her-own-frame-of-reference; or a pre-Parsonian as quantifying over events when saying 'I walked quickly down the street' (Parsons, 1990). Thus, since platonism may well be true, second-order quantification may well 'semantically commit' one to sets. This is neither here nor there because the question is whether it can be *established* in the current dialectical context that one cannot use higher-order quantification without believing in sets.

---

[29] What is behind this opinionated remark is opposition to leading attempts to explain first-order logical knowledge: logical conventionalism (against which see Quine, 1936; Sider, MS) and the view that logical knowledge is fully explained by linguistic knowledge (against which see Prior, 1960; Horwich, 1997; Williamson, 2003; Field, 2006).

[30] See, for instance, Rayo and Yablo (2001).

So how should we approach the question of whether innocent second-order quantification is possible? The following move sharpens the debate. Let our neo-Fregean *stipulate* that her second-order quantifiers are to be understood innocently, as not quantifying over sets. What form must opposition to innocent second-order quantification now take?

It must turn into the charge that the second-order quantifiers are semantically defective by virtue of underspecification. The second-orderist's usage of the allegedly innocent quantifiers settles *some* things about how they are to behave. For instance, the second-orderist's usage might settle that every sentence of the form $\ulcorner Ga \urcorner$, with G a predicate constant, is to imply $\ulcorner \exists F Fa \urcorner$. But, the criticism would be, when we reach second-order quantifications whose truth values are not settled by the actual usage of second-orderists, then everything goes fuzzy: there are no determinate truth values. In essence, if there are no sets, then no other Wittgensteinian (1958, §218) 'rails to infinity' are available to supply semantic determinacy in cases that are not settled by usage.

Conversely, since the neo-Fregean who stipulates an innocent usage of second-order quantifiers is committed to the semantic determinacy of her language, she is committed to there being sufficient structure in the world to provide the Wittgensteinian rails.[31]

IV

The Maximalist Interpretation. Before discussing the quantifier variance interpretation of neo-Fregeanism further, I want to distinguish it from another interpretation: the 'maximalist' interpretation.[32] The distinction can be brought out by asking the question, if Hume's principle is to be a definition, then what expression or expressions does it define? As we'll see, the quantifier variantist thinks that it defines the quantifiers. The maximalist denies this.[33] According to the maximalist, in laying down Hume's Principle as a definition, we

---

[31] The question of how exactly to articulate this commitment to structure is a difficult one; but there is no question that there is indeed such a commitment. See Sider (2007).

[32] Here I am indebted to Eklund (MSa; MSb). The term 'maximalist' is his.

[33] And therefore has no need for quantifier variance. The maximalist could, for instance, be an ontological realist.

keep the quantifiers meaning exactly what they did before, and stipulate that '#' is to be interpreted so that Hume's Principle comes out
true.

In that case, one might ask, how could we be certain that the implicit definition succeeds? Mightn't the requisite objects be missing?

Well, suppose it's just a fact about the nature of existence that, in
a sense to be explored, anything that can exist, does exist. That is,
existence is quite generally maximal—maximalism. Then if Hume's
Principle is consistent, there must be objects satisfying Hume's Principle.[34]

Of course, the *truth* of maximalism wouldn't on its own dispel all
ontological doubts about arithmetic, for one could doubt that maximalism is true. But as I explained in section 3.2, modest epistemic
progress would be made if an attractive general hypothesis about
metaontology were found on which stipulations like Hume's Principle invariably succeed.

And—perhaps contrary to appearances—maximalism is indeed a
reasonably attractive hypothesis. Maximalism is tempting (to the
degree that it is) because it minimizes arbitrariness. If maximalism is
false, and some consistent objects are present while others are missing, there's a why-question without an answer: why do these objects, but not those, exist? Whereas if maximalism is true, we have a
nicely rounded picture of the world, and fewer why-questions go
unanswered. Maximalism is attractive for the same reason that
plenitudinous views about material ontology are attractive.

The more general the maximalism, the more it minimizes arbitrariness. For instance, maximalism might be extended beyond the
realm of the abstract into the realm of the concrete: temporally (B-
theory, perdurance), modally (modal realism), and/or existentially
(Meinong). Of course, this may be taking things too far—there's
more to epistemic life than minimizing arbitrariness. (For my money, modal, existential and abstract maximalism go too far, but I'm
not going to try to evaluate maximalism here; my point is just that it
has its charms.)

---

[34] A maximalist could bypass Hume's Principle and infer the truth of the Peano Axioms
directly (though perhaps the abstraction principles are better candidates to be partial definitions of natural language number terms). Similar remarks apply to the quantifier variance
interpretation of the next section. Hume's Principle fails to be central on my interpretations
of neo-Fregeanism because I refused in section 1.3 to view the priority of syntax as an
important issue. Thanks to Matti Eklund here; and see Eklund (MSb, §III).

'Everything that can exist, does exist'—what exactly does that amount to, even confining our attention to mathematics? Here are three unacceptable interpretations:

(M1)Every abstraction principle can be truly interpreted.

(M2)Every consistent abstraction principle can be truly interpreted.

(M3)Every conservative consistent abstraction principle can be truly interpreted.

An abstraction principle is a principle of the form:

$$\forall F \forall G (ax{:}Fx = ax{:}Gx \leftrightarrow \phi(F,G))$$

where ϕ expresses an 'equivalence relation between the concepts F and G'. But some abstraction principles are contradictory. Frege's Basic Law V is an example. So (M1) is false.

(M2) is false because there are pairwise consistent abstraction principles that are jointly inconsistent. Let's take George Boolos's (1990) example of parity:

Definition: F and G *differ evenly* iff the things, x, such that $(Fx \wedge \neg Gx) \vee (Gx \wedge \neg Fx)$, are even (and finite) in number.

Parity abstraction principle:
$\forall F \forall G (Px{:}Fx = Px{:}Gx \leftrightarrow F$ and G differ evenly$)$.

Boolos shows that the Parity abstraction principle is consistent, but is only true in finite domains. Hume's Principle is consistent, but is only true in infinite domains. So each is consistent, but they can't be true together.

In response to Boolos, Wright proposed that acceptable abstraction principles must be conservative, in a certain sense. Not the usual sense (namely, that nothing in the old vocabulary that was unprovable before the introduction of the abstraction principle becomes provable after its introduction), for Hume's Principle isn't conservative in that sense: 'there are infinitely many things' is stateable in second-order logic, isn't a logical truth, but is a consequence of Hume's Principle. Wright's conservativeness requirement is rather that nothing about the extensions *of old concepts* can follow from the added abstraction principle. The parity principle implies, with respect to each primitive predicate F, that its extension must be finite, and so is not conservative in the relevant sense. However, it turns out that there are inconsistent pairs of individually conservative abstractions.[35]

So the view will have to be much more subtle. Kit Fine (2002) develops a sophisticated theory of when abstractions succeed, which could be taken over by maximalists in order to articulate the precise sense in which mathematical existence is maximal. Matti Eklund (MSa) discusses the prospects of a general maximalism.

V

The Quantifier Variance Interpretation. Return to the question: if Hume's principle is a definition, then what expressions does it define? According to the quantifier variance interpretation, the answer is that Hume's principle constrains the interpretation of the quantifiers, as well as 'the number of'. (Given section 2.7, it thereby constrains the interpretation of every other predicate logic expression.) The idea is to stipulate that the quantifiers are to be interpreted so that Hume's Principle comes out true. And an appropriate version of the doctrine of quantifier variance will guarantee that the quantifiers *can* be so interpreted.

In light of section three, the goal is not to make the epistemology of mathematics utterly unproblematic. To erase all doubts, one would need to know that quantifier variance is true. Still, if quantifier variance has independent plausibility, the neo-Fregean will have integrated mathematics into a plausible general metaontology, thus making epistemic progress. And quantifier variance does indeed have independent plausibility: like maximalism, it minimizes arbitrariness.

5.1. *Neo-Fregean Quantifier Variance Stated.* On the quantifier variance interpretation, when we lay down Hume's Principle as a definition, we're no longer assuming that the principle can be rendered true under the old meaning of the quantifiers. The idea is to *change* what the quantifiers mean.

---

[35]See Shapiro and Weir (1999); and see MacBride (2003, pp. 145–6) for further discussion and references.

The view is *not* that, after introducing Hume's Principle, the quantifiers in mathematical sentences mean something different from the quantifiers in non-mathematical sentences. The idea is rather that all quantifiers throughout the language have changed. In the new language, one can say that mathematical entities and physical entities exist in the same sense.

But we *don't* want to say that statements about non-mathematical entities change their truth values. The meaning shift ought to be conservative, in a certain sense. Not of course in the strictest sense, for as noted above, Hume's Principle forces an infinite domain. And in fact, we can't even say quite what Wright says about the conservativeness of acceptable abstractions: that no constraints may be put on the extensions of primitive non-mathematical (and non-logical) predicates. Since the notion of an extension is defined using quantifiers, after the quantifiers change meaning one cannot strictly speak of the old predicates as having extensions at all (they may not even be rightly called predicates). Instead we can offer an appropriate account of quantifier variance using the apparatus of section two. Here is a stab at it:[36]

> *Neo-Fregean quantifier variance*: There is a nonempty class of models, $\mathcal{M}$, and a class of meanings, E, such that:
> (1) $\mathcal{M}$ obeys upward $\langle\{\text{'\#'}\},\varnothing\rangle$-closure.
> (2) Every member of E is as natural as every other, and no meaning not in E is as natural as any meaning in E.
> (3) Strong $\mathcal{M}/E$-$\langle\{\text{'\#'}\},\varnothing\rangle$-quantifier variance is true.

Some help in unpacking. $\mathcal{M}$ is nonempty, so it contains at least one 'initial' quantifier world. Upward $\langle\{\text{'\#'}\},\varnothing\rangle$-closure will then force it to include all $\langle\{\text{'\#'}\},\varnothing\rangle$-supermodels of the initial world, which 'add' new entities to those present in the initial world. For each of

---

[36] How far beyond the bounds of this thesis does quantifier variance extend? As Joshua Brown pointed out to me, quantifier variantists face hard questions here. Is there, for example, a maximally natural quantifier meaning on which nothing at all exists? Is there one on which gods exist? There is a continuum of available positions here. At one end, maximally natural quantifier meanings proliferate; the more alien-seeming ones are merely semantically deficient; their only sin is that they do not fit our actual *use* of quantificational language. On the other, there are fewer maximally natural candidate meanings, perhaps only those guaranteed by the thesis stated in the text. The first end of the continuum best minimizes arbitrariness, but at a terrible cost: surely *some* ontological questions (e.g. 'Are there gods?', 'Are there extra-terrestrials?') have 'objective' answers!

these worlds, according to the claim, there is a corresponding (i.e. depicted) quantifier. Recall that restricting a quantifier variance claim to the ordered pair $\langle K, L \rangle$ constrains what non-logical expressions can apply to the 'newly introduced objects'. A restriction to $\langle \{`\#'\}, \varnothing \rangle$ means that the newly introduced entities may not enter into the extensions of non-logical predicates occurring in the initial world; they can only be semantic values of '#'.

5.2. *Which Abstraction Principles Are Acceptable?* The problem of incompatible stipulations—individually consistent but pairwise inconsistent abstraction principles—undermined reading (M2) of maximalism. The quantifier variance neo-Fregean has a little more latitude.

Hume's Principle is true only in infinite domains. The parity abstraction principle is true only in finite domains. So under no one quantifier meaning can both be true. But they can be true under different quantifier meanings. Thus, more abstraction principles are available to the quantifier variantist, so long as they are not all introduced at the same time.

Quantifier variantists could investigate the conditions under which abstractions succeed—that is, the conditions under which there exists a quantifier meaning on which a given abstraction principle comes out true. The following simple theorem is a start:[37]

> *Success*: Suppose neo-Fregean quantifier variance is true. Suppose a certain abstraction principle A, in which the only non-logical expression is '#', is consistent. Then there is some maximally natural meaning m and context c such that A is true$_m^c$.

5.3. *Give the People What They Want.* The quantifier variance interpretation gives neo-Fregeans all they can reasonably hope for, if not absolutely everything they want. It lets them say that abstract objects exist and are mind-independent, while claiming that in some

---

[37] Proof: understand talk of supermodels, etc., as relativized to $\langle \{`\#'\}, \varnothing \rangle$ throughout. Let M_0 be a member of $\mathcal{M}$. Let M be a model of A (choose M so that its domain does not overlap that of M_0). Construct model M^+ by combining the domains of M and M_0, and keeping the extensions of all non-logical expressions fixed. M^+ is a supermodel of M_0; thus, by upward closure, $M^+ \in \mathcal{M}$, and so by strong $\mathcal{M}/E$-quantifier variance, M^+ depicts $\langle m, c' \rangle$ for some (maximally natural) $m \in E$ and context c'. Now, M^+ is a supermodel of M as well; so by closure under restrictions, M depicts $\langle m, c \rangle$ for some c. A is true in M, and so is true$_m^c$.

sense the definitions that 'introduce' them are bound to succeed.

Neo-Fregean quantifier variance is an underlying metaontology on which consistent abstraction principles can invariably be truly interpreted. These abstraction principles may be put forward as implicit definitions of mathematical expressions plus the apparatus of predicate logic (quantifiers, names, predicates, function symbols). The resulting quantificational language will be at least as good as any other quantificational language, and the propositions expressed in the new language will be perfectly mind-independent.

Individually consistent but pairwise inconsistent abstractions can be truly interpreted on different interpretations of the quantifiers, even though they cannot be simultaneously truly interpreted.

The quantifier variance interpretation makes sense of the neo-Fregean idea that quantification is 'light', not a big deal. If there were a single distinguished quantificational meaning, then it would be an open possibility that numbers, directions, and other abstracta are simply *missing* from existence in the distinguished sense of 'existence', even though we speak in a perfectly consistent way about them. We would have to approach the question of whether they exist by some means other than assessing the consistency of their postulation—we would need the dreaded 'philosophical science of ontology'. That's heavy. But if quantifier variance is true, then this is not an open possibility.

Regarding the epistemology of arithmetic, once you spot yourself the truth of neo-Fregean quantifier variance (and spot yourself second-order consequence!), the introduction of numbers becomes relatively epistemically unproblematic. Now, I see no hope of establishing neo-Fregean quantifier variance itself beyond a shadow of a doubt. But that thesis is an attractive general thesis about metaontology. Integration of mathematics into an attractive and general theory is the most epistemic progress we can hope for.

Most importantly, the quantifier variance interpretation is a way—the *only* way, as far as I can see—of making sense of the idea that abstraction principles 'reconceptualize' facts about, for example, parallelism and equinumerosity. The core of quantifier variance is that the facts do not demand a unique description in the language of quantifiers. The facts about parallelism can be described by saying 'there are only lines', or they can be described by saying 'there are lines and directions'. Just as one can describe the facts of distance using any chosen unit of measure, one can describe the facts of ontology using any chosen quantificational meaning.

And the content of the quantifier variance interpretation is clearer than the intriguing but elusive texts of real live neo-Fregeans. That's not to say that it is *true*. I myself reject it, because I reject quantifier variance.[38] But I prefer an enemy that I can understand.[39]

REFERENCES

Boolos, G. 1985: 'Reading the *Begriffsschrift*', *Mind*, 94, pp. 331–44; reprinted in Boolos (1998, pp. 155–70).
——1990: 'The Standard of Equality of Numbers', in G. Boolos (ed.), *Meaning and Method: Essays in Honor of Hilary Putnam*, pp. 261–78 (Cambridge: Cambridge University Press); reprinted in Boolos (1998, pp. 202–19).
——1997: 'Is Hume's Principle Analytic?', in Heck (1997, pp. 245–62); reprinted in Boolos (1998, pp. 301–14).
——1998: *Logic, Logic, and Logic* (Cambridge, MA: Harvard University Press).
Burgess, J. P. 1984: 'Review of Crispin Wright, *Frege's Conception of Numbers as Objects*', *Philosophical Review*, 93, pp. 638–40.
Carnap, R. 1950: 'Empiricism, Semantics and Ontology', *Revue International de Philosophie*, 4, pp. 20–40; reprinted in *Meaning and Necessity: A Study in Semantics and Modal Logic,* 2nd edn. (Chicago: University of Chicago Press, 1956).
Demopoulos, W. (ed.) 1995: *Frege's Philosophy of Mathematics* (Cambridge, MA: Harvard University Press).
Eklund, M. 2006: 'Metaontology', *Philosophy Compass*, 1, pp. 317–34.
——forthcoming: 'The Picture of Reality as an Amorphous Lump', in Sider, Hawthorne and Zimmerman (forthcoming).
——MSa: 'Maximalist Ontology'.
——MSb: 'Neo-Fregean Ontology'. Available online at <http://www.people. cornell.edu/pages/me72/pnfo.pdf>.
Field, H. 1984: 'Platonism for Cheap? Crispin Wright on Frege's Context

---

[38] See Sider (2007).

[39] Matti Eklund's work (MSb; 2006) connecting neo-Fregeanism to questions about the ontology of material objects sparked my interest in these topics. Thanks to Matti for helpful comments, and to Frank Arntzenius, Deniz Dagci, Kit Fine, John Hawthorne, Eli Hirsch, Anders Strand, Jason Turner, Dean Zimmerman, attendees of the 2006 BSPC conference (especially Joshua Brown, my commentator), and participants in my Spring 2006 seminar on metaontology.

Principle', *Canadian Journal of Philosophy*, 14, pp. 637–62; reprinted in Field (1989, pp. 147–70).

——1989: *Realism, Mathematics and Modality* (Oxford: Blackwell).

——2006: 'Recent Debates about the A Priori', in T. S. Gendler and J. Hawthorne (eds.), *Oxford Studies in Epistemology*, Vol. 1 (Oxford: Oxford University Press).

Fine, K. 2002: *The Limits of Abstraction* (Oxford: Clarendon Press).

Hale, B. 1987: *Abstract Objects* (Oxford: Basil Blackwell).

——and C. Wright 2001: *The Reason's Proper Study: Essays Towards a Neo-Fregean Philosophy of Mathematics* (Oxford: Oxford University Press).

Harris, J. H. 1982: 'What's So Logical About the Logical Axioms?', *Studia Logica*, 41, pp. 159–71.

Hart, W. D. 1982: 'Prior and Belnap', *Theoria*, 48, pp. 127–38.

Hawthorne, J. 2006: 'Plenitude, Convention, and Ontology', in *Metaphysical Essays*, pp. 53–70 (Oxford: Oxford University Press).

Hazen, A. 1985: 'Review of Crispin Wright's *Frege's Conception of Numbers as Objects*', *Australasian Journal of Philosophy*, 63, pp. 251–54.

Heck, R. G. (ed.) 1997: *Language, Thought, and Logic: Essays in Honour of Michael Dummett* (Oxford: Oxford University Press).

Hirsch, E. 2002a: 'Against Revisionary Ontology', *Philosophical Topics*, 30, pp. 103–27.

——2002b: 'Quantifier Variance and Realism', *Philosophical Issues*, 12, pp. 51–73.

——2005: 'Physical-Object Ontology, Verbal Disputes, and Common Sense', *Philosophy and Phenomenological Research,* 70, pp. 67–97.

——forthcoming: 'Ontological Arguments: Interpretive Charity and Quantifier Variance', in Sider, Hawthorne and Zimmerman (forthcoming).

Horwich, P. 1997: 'Implicit Definitions, Analytic Truth and Apriori Knowlege', *Noûs*, 31, pp. 423–40.

Lewis, D. 1983: 'New Work for a Theory of Universals', *Australasian Journal of Philosophy*, 61, pp. 343–77; reprinted in Lewis (1999, pp. 8–55).

——1984: 'Putnam's Paradox', *Australasian Journal of Philosophy*, 62, pp. 221–36; reprinted in Lewis (1999, pp. 56–77).

——1986: *On the Plurality of Worlds* (Oxford: Basil Blackwell).

——1999: *Papers in Metaphysics and Epistemology* (Cambridge: Cambridge University Press).

MacBride, F. 2003: 'Speaking with Shadows: A Study of Neo-Logicism', *British Journal for the Philosophy of Science*, 54, pp. 103–63.

Parsons, C. 1965: 'Frege's Theory of Number', in M. Black (ed.), *Philosophy in America* (Ithaca: Cornell University Press), pp. 180–203; reprinted in Demopoulos (1995, pp. 182–210).

Parsons, T. 1990: *Events in the Semantics of English* (Cambridge, MA: MIT Press).

Prior, A. N. 1960: 'The Runabout Inference Ticket', *Analysis*, 21, pp. 38–39.

Putnam, H. 1987a: *The Many Faces of Realism* (La Salle, IL: Open Court).

——1987b: 'Truth and Convention: On Davidson's Refutation of Conceptual Relativism', *Dialectica*, 41, pp. 41–67.

Quine, W. V. O. 1936: 'Truth by Convention', in O. H. Lee (ed.), *Philosophical Essays for A. N. Whitehead*, pp. 90–124 (New York: Longmans); reprinted in Quine (1966, pp. 70–99).

——1966: *The Ways of Paradox* (New York: Random House).

——1970: *Philosophy of Logic* (Cambridge, MA: Harvard University Press); 2nd edn., 1986.

Rayo, A. and S. Yablo 2001: 'Nominalism through De-Nominalization', *Noûs*, 35, pp. 74–92.

Rosen, G. 1993: 'The Refutation of Nominalism(?)', *Philosophical Topics*, 21, pp. 149–86.

Schiffer, S. 2003: *The Things We Mean* (Oxford: Clarendon Press).

Shapiro, S. and A. Weir 1999: 'New V, ZF and Abstraction', *Philosophia Mathematica*, 7, pp. 293–321.

Sider, T. 2007: 'Ontological Realism', in D. Chalmers, D. Manley and R. Wasserman (eds.), *Metametaphysics* (Oxford: Oxford University Press).

——MS: 'Reducing Modality'. Available online at <http://fas-philosophy. rutgers.edu/sider/papers/reducing_modality.pdf>.

——J. Hawthorne and D. W. Zimmerman (eds.) forthcoming: *Contemporary Debates in Metaphysics* (Oxford: Blackwell).

Turner, J. 2008: *Ontology, Quantification, and Fundamentality*. Ph. D. thesis, Rutgers University.

van Inwagen, P. 1987: 'When Are Objects Parts?', in J. Tomberlin (ed.), *Philosophical Perspectives 1: Metaphysics*, pp. 21–47 (Atascadero, CA: Ridgeview).

——1990: *Material Beings* (Ithaca, NY: Cornell University Press).

——1998: 'Meta-Ontology', *Erkenntnis*, 48, pp. 233–50; reprinted in van Inwagen (2001, pp. 13–31).

——2001: *Ontology, Identity and Modality* (Cambridge: Cambridge University Press).

Williamson, T. 1988: 'Equivocation and Existence', *Proceedings of the Aristotelian Society*, 88, pp. 109–27.

——2003: 'Understanding and Inference', *Proceedings of the Aristotelian Society Supplementary Volume*, 77, pp. 249–93.

Wittgenstein, L. 1958: *Philosophical Investigations*, 3rd edn., trans. G. E. M. Anscombe (Oxford: Basil Blackwell & Mott).

Wright, C. 1983: *Frege's Conception of Numbers as Objects* (Aberdeen: Aberdeen University Press).

——1997: 'The Philosophical Significance of Frege's Theorem', in Heck, 1997, pp. 201–44; reprinted in Hale and Wright (2001, pp. 272–306).

Neo-Fregeanism and Quantifier Variance
Theodore Sider and Katherine Hawley

II—Katherine Hawley

Neo-Fregeanism and Quantifier Variance

Sider argues that, of maximalism and quantifier variance, the latter promises to let us make better sense of neo-Fregeanism. I argue that neo-Fregeans should, and seemingly do, reject quantifier variance. If they must choose between these two options, they should choose maximalism.

I

Introduction. Benacerraf's problem lies at the heart of philosophy of mathematics: the truth of mathematical statements appears to require the existence of infinitely many abstract mathematical objects, yet we seem to know these truths without having perceptual access to abstracta. What grounds our knowledge of mathematics? Philosophical responses typically take one of two paths, attempting either to dispense with abstract objects, or else to show how we can have knowledge of them.

Neo-Fregeans take the second path, arguing that our knowledge of logic together with our knowledge of a definitional fact about the word 'number' secures our knowledge of abstracta and arithmetic. The definitional fact is Hume's Principle:

$\forall F \forall G$ [the number of Fs = the number of Gs iff the Fs stand in one-one correspondence with the Gs].

We know that there are concepts which stand in one-one correspondence with each other (e.g. the concept *being non-self-identical* stands in one-one correspondence with itself); via the biconditional, we can thus establish that there are numbers. Moreover, we can derive the axioms of Peano Arithmetic from this starting point using logic alone.

To those of us who make a living out of the 'philosophical science of ontology' (Wright, 1983, p. 52), this looks like audacious sleight of hand. Of course we can stipulate that 'the number of Fs = the number of Gs' is true iff the Fs stand in one-one correspondence with the Gs, but can we really then treat that phrase as referring to entities called 'numbers'? There is apparently no commitment to the existence of numbers on the right-hand side of Hume's Principle: can stipulation create such a commitment on the left?

Ted Sider believes that our disagreement with neo-Fregeans can be traced to broader disagreements about the nature of language and reality, and the proper constraints upon metaphysics; I agree. He discusses two rival metaontologies—quantifier variance and maximalism—and tries out each as an underpinning for neo-Fregeanism. He doesn't attribute either view to actual neo-Fregeans, though he does argue that quantifier variance at least supplies all that neo-Fregeans can reasonably hope for.

In response, I will attempt the following. First, I will argue that one of Sider's attempts to simplify the debate—by shifting attention away from the 'syntactic priority' thesis and the role of singular terms—manages instead to distort the debate. Second, I will argue that maximalism is a closer match to actual neo-Fregeanism than is quantifier variance, and that if neo-Fregeans must choose between these two options, maximalism is the right choice to make. One apparent difficulty for my argument is that it is not clear how maximalism can make sense of neo-Fregean talk of 'reconceptualization' or 'recarving content'; I address this difficulty by drawing upon the work of David Armstrong and David Lewis.

II

The Importance of Singular Terms. Taken in isolation the stipulation of Hume's Principle would seem unobjectionable: we could read 'the number of Fs is identical to the number of Gs' as a semantically-simple synonym for 'the Fs are in one-one correspondence with the Gs'. Moreover, taken in isolation, the neo-Fregean claim that 'the number of Fs is identical to the number of Gs' really does have the logical form of an identity statement would also seem unobjectionable: we could understand Hume's Principle as a bold hypothesis about numbers.

The power and the mystery of neo-Fregeanism derives from combining these two claims: Hume's Principle may be stipulated true, *and* its apparent logical form is genuine, so that if there are any con-

cepts in one-one-correspondence, then there are numbers. Consequently, much effort has been devoted to the question whether 'the
number of Fs' and 'the number of Gs' really function as singular
terms on the left-hand side of Hume's Principle.[1]

Sider, however, suggests that this particular debate is a mere dis-
traction. What's crucial is whether sentences like 'the number of Fs
is identical to the number of Gs' are susceptible to the usual quantificational laws. For example, suppose that we establish via the biconditional that 'the number of non-self-identical things is identical
to the number of non-self-identical things' is true. Neo-Fregeans
want to infer from this that there is something which is identical to
the number of non-self-identical things. Sider recommends that they
simply stipulate that 'the number of Fs' and similar terms are liable
to such quantificational treatment and, moreover, that the components of such terms are semantically significant, so that we can infer
from the existence of something which is identical to the number of
non-self-identical things to the existence of a number.

'The debate can then focus on the real issue: on whether the joint
stipulation of [Hume's Principle] and [the logical form claim] is coherent' (Sider, 2007, p. 205).

This account of neo-Fregeanism as founded upon a joint stipulation does make sense of some critical reactions to the view. Reduc-
tionists accept the stipulation of Hume's Principle, but deny that the
left-hand side reveals any ontological commitment to numbers; re-
jectionists accept that the left-hand side has its apparent logical
form, but reject the stipulation of Hume's Principle.

But there are two problems with Sider's attempt to re-frame neo-
Fregeanism in this way. First, the issues at stake in the debate about
whether 'the number of Fs' is a singular term will simply reappear in
debate about whether the left-hand side of instances of the biconditional satisfy semantic compositionality and penetrability by quantifiers. For neo-Fregeans, all it takes for something to be a singular
term is for it to behave like a singular term (for example, to stand on
one side of a genuine identity sign), and all it takes for such a term
to refer is for it to feature in a true atomic statement. The fact that
we can consistently stipulate Hume's Principle to be true reveals that
we were already committed to the existence of numbers by our ac-

---

[1] See MacBride (2003, pp. 103–63) for discussion and references.

©2007 The Aristotelian Society
Proceedings of the Aristotelian Society Supplementary Volume LXXXI

ceptance of one-one correspondences. Second, taking the logical form claim to be a matter of stipulation obscures the fact that it flows directly from neo-Fregeans' metaontological views about syntax, semantics, extra-linguistic reality, and the connections amongst them.

Perhaps my difference with Sider here is just a difference of emphasis: I say that the neo-Fregeans' claim about the logical form of Hume's Principle is a consequence of their metaontology, whereas Sider takes it to be a stipulation whose joint stipulability with the truth of Hume's Principle is supposed to be licensed by the metaontology. Still, I think this difference of emphasis is significant, for two reasons. First, it shows that the debate about singular terms which Sider recommends sidestepping is integral to the debate about neo-Fregean metaontology; this in turn reminds us that neo-Fregeans do not separate language and world in the neat fashion we scientific ontologists prefer. Second, the reduction of neo-Fregeanism to a joint stipulation naturally prompts the hostile thought that neo-Fregeans are trying to stipulate numbers into existence, rather than, as they see it themselves, revealing our existing ontological commitments.

III

Quantifier Variance or Maximalism? Sider suggests two possible metaontologies for neo-Fregeanism—quantifier variance and maximalism—and while he doesn't attribute either of these to actual neo-Fregeans, he does recommend that they adopt quantifier variance. In contrast, I will argue both that maximalism is closer to the view of actual neo-Fregeans, and that it provides them with a stronger position. In the first of these, at least, I side with Matti Eklund (2006), who has provided more detailed arguments for assimilating neo-Fregeanism to maximalism, whilst highlighting some pitfalls for this view. I will outline the two metaontologies then explain why neo-Fregeans should (and perhaps do) favour maximalism.

The core claim of quantifier variance is that there is a range of equally good meanings for the existential quantifier, none of which is simply a restriction of the others. Central to Sider's paper is the welcome development of a formal framework for understanding this 'neo-Carnapian' idea, which is derived from Eli Hirsch (2002). Quantifier variance is intended to make sense of 'no-fault' disagreements about ontology where neither party appears to be quantifying over a domain which is simply a restriction of that intended by the other. Hirsch's focus is the metaphysics of material objects, and in particular the question of whether arbitrary sums of familiar objects exist: in one sense of 'exist' they do, in another sense they don't, and there's no deeper meaning to the question whether they *really* exist. But Sider shows how the same framework may cohere with neo-Fregeanism.

A standard objection to neo-Fregeanism is that there just might not be any objects which satisfy the definition of 'number' laid down by the stipulation of Hume's Principle. Surely the most we can stipulate is that *if* there are numbers, then they satisfy Hume's Principle? (Field, 1984). On the quantifier variance interpretation, neo-Fregeans take the stipulation of Hume's Principle to shift the meaning of the quantifiers such that it becomes true to say that numbers exist. Roughly speaking, pre-stipulation, 'numbers exist' is false but post-stipulation 'numbers exist' is true, because the meaning of 'exist' shifts at stipulation. Crucially, neither of these meanings of 'exist' is objectively better or more natural than the other; there's no deeper meaning to the question whether numbers *really* exist.

This is only a rough formulation, since strictly speaking 'numbers exist' is meaningless, rather than false, before the stipulation of Hume's Principle. A little more carefully: anyone who said pre-stipulation 'there are infinitely many objects' would have spoken falsely; anyone who made the homophonic claim post-stipulation would speak truly.

The second metaontology, maximalism, is the luxurious view that everything which can exist does exist. Neo-Fregeans apparently only need maximalism about the abstract; on this interpretation, the consistency of Hume's Principle shows that numbers can exist, then maximalism guarantees that they do.[2] (Maximalism about the abstract is much like 'full-blooded Platonism': this is the view, as formulated by Mark Balaguer (1998), that every mathematical object which could possibly exist does exist.)

---

[2] Eklund (2006) argues, however, that it will prove difficult for neo-Fregeans to restrict their maximalism to the abstract: the views about language and reality which underwrite the method of abstraction also apply to the concrete realm.

If maximalism is to be straightforwardly incompatible with quantifier variance, it must include the rejection of the quantifier variance thesis, as well as the positive claim about what objects there are. Without this, debate about the truth of maximalism would look like just the sort of ontological 'disagreement' which Hirsch's quantifier variance is intended to deflate, and it would not be clear that the views were genuine rivals.

Suitably understood, maximalism and quantifier variance are competing answers to at least three different questions. First, which metaontology is true? Second, what is the intended metaontology of actual neo-Fregeans? Third, which metaontology best serves the goals of neo-Fregeanism? The first question is explicitly sidelined in Sider's paper, except for passing remarks about the falsity of both views; I too will ignore it. Sider also sets aside the second question; I will give it a little more attention. The third question gets most airtime, and Sider's conclusion is that 'Neo-Fregeans should embrace quantifier variance' (2007, p. 201). I will disagree.

My method is the following: I will examine several different aspects of neo-Fregeanism, including some positive features and some difficulties for the view; in each case I will discuss which of maximalism and quantifier variance would be most advantageous to neo-Fregeans, and which, if either, seems close to the views of actual neo-Fregeans. I do not claim that this procedure is conclusive, but it does tend to favour maximalism.

IV

Mutually Incompatible Abstraction Principles. I will confront a key difficulty for maximalism first. As Sider points out in his sections 4 and 5.2, individually consistent but pairwise inconsistent abstraction principles are a problem for neo-Fregeanism under the maximalist interpretation but not under the quantifier variance interpretation. An extended version of this argument is central to Eklund's criticism (2006, §VI) of maximalist neo-Fregeanism. I concede that this problem does provide a good reason for neo-Fregeans to adopt quantifier variance rather than maximalism, if they cannot solve the problem otherwise.

That said, the responses of actual neo-Fregeans to the problem do suggest that their intended metaontology is closer to maximalism than to quantifier variance. In their prospectus Hale and Wright (2001, p. 426) consider (i) rejecting all abstraction principles which require the universe to have a determinate cardinality; (ii) holding 'that *either* (though not of course both) of such a pair of [mutually inconsistent] abstractions is acceptable ... there is simply no fact of the matter with which an otherwise acceptable abstraction might conflict and we are in effect merely presented with choices about in which of two incompatible directions we should develop the notion of set'; and (iii) 'A third, as it seems to us attractive, line of response, would be to argue that [an abstraction is unacceptable] unless there is no other abstraction incompatible with it which has exactly the same other virtues.' It's hard to be certain, but (ii) does sound like quantifier variance, with its various distinct domains of existents, whilst the 'attractive' (iii) suggests a single domain, as entailed by maximalism.

V

Duds. Richard Heck (2000) points out that first-order equivalence relations are easily gerrymandered: if we do not place restrictions on which relations are suitable for abstraction, we will be lumbered with all sorts of peculiar abstracta. Consider an arbitrary equivalence relation, Q, one of whose equivalence classes contains just Heck's shoes, Queen Victoria, and the blackboard in 104 Emerson Hall. Now Dud(a) = Dud(b) iff aQb.

Hale and Wright are rather sanguine about Duds:

> Why, after all, shouldn't Fregean abstracts be just as 'proliferated' as sets? This not to deny that if any well-defined first-order equivalence relation is allowed to sustain an abstraction, then some of the result-ing abstracts—like Duds—will rightly impress as frivolous. But there seems no good reason why that impression should issue in scepticism about such entities, or why tolerance of them should somehow trivial-ize the abstractionist account in more serious cases. As an analogy: someone whose notion of set is initially grounded in predication will

be inclined to find sets to which no naturally conceived property or relation corresponds equally bizarre on first encounter. (Hale and
Wright, 2001, p. 424, n. 8)

Again this isn't decisive, but both the lack of concern and the analogy with sets are a poor match with quantifier variance. Sets are out
there and quantified over, regardless of whether and when we define
predicates to match them; systematicity pushes us to recognize the
full set-theoretical universe, moving beyond our initially restricted
view of what exists. Similarly, according to maximalist neo-Fregeanism, abstracta are out there, and quantified over, regardless of
whether and when we implicitly define concepts to match them;
Heck and systematicity push us to move beyond our initially restricted view of what exists. But according to quantifier variance
doesn't fit so well here: at any time, it's true to say that only those
abstracta exist which are required by abstraction principles already
stipulated true. So the discussion of Duds provides good reason for
thinking neo-Fregeans do not intend to endorse quantifier variance.

Is this a wise choice? The quantifier variance interpretation might
seem preferable to maximalism on this count, since it would in some
sense reduce the number of Dud-like entities in our ontology: before
the relevant abstraction principle is rustled up, the peculiar entities
do not fall within the scope of our quantifiers, and it's true then to
say that they don't exist. This is a meagre advantage, however, given
that merely stipulating a gerrymandered abstraction principle is
enough to bring the relevant objects into the domain of our quantifiers, making it true to say that they exist.

VI

Impredicativity. Neo-Fregeans want to use Hume's Principle to establish the existence of infinitely many numbers, and to do so without relying on the assumption that there are infinitely many non-
numerical objects. This means that Hume's Principle must be interpreted in such a way that numbers are amongst the objects falling
under the concepts whose one-one correspondence is discussed on
the right-hand side. So Hume's Principle is impredicative: 'Its first-
order quantifiers must be construed as ranging over, *inter alia*, ob-

jects of that very kind whose concept it is intended to introduce'
(Hale and Wright, 2001, p. 21).

A more explicit, second-order formulation of Hume's Principle
makes this clear:

$$\forall F \forall G[(\text{the number of } Fs = \text{the number of } Gs) \text{ iff}$$
$$\exists R \, \forall x((Fx \rightarrow \exists! y(Gy \wedge Rxy)) \wedge (Gx \rightarrow \exists! y(Fy \wedge Ryx)))].$$

If impredicativity is a problem, it is because impredicative definitions are viciously circular. The apparent circularity here is not metaphysical: Hume's Principle is not supposed to show how numbers
themselves are somehow composed out of non-numerical objects.
Any ban on impredicativity must instead arise from a requirement
for epistemic noncircularity. Hume's Principle is supposed to function as an introduction to, or explanation of, the concept 'number'
for those who are already familiar with the sorts of facts described
on the right-hand side of the biconditional. Thus it is crucial to the
success of neo-Fregeanism that it be possible to grasp the content of
the right-hand-side without already having a grasp of 'number', even
though numbers fall under the concepts whose equinumerosity is
discussed on the right-hand side. Recognizing the importance of the
issue, Hale (1994) and Wright (1998) argue that one can understand
a concept, understand it well enough to know whether the objects
falling under it stand in a one-one correspondence with the objects
falling under some other concept, without knowing whether numbers fall under that concept.

If maximalism is true, the neo-Fregeans must be right about what
it takes to grasp a concept. Given maximalism, all sorts of things exist, things which no-one has ever explicitly considered (including
lots of Dud-like entities). Presumably many of these things fall under concepts which we all understand (like *being self-identical*), so it
must be possible to understand a concept without having a firm
grasp on all the things which fall under it. Maximalism makes it
compulsory to think of our understanding of concepts roughly as
the neo-Fregeans do, on pain of our not understanding even very familiar concepts. So if we grant maximalism to the neo-Fregeans, the
problem of impredicativity dissolves.

But the quantifier variance interpretation makes impredicativity
look more worrying. Recall the central idea: by stipulating the truth

of Hume's Principle, we shift the meanings of the quantifiers in a way which makes the biconditional true. So the stipulation of Hume's Principle changes the meaning of the one-one correspondence claim on the right-hand side of the biconditional:

> The view is *not* that, after introducing Hume's Principle, the quantifiers in mathematical sentences mean something different from the quantifiers in non-mathematical sentences. The idea is rather that all quantifiers throughout the language have changed. (Sider, 2007, p. 227)

Given this quantifier variance interpretation, it is less clear whether someone could be introduced to the concept of number as the neo-Fregeans say. Before the stipulation of Hume's Principle, one-one correspondence claims do *not* quantify over numbers; after stipulation they do. We lose the cosy picture of our Hero (Wright, 1998), extending his language by correlating claims involving new words (like 'number' or 'direction') with claims involving old words (like 'one-one correspondence' or 'parallel'), whose meaning he already grasps. Instead, Hero must somehow first grasp the *shifted* meaning of the old words, then use this to grasp the meaning of the new words. Moreover we lose the cosy picture of a Hero who already knows that the concept *being-non-self-identical* is equinumerous with itself, and can use this knowledge, via the stipulation of Hume's Principle, to acquire knowledge of numbers. Instead, Hero must somehow work out that '*being-non-self-identical* is equinumerous with itself' expresses a truth in the new language, before he can use this knowledge to acquire knowledge of numbers.

Now, this difficulty should not be overstated, since the change in meaning induced by quantifier variance should not be overstated. As Sider points out, if quantifier variance is not to collapse into the uninteresting claim that the string of letters 'exists' could have meant something else, then the various available meanings for the existential quantifier must all in some sense be *existential* meanings, related in some significant way (perhaps their shared inferential role is key). So Hero doesn't face the difficult task of translating his knowledge into an entirely novel language. But recall that, for the purposes of neo-Fregeanism, Hero's epistemic position must be extremely secure. Adopting a quantifier variance interpretation makes this more difficult to demonstrate; adopting maximalism makes it rather easy.

VII

Pre- and Post-Stipulation Asymmetry. As Sider shows, a crucial feature of the quantifier variance approach is that it treats the various meanings for the quantifiers as equally good, and thereby dissolves many apparent disagreements about what exists. This feature distinguishes quantifier variance from certain other attempts to resolve ontological disagreements, those which invoke quantification over a restricted domain. Everyday folk deny that there is any such thing as Noel's-nose-plus-Liam's-fist; rather than class these everyday beliefs false, advocates of unrestricted composition may argue that everyday quantifiers range over the restricted domain of ordinary objects, not the universal domain.

Here is Hirsch on such attempts to defend unrestricted composition:

> This suggestion is misguided, I think. Ordinary people must have a concept of 'existence *simpliciter*'. They must understand how to use the quantifier unrestrictedly; otherwise no such use could be part of the English language ... if we explain to ordinary people that the [arbitrary sum] in question need not be any kind of familiar thing, it need not be an interesting thing or the sort of thing one would normally talk about, they still regard the sentence [which claims that it exists] as insanely false. (Hirsch, 2002, p. 65)

According to Hirsch and his quantifier variance view, philosophical advocates of unrestricted composition use quantifiers which are simply *different* from those used in everyday speech; these quantifiers are not better, less restricted, more encompassing versions of those used by ordinary people.

So quantifier variance encapsulates a kind of symmetry amongst the different meanings for the quantifiers. Maximalism is at odds with this: the speaker who denies the existence of objects which *could* exist either speaks falsely (though perhaps forgivably), or else speaks truly only by virtue of using a quantifier which fails to range over the entire universal domain.

How does this disagreement play out for neo-Fregeanism? Suppose that, before the stipulation of Hume's Principle, Hero denies that there are infinitely many objects (he's not equipped to deny that there are numbers, as such). According to the quantifier variance in-

terpretation, Hero speaks the truth, as indeed he would if he added
'and I mean that absolutely, not even if we include all the things we
don't normally talk about'. Maximalists, in contrast, count his denial as false, at least if it is intended to have entirely general scope; Hero's quantifiers already range over numbers (and much else), even if
he can be forgiven for not yet realizing this.

According to neo-Fregeans, however, abstraction merely reveals
the ontological commitments which are already present in claims
about one-one-correspondence between concepts (or parallelism between lines, as the case may be).

> The Fregean platonist holds ... that the ontological commitments of
> the right-hand sides are just what are displayed in the surface gram-
> mar of the left-hand sides—an ontology of both directions and lines.
> But that seems to imply that even if we speak exclusively in the vocab-
> ulary of the right-hand sides, we nevertheless refer, willy-nilly, to di-
> rections as well. Indeed, this would be so even if we had no inkling of
> the concept of direction and never introduced direction terminology.
> (Wright, 1990; p. 164 in Hale and Wright, 2001)

(It's only 'seems to imply' because Wright goes on to argue that although claims about parallel lines ontologically commit us to
directions—even if we have no inkling of this—they do not thereby
involve *reference* to directions.)

On this view, concept-formulation via stipulation reveals aspects
of the world which might otherwise have remained hidden. We improve our epistemic position, our knowledge of what (already) exists, by stipulating Hume's Principle, thereby acquiring a new
concept, and by employing logic; post-stipulation we know more
about the world. There seems to be an asymmetry between pre- and
post-stipulation positions which cannot be captured by the quantifier variance interpretation, according to which no particular meaning of the existential quantifier is the most natural, or objectively
best.

As Sider points out, a great advantage of quantifier variance is
that it provides neo-Fregeans with a guarantee that existence claims
about numbers are true:

> If [contrary to quantifier variance] there were a single distinguished
> quantificational meaning, then it would be an open possibility that
> numbers, directions, and other abstracta are simply *missing* from ex-

istence in the distinguished sense of 'existence', even though we speak in a perfectly consistent way about them ... But if quantifier variance is true, then this is not an open possibility. (Sider, 2007, p. 229)

This is true; my claim is that maximalism also closes off this worrying possibility, as Sider himself shows, whilst staying closer to the spirit of neo-Fregeanism.

VII

Conceptual Recarving. Finally, Sider argues that quantifier variance makes best sense of the neo-Fregean 'recarving' or 'reconceptualization' idea. According to Hale and Wright this is:

> Frege's idea at *Grundlagen* 64 that the two halves of an instance of an abstraction principle may be seen as 'recarvings' of a single content: specifically, that we are free to reconceive the obtaining of an equivalence relation on objects of a certain kind as the identification of objects of a new kind. (Hale and Wright, 2001, p. 421)

In concluding his paper, Sider writes:

> Most importantly, the quantifier variance interpretation is a way—the *only* way, as far as I can see—of making sense of the idea that abstraction principles 'reconceptualize' facts about, for example, parallelism and equinumerosity. The core of quantifier variance is that the facts do not demand a unique description in the language of quantifiers. The facts about parallelism can be described by saying 'there are only lines', or they can be described by saying 'there are lines and directions'. (Sider, 2007, p. 229)

The mapping of quantifier variance onto recarving is not especially smooth. The Fregean claim is that, for any *instance* of the biconditional, the description on the left is equivalent to the description on the right: in some sense, the fact that these two particular lines are parallel just is the fact that they have the same direction. Recarving is something that can be done to parallelism facts one at a time, though it is the abstraction principle which gives us the general recipe for doing so.

In contrast, Sider's quantifier variance explicitly turns recarving into something that is done just once for the whole realm, by stipulating the abstraction principle: '[T]he totality of states of affairs about equinumerosity can be reconceptualized as states of affairs involving the existence of a domain of numbers' (p. 206). This is no accident: no one should think that directions enter the scope of our existential quantifier piecemeal as we consider various pairs of parallel lines.

So there's some awkwardness here: quantifier variance doesn't quite capture reconceptualization as neo-Fregeans intend it. But does it do better than maximalism, at least? You might very well think so. If maximalism is true, then Hume's Principle merely introduces a term for those entities (numbers) which, whilst being entirely distinct from concepts, are correlated with them in a certain way. Sure, maximalism guarantees that there are such entities, but how could this process be described as 'reconceptualization' or 'recarving'? I think there are two questions here. First, how can commitment to a fact about entities of one sort involve commitment to a fact about entities of another, distinct sort? Second, how can such a relation between distinct entities have anything to do with 'reconceptualization'?

In considering the first question, we may consult two noble laureates of the philosophical science of ontology: David Armstrong and David Lewis. Armstrong writes, repeatedly and notoriously, that supervenient entities are an 'ontological free lunch', and that 'what supervenes is no addition of being' (1997, p. 12). Lewis wrote, not so often, but notoriously nevertheless, that once we are committed to the existence of some objects, commitment to their fusion is no further commitment. 'It just *is* them. They just *are* it' (1991, p. 81).

Consider your ontological commitments. Now 'add' an object which is identical (numerically identical) to one of the objects you already accept; clearly this is no further commitment, no addition to being. Indeed, you could stipulate that 'Robert' be another name for Lucy, an object you're already committed to; then a commitment to the existence of Robert is no further commitment, it's just another way of expressing your existing commitments.

For Lewis (1991, p. 82), mereological fusion is ontologically innocent because 'it commits us only to things that are identical, so to speak, to what we were committed to before'. That 'so to speak' must do some delicate work, as Sider himself has shown elsewhere (forthcoming). Lewis doesn't accept the strong view that many-one composition and one-one identity are the very same relation; rather, he accepts an 'analogical' version of the thesis, according to which one-one identity is one kind of identity, while composition, and indeed parthood, are other kinds of identity.

Armstrong is bolder. A commitment to supervenient entities is not anything additional to a commitment to the subvening entities, whether or not the superveners are identical to the subveners. Moreover, in the special case of composition, the whole is nothing in addition to its parts, and the parts are nothing in addition to the whole, so 'mereological wholes are identical with all their parts taken together. Symmetrical supervenience yields identity' (1997, p. 12). A paragraph later, Armstrong writes 'Like other free lunches, this one gives and takes away at the same time. You get the supervenient for free, but you do not really get an extra entity'. Again, this is a delicate matter: it seems that supervening entities are identical to subveners only where supervenience is symmetric, yet somehow superveners are not really extra entities, even where they fail to be identical to subveners.

Lewis and Armstrong's views are hardly pellucid, but they do have the sociological advantage of being familiar to many contemporary metaphysicians. And they provide a model for the idea that facts about distinct objects can in some sense be the same fact. The sum is not, for Lewis, literally identical with its many parts, but commitment to the parts already involves commitment to the whole. For Armstrong, supervening entities are real, and are not in general identical to subveners, but a commitment to them is somehow no additional commitment.

This is strongly reminiscent of the neo-Fregean idea that we are already ontologically committed to numbers by our commitment to equinumerous concepts. Recall Wright's efforts to establish that, despite this, equinumerosity claims do not involve *reference* to numbers; likewise, Lewis and Armstrong would presumably accept that I do not *refer* to a complex object when I refer to the objects which are its parts, even though I thereby commit myself to its existence.

The Australian free lunch resembles the Scottish generosity about ontology, but neither Lewis nor Armstrong suggests that supervenient entities are in any sense constructed by our 'conceptualization' of them. But nor do neo-Fregeans endorse such an anti-realism. Their picture involves a single fact (or content, or state of affairs) which includes both a pair of parallel lines and a 'pair' of identical directions. Which of these entities we 'see' depends upon the perspective from which we consider the fact; it is the shift between perspectives which involves recarving or reconceptualizing the fact.

Consider an analogy. Suppose that a cat is ontologically more basic than any of its parts. What does this mean? Hard to say exactly, but perhaps the cat is 'more than the sum of its parts', or the parts are ontologically dependent upon the cat, or it is essential to the parts that they are parts of the cat, yet inessential to the cat that it have those very parts. Perhaps it's the converse of whatever philosophers have in mind when they think that macroscopic entities exist, but are less basic than the microscopic entities which compose them.

Now, think of the cat as divided into parts. Which parts? You might consider: head, torso, limbs, tail. Then: cells. Then: left half, right half. Then: front half, back half. No particular decomposition is the most fundamental; the most complete account is the one which includes every part, though this may not be the most useful account; there is a good sense in which commitment to the parts involved in one decomposition just is commitment to the parts involved in every other, as indeed is commitment to the cat. All of the parts exist before you think of them: to say that the parts are secondary to or dependent upon the cat is not to say either that they fail to exist, nor that their existence depends upon our recognizing them.

My suggestion, of course, is that on this picture the parts stand to the cat as do the components of the fact to the fact itself. Are you recarving the cat as you idly contemplate it? You're not physically chopping it up, merely shifting your attention between its various parts; indeed I can think of nothing—concept, thought, whatever— which is literally segmented during this process. Yet the metaphor seems reasonable.

So maximalism offers neo-Fregeans the opportunity to get (more or less) what they want, and, provided we adopt certain other views about ontological free lunches and the primacy of facts, then maximalism even promises to make sense of recarving. But do neo-Fregeans feel the need for *any* explicit metaontology?[3]

---

[3] This paper was written during research leave funded by a Philip K. Leverhulme Prize: I am very grateful to the Trust and to my St Andrews colleagues for making this possible. For useful discussions, I thank Herman Cappelen, Peter Clark, Matti Eklund, Paul McCallion, James McKinna, Marcus Rossberg, Ted Sider, Crispin Wright, Elia Zardini, and, in particular, Fraser MacBride.

REFERENCES

Armstrong, D. M. 1997: *A World of States of Affairs* (Cambridge: Cambridge University Press).

Balaguer, M. 1998: *Platonism and Anti-Platonism in Mathematics* (New York: Oxford University Press).

Eklund, M. 2006: 'Neo-Fregean Ontology', *Philosophical Perspectives*, 20, pp. 95–121.

Field, H. 1984: 'Critical Notice of Wright's *Frege's Conception of Numbers as Objects*', *Canadian Journal of Philosophy*, 14, pp. 637–62.

Hale, B. 1994: 'Dummett's Critique of Wright's Attempt to Resuscitate Frege', *Philosophia Mathematica*, (3) 2, pp. 122–47.

——and C. Wright 2001: *The Reason's Proper Study* (Oxford: Oxford University Press).

Heck, R. 2000: 'Syntactic Reductionism', *Philosophia Mathematica*, (3) 8, pp. 124–49.

Hirsch, E. 2002: 'Quantifier Variance and Realism', *Philosophical Issues*, 12, pp. 51–73.

Lewis, D. 1991: *Parts of Classes* (Oxford: Blackwell).

MacBride, F. 2003: 'Speaking with Shadows: A Study of Neo-Logicism', *British Journal for the Philosophy of Science*, 54, pp. 103–63.

Sider, T. 2007: 'Neo-Fregeanism and Quantifier Variance', *Proceedings of the Aristotelian Society Supplementary Volume* 81, pp. 201–232.

——forthcoming: 'Parthood', *Philosophical Review*.

Wright, C. 1983: *Frege's Conception of Numbers as Objects* (Aberdeen: Aberdeen University Press).

——1998: 'On the Harmless Impredicativity of N$^=$ (Hume's Principle)', in M. Schirn (ed.), *Philosophy of Mathematics Today* (Oxford: Clarendon Press), pp. 339–68.

ACTUALITY
SCOTT SOAMES AND KEITH HOSSACK

I—SCOTT SOAMES

ACTUALLY

The paper presents a theory of the metaphysics and epistemology of actuality and possibility, plus the language we use to talk about them. World-
states—which are consistent, maximally informative properties attributed to the universe—include the actual world-state, which is instantiated,
metaphysically possible states, which could have been instantiated, plus
additional, epistemically possible states, which can coherently be conceived to be instantiated. Although the contents of these properties are
knowable a priori, empirical knowledge of the actual world-state also
arises when it is given to us indexically. This duality is the key to understanding the rigidifying actuality operator, and to solving the philosophical puzzles about the necessary a posteriori and the contingent a priori to
which it gives rise.

My topic is the metaphysics and epistemology of actuality and possibility, plus the semantics and pragmatics of the language we use to
talk about it. By *actuality* I mean the actual world-state. By *possibility* I mean all possible world-states, both the metaphysically and the
epistemically possible. The actual world-state is the way the world
is. Metaphysically possible states are ways the world could have
been. Epistemically possible states are ways the world can coherently be conceived to be. In what follows I will sketch a conception of
what these world-states are, and explore how we know about them.

To that end I will examine two characterizations of epistemic possibility.

(EP1) A world-state w is epistemically possible iff w is a way
the world can coherently be conceived to be, which it
cannot be known a priori not to be.

(EP2) A world-state w is epistemically possible iff w is a way
the world can coherently be conceived to be, and one
cannot know a priori that w is not a way the world could
be (or have been).

Since knowing that w is a way that the world could not be (or have been) involves knowing that w is a way that the world is not, but not vice versa, EP1 is more restrictive than EP2. I will, therefore, take it to be the default definition.[1] One of my tasks will be to determine whether or not it needs to be liberalized.

In addition to limning the nature of world-states, and distinguishing different types of possibility, I will also explain the semantics and pragmatics of our talk about actuality and possibility. All of this, I will argue, leads to the resolution of certain puzzling problems about the necessary a posteriori and the contingent a priori.

I

Two Uses of 'Actually'. I begin with the standard philosophical semantics of the actuality operator. This semantics presupposes that sentences are evaluated for truth or falsity at pairs of world-states—one, the designated 'actual state', which provides the interpretation of 'actually', and the other, which may be any possible state, which is needed to evaluate sentences containing 'necessarily' and 'possibly'. As David Kaplan (1989) taught us, the first of these states may be thought of—along with a designated time, place and agent—as a *context of utterance*, which, together with the meaning of the sentence uttered, determines the proposition the sentence expresses. The second world-state is a *circumstance of evaluation* at which that proposition is assessed for truth or falsity.[2]

Syntactically, the actuality operator combines with a formula to form a more complex formula. Semantically, it is an indexical, the content of which it varies from context to context. For example, the sentence 'Actually Kaplan wrote "Demonstratives"', used by anyone at the actual world-state, @, expresses the proposition *that Kaplan wrote 'Demonstratives' at @*, while the same sentence used by a speaker at a world-state w expresses the proposition *that Kaplan wrote 'Demonstratives' at w*. In this way, 'actually' stands for the

---

[1] This is the definition I adopted in Soames (2005a; 2006a; forthcoming).

[2] Whereas Kaplan takes circumstances of evaluation to be time/world-state pairs (because he takes the truth-values of propositions to be temporally changeable), I take circumstances to be world-states (because I agree with Nathan Salmon (1989a) that propositions have their truth-values eternally).

world-state C_w of the context in a manner analogous to the way in which 'now' stands for the time, and 'I' stands for the agent, of the context. When p is the proposition expressed by S in C, $\ulcorner$Actually $S\urcorner$ expresses the proposition *that p is true at C_w* (which predicates, of C_w, the property of being a world-state at which p is true). Since this proposition doesn't change truth-value from state to state, $\ulcorner$Actually $S\urcorner$ is true at an arbitrary pair C, w iff S is true at C, C_w.[3] Thus, when S is true at C_w, $\ulcorner$Actually $S\urcorner$ is a necessary truth, and when $\ulcorner$the x: $Fx\urcorner$ denotes a unique individual o at C_w, $\ulcorner$the x: actually $Fx\urcorner$ denotes o at C, w, for all world-states w at which o exists, and never denotes anything else at C, w^*, for any w^*. Hence, 'actually' is a rigidifier. However, $\ulcorner$the x: actually $Fx\urcorner$ is not directly referential, since its content is not an object but a descriptive condition, (expressed by) $\ulcorner$the unique object which is F at $C_w\urcorner$.[4]

So understood, the actuality operator is a useful logical tool. However, does it capture the ordinary meaning of the English word 'actually'? Initially, there appears to be evidence on both sides. On the positive side, (1) provides evidence that both the adverb 'actually', and its adjectival cousin 'actual', are rigidifiers.

(1)   It could have been the case, had just a few things gone differently, that the actual winning general (the general who actually won) at Chancellorsville lost that battle.

What I say in assertively uttering (1) is true iff the general who won the battle at the actual world-state @—Robert E. Lee—lost the battle at a world-state w differing in only a few respects from @. This is just what we should expect, if 'actual' and 'actually' are rigidifiers. On the negative side, (2a) and (2b) seem to provide evidence that S and $\ulcorner$Actually $S\urcorner$ differ only rhetorically.

(2a) Actually, I live in California.

(2b) I live in California.

---

[3] To say that S is true at C, w is to say that the proposition expressed by S at C is true when evaluated at w.

[4] If, when evaluating $\ulcorner$the x: actually $Fx\urcorner$ at w, 'x' ranges over all possible individuals, then its denotation at C, w need not exist at w. If the range of 'x' at w is restricted to things existing at w, this is not so, leading to complications noted in Soames (2005a, pp. 29–30). For simplicity, I let 'x' be unrestricted, unless otherwise indicated.

In uttering (2a), I assert the information carried by (2b), while sign-aling that it may be unexpected. In general, ⌜Actually S⌝ is used rhe-torically to indicate that the information expressed by S, which one is asserting, may contrast with possibilities that one's hearers find salient.

   Thus, we are faced with a dilemma. The all-too-ubiquitous rhe-torical use of 'actually' seems to suggest that, in ordinary language, it is a purely rhetorical device that is logically and semantically in-ert, while its apparently rigidifying use points in the opposite direc-tion. In what follows, I will show that this dilemma is merely apparent: the rhetorical use is fully explainable on the hypothesis that the ordinary word 'actually' is simply the actuality operator of philosophical semantics. However, there is more to be done before we reach that result.

II

'Actual' and 'Actually'. First, a word about the relationship between the adverb 'actually'—which can be prefixed to a sentence, ⌜Actually S⌝—the adjective 'actual'—which modifies a noun, ⌜the actual N⌝—and the predicate, 'is actual'. To the extent that these forms are interdefinable, their grammatical differences are philo-sophically unimportant. Taking the indexical semantics of 'actually' as basic, one naturally understands ⌜the actual N⌝ as equivalent to ⌜the x: actually x is N⌝, thereby explaining the apparent rigidity of the former. However, the predicate 'is actual', used by philosophers to express the property of being a world-state that obtains (or is in-stantiated), is another matter. Although it applies only to the way the world is, it could have applied to any way the world could have been, thereby making (3a) and (3b) true.

   (3a) Every metaphysically possible world-state is one that could have been actual.

   (3b) No world-state can be known a priori to be actual.

Though equivalent to (4a), this predicate is not equivalent to (4b), which—when used at @—expresses the property (4c), which is equivalent to the property *being @*.

(4a) 'is a world-state that obtains (is instantiated)'

(4b) 'is a world-state that actually obtains (is instantiated)'

(4c) being a world-state that obtains (is instantiated) at @—
i.e. being a world-state that would obtain (be instantiated), if @ obtained (were instantiated).

Since this property would make (3a) and (3b) trivially false, 'is actual' —as used by philosophers—is not definable in terms of the actuality operator.

Given this use of 'is actual', one can, of course, define a corresponding use of ⌜the actual N⌝ in which it is synonymous with ⌜the
thing that is N at whatever world-state is actual⌝. However, on this
use, 'actual' is not a rigidifier, and ⌜the actual N⌝ is trivially equivalent to ⌜the N⌝. Since this interpretation doesn't explain the apparently rigidifying effect of adding 'actual' or 'actually' to descriptions
in English, I will assume that these descriptions contain the indexi-
cally-defined operator. I will further assume that this is the operator
in ⌜Actually S⌝, since, as I will show, the rhetorical effects of assertively uttering that sentence pose no problem for this hypothesis. I
use the phrase 'the actual world-state' to name the way, @, that the
world is. A different, but referentially equivalent, understanding assimilates it to 'the world-state w such that actually w is instantiated'—which, when used at @, has the same content as 'the
world-state w such that if @ were instantiated, then w would be instantiated'. On this understanding, it is knowable a priori that @ is
the actual world-state—even though it is not knowable a priori that
@ obtains (or is instantiated).[5]

III

Actuality, Necessity, and Apriority. With these linguistic matters in
place, I turn to the metaphysics and epistemology of actuality and
possibility. Since adding the actuality operator to a contingent truth
produces a necessary truth, and since it is widely assumed that adding it to a truth that is knowable only a posteriori preserves aposte-

---

[5] If 'the actual world-state' were understood as 'the world-state that is actual (i.e. obtains)',
then it would be non-rigid, referring, at each w, to w itself. On that construal, one can't
know a priori that @ is the actual world-state.

riority, the actuality operator is often seen as a rich source of the necessary a posteriori. A related point is made about the contingent a priori. When S is contingent, the proposition expressed by ⌜S iff actually S⌝ is also contingent, even though it is knowable a priori. Although these results appear obvious, it is wise to withhold judgement on them until we have a clearer picture of what the actual world-state really is. Since the proposition expressed by ⌜Actually S⌝, is a singular proposition that attributes the property of being a world-state at which p is true to @, knowing it, and thereby satisfying ⌜x knows that actually S⌝, involves having *de re* knowledge of @. Surely, the nature of @ is relevant to whether we have such knowledge, and, if so, how we come by it. Thus, in order to assess the role of the actuality operator in generating instances of the necessary a posteriori and the contingent a priori, we need to clarify what world-states are.

IV

The Nature of World-States. My account is based on three leading ideas. From Robert Stalnaker (1976), I take the idea that world-states are not Lewisian alternative concrete worlds (universes), spatially and temporally disconnected from ours. Rather, they are properties specifying ways the world could be, or be coherently conceived to be.[6] From Saul Kripke, I take the idea that world-states may be specified in terms of the objects and properties we find around us, and so need not be given purely qualitatively. As Kripke puts it:

> Don't ask: how can I identify this table in another possible world, except by its properties? I have the table in my hands, I can point to it, and when I ask whether it might have been in another room, I am talking, by definition, about it. I don't have to identify it after seeing it through a telescope. (Kripke, 1980, pp. 52–3)

From Nathan Salmon (1989b), I take the idea that the space of world-states includes not only the actual and genuinely possible, but

---

[6] Whereas Stalnaker identifies ways the world could be with ways they can be conceived to be, I distinguish the two.

also some that are metaphysically impossible. The actual world-state is the maximal, world-constituting property that the world really instantiates. Metaphysically possible world-states are maximal, world-constituting properties that could have been instantiated. Epistemically possible world-states are maximal, world-constituting properties that we can coherently conceive to be instantiated, and (assuming EPI) that we cannot know a priori not to be instantiated.

For insight into these properties, I turn to Rudolf Carnap's (1947) classic notion of a *state description*, used in giving the semantics of an elementary first-order language L. Details aside, a Carnapian state description is a complete, consistent set of atomic sentences of L, or their negations (resulting in a complete assignment of truth-values to atomic sentences). Truth-values of complex sentences relative to a state description are determined using familiar recursive clauses for quantifiers, truth functions, and modal operators. In updating this picture, I replace Carnap's atomic sentences with structured, Russellian propositions expressed by atomic formulas, relative to assignments of objects to variables. Complete, consistent sets of such propositions, and their negations, are used to define world-states, at which complex sentences, and the propositions they express, are evaluated.

Let D be the domain of objects talked about, and B the set of properties expressed by simple predicates of L, including an existence predicate. A world-description S_w is a set each member of which is either an atomic proposition, consisting of an n-place property from B plus an n-tuple of objects from D, or the negation of such. S_w is complete iff for every atomic proposition, either it or its negation is a member of S_w. It is consistent iff its members cannot be known a priori not to be jointly true. The world-state w corresponding to S_w is *the property of making the propositions in S_w true*. To conceive of w as instantiated is to conceive of every member of S_w being true, while taking the objects in the universe to include only those the existence of which is required by S_w. The propositions in S_w are, of course, not the only ones true at w. Others include those expressed by non-atomic, non-modal sentences the truth of which is determined from S_w by recursive clauses for quantifiers and truth-functional operators.

All states in the structure are epistemically possible. The one that is instantiated is *actual*. The ones that could have been instantiated

are *metaphysically possible*. The rest are *metaphysically impossible*.
⌜Possibly S⌝ is true at *w* iff *S* is true at some world-state that is metaphysically possible from *w*—similarly for ⌜Necessarily S⌝. World-states that are metaphysically possible from one state may differ from those that are possible from another. For example, suppose that P_1 and P_2 are mutually exclusive, essential properties of anything that has them (so that having one precludes having the other). Suppose further that one can determine whether an object has these properties only by empirical investigation. It follows that if it is true at w_1 that *o* has P_1, and true at w_2 that *o* has P_2, then the world-states metaphysically possible from the two states are different.

Since each world-state is epistemically possible, it can coherently be conceived to be instantiated. For each such state w_1, there is a set of states w_2 that would be metaphysically possible, if w_1 were instantiated. These are properties the universe could have had, if it had had w_1. For each such w_2 there is a set of states w_3 that would be metaphysically possible, if w_2 were instantiated. These are properties that it could have been the case that the universe could have had.[7] This process is repeatable. The truth-values, at *w*, of the propositions expressed by sentences containing modal operators are determined not by *w* itself, but by its position in the overall space of world-states.

Finally, we introduce the actuality operator, allowing each metaphysically possible world-state to be the designated state of a possible context.[8] Taking @ to be designated in our present context, and *S* to express *p*, our use of ⌜Actually S⌝ expresses the proposition *that p is true at* @. The truth-value of this proposition at an arbitrary state *w* is determined, not by the content of the world-describing set S_w, nor by the world-states metaphysically possible from *w*, but simply by the truth-value of *p* at @. ⌜Actually S⌝ is true at any world-state iff the proposition expressed by *S* is true at @.

To sum up, a world-state *w* is a property that gives a complete story of what the universe would be like if *w* were instantiated. Since it is no part of that story to specify what the universe would be

---

[7] This is not a stutter. As Nathan Salmon (1989b) argues, (for ship of Theseus-type examples) it should not be assumed that if *w* is (metaphysically) possibly possible, then *w* is (metaphysically) possible.

[8] There are some niceties excluding certain world-states from playing this role. However, these won't matter to us.

like if other world-states were instantiated, the propositions in terms of which w is defined don't contain explicit information about other world-states. This is compatible with the fact that, for any world-state w^* and proposition p, we can always evaluate the truth-value of the proposition *that p is true at w^** at any world-state whatsoever. We need only remember that a proposition can be true at a world-state without being one of the propositions that define it.

There are, of course, limitations to this framework. Like Carnap, I have introduced a space of states to evaluate sentences of a simple, first-order, modal language L (and the propositions they express). As a result, some features of this space are tied to features of L. The properties in terms of which world-states are defined are those expressed by simple predicates of L, and the objects mentioned in the definition are those that L is used to talk about. If richer languages had been chosen, the world-states would have been richer, and the rules for determining truth at a state would have been more complex. This raises two questions.

Q1. Would the choice of a more complex language invalidate essential features of this framework?

Q2. Should the relativization of the space of world-states to particular languages, and contextually varying inquiries involving them, be discarded in favour of an absolute space of world-states, equally relevant for all inquiries in all languages?

Stalnaker addresses Q2.

One might ask, are there such things as possibilities, or possible worlds, in this sense [maximal properties that the world might have had]? I doubt that it is plausible to believe that there is, independent of context, a well-defined domain of absolutely maximally specific possible states of the world, but I do not think the proposed conception ... requires such a domain. The alternative possibilities ... must be exclusive alternatives made in the context at hand. But one can make sense of this requirement even if there is no ultimate set of possibilities relative to which any possible distinctions might be made. One might think of possible worlds as something like the elements of a partition of a space, rather than as the points of the space. The space might be partitioned differently in different contexts, and there might be no maximally fine partition. (Stalnaker, 1999, p. 136)

There is, I think, something right about this. World-states are properties attributed to the universe. When attributed, they are taken to capture everything relevant to the inquiry at hand. However, it is reasonable to suppose that for every inquiry that might be undertaken, there is another requiring a finer level of detail and specificity, for which a more fine-grained and fully articulated set of world-states would be needed. If so, then there may be no absolute sense in which a world-state is a maximally informative story about the universe that answers every conceivable question, and evaluates every conceivable proposition. Rather, world-states are properties treated as maximal for particular purposes. The stories they tell are maximally informative in the sense of answering every question relevant to a given inquiry. This doesn't mean that world-states are made up to suit our interests. The properties are there independently. It is the use to which we put them that is relative to us.

Thus, it is no defect in the framework I have sketched that it doesn't provide an absolute conception of maximality for world-states. It would be a defect, however, if the framework couldn't be liberalized to overcome limitations of the simple Carnapian conception of world-states, and generalized to accommodate languages richer than L. Later, I will discuss ways of doing so. However, we already have enough to resolve some puzzles, and record some results.

V

The Necessary A Posteriori Revisited. Kripkean instances of the necessary a posteriori are propositions that predicate essential properties or relations of objects that can be known to possess them only empirically.[9] The function of empirical evidence needed for knowledge of these propositions is to rule out epistemically possible, but metaphysically impossible, world-states at which they are false. The same cannot be said for what are widely taken to be examples of the necessary a posteriori involving the actuality operator. Whenever S expresses a contingent truth p, ⌜Actually S⌝ expresses the necessary truth *that p is true at @*. However, since ⌜Actually S⌝ is trivially inferable from S, and since the proposition it expresses often doesn't

---

[9] See Soames (2006b; forthcoming).

seem to be knowable in any other way, it has seemed to be knowable only a posteriori, whenever p is. This is problematic. If p is true at @, then the proposition *that p is true at @* is true, not just at every metaphysically possible world-state, but at every epistemically possible state as well. What, then is the role of empirical evidence needed for a posteriori knowledge? If there are *no* possible world-states at which this proposition is false, why is empirical evidence required to know it?

Strictly speaking, it isn't. World-states are properties we can conceive the universe as having—properties of making certain world-describing sets of propositions true. Imagine, then, a tiny universe consisting of two blocks side by side, with a third on top. This world-state, Tiny, is (in effect) *the property of containing blocks 1 and 2 side by side, with block 3 on top*. Since we have no trouble comprehending the content of this property, we can know, just by thinking about it, that if it were instantiated, then block 3 would be sitting on blocks 1 and 2. So, when p is the proposition that block 3 is sitting on those blocks, it is knowable a priori *that p is true at Tiny*.

The point generalizes. If, as often seems plausible, the world-states relevant to an inquiry are finitely specifiable, then, for every such state w, and every proposition p the truth of which is calculable from those defining w, the proposition *that p is true at w* is knowable a priori. Since this result applies to the actual world-state (relative to an inquiry), as much as to any other, the proposition expressed by uses of ⌜Actually S⌝ is often knowable a priori. *Knowable*, though not, necessarily, *known* a priori. Since the actual world-state, relative to many inquiries, will be much more complex than Tiny, we may not be able grasp it in the non-demonstrative way we grasp Tiny—in which case we won't have any way of calculating the truth-values of propositions from a complete specification of @. In such cases, our only practical way of coming to know *that p is true at @* is by inferring it from p. Thus, when p is a posteriori, our knowledge of the proposition expressed by ⌜Actually S⌝ may be a posteriori, even though *what we know* can, abstracting away from our cognitive limitations, also be known in another way.[10]

---

[10] This position is suggested in Soames (2005a, pp. 304–5, n. 16; 2006c, pp. 231–2).

How, for example, do I come to know the necessary truth that actually over 600,000 soldiers died in the American Civil War? I derive it indexically. To say that *actually* over 600,000 soldiers died is just to say that *at this very world-state*—the one that is instantiated—over 600,000 died. Hence, if I know from historical research how many soldiers died in the Civil War, I know how many died *at this very world-state*, and I can express this knowledge by saying: 'Actually, over 600,000 soldiers died in the Civil War'. In so doing, I demonstrate @, and say of it that a certain proposition is true at it, in something like the way in which, in another context, I demonstrate Southern California, and say of it that it is warm there, by uttering: 'It is warm here'. Just as in the latter case, I demonstrate a certain large territory, and say something about it, on the basis of my limited acquaintance with it—even though my ignorance of the territory greatly exceeds my knowledge of it—so, in the former case, my limited familiarity with the way the world is allows me to refer to it indexically, and say something about it, despite being ignorant of much of its content. In this way, I come to know, a posteriori, the necessary truth *that at @, over 600,000 soldiers died in the Civil War*, by deriving it from a contingent truth that I know a posteriori.

The inference also runs in the other direction. To know that *actually* over 600,000 soldiers died in the Civil War is to know that over 600,000 soldiers died in the Civil War, *at this very world-state*—from which one may trivially conclude that over 600,000 soldiers died then. Why, then, isn't it knowable a priori *that over 600,000 soldiers died in the Civil War*? After all, I have argued, (i) that the necessary truth *that at @, over 600,000 soldiers died in the Civil War* is, in principle, knowable a priori, and (ii) that there is a certain way of knowing this truth, when @ is presented indexically, such that when one knows it this way, one can derive the contingent truth *that over 600,000 soldiers died in the Civil War* from it. Thus, the contingent truth is an a priori consequence of an a priori truth. How, then, can it fail to be knowable a priori?

It fails to be knowable a priori because the route to it from the necessary proposition *that at @, over 600,000 soldiers died in the Civil War* is different from, and at odds with, the route to the apriority of the latter. In order to derive *p* from the proposition *that p is true at @*, @ must be given as *this very world-state* (the one that is instantiated). However, in order for one to know a priori *that p is true at @*, @ can't be given in this way, but must be known by grasping the propositions that define it. The proposition *that p is true at @* is entertainable in two radically different ways. One way—which, as a practical matter, may exceed our cognitive abilities—involves grasping the propositional content of @. One who entertains the proposition in this way can know it a priori—by deriving p from the propositions that define @. But when @ is presented in this way, there is no way of knowing that it is instantiated. Hence, when one entertains the proposition *that p is true at @* in a way that allows one to know it a priori, there is nothing in one's knowledge that allows one to infer p from it. The second, indexical, way of entertaining the proposition *that p is true at @*—which is how it is presented using the actuality operator—does not involve grasping the full propositional content of @. When presented with the proposition in this way, we cannot determine it to be true a priori, though we can move a priori from it to p, and vice versa. Since on neither way of knowing *that p is true at @* is there a way of establishing p a priori, p is knowable only a posteriori.

Is it strange that the proposition *that p is true at @* should, in principle, be knowable a priori, even though, in practice, our knowledge of it is often a posteriori? Not when one realizes the kind of proposition it is—namely, one that relates one propositional content (a particular proposition) to another propositional content (a particular world-state that is itself propositionally defined). As the example about the miniature world-state Tiny shows, propositions of this kind are, in general, knowable a priori. The fact that the complexity of world-states often exceeds our psychological limitations is balanced by the fact that many other a priori truths do, too. Some arithmetical truths are too complex for us to effectively evaluate, even though they are expressed by theorems of correct arithmetical theories. We shouldn't deny that these propositions are knowable a priori—even if our psychological limitations afford us no way of knowing them, short of using a posteriori methods, like running a reliable computer program for a long time. The point about propositions expressed by uses of ⌜Actually S⌝ is similar.

VI

A Puzzle About the Contingent A Priori. In explaining Kripkean instances of the necessary a posteriori, I argued that the function of empirical evidence required to know them is to rule out metaphysically impossible, but epistemically possible, world-states in which they are false. This may seem to suggest (5).

> (5) If p is false at some epistemically possible world-state, then p isn't a priori. So, if p is a priori, then p isn't false at any epistemically possible world-state, and so (we may assume) p is true at every such state.

But then, if p is contingent a priori, it will follow that p is true at all epistemically possible world-states, while being false at some metaphysically possible state. Thus, if (5) is correct, some metaphysically possible world-states are epistemically impossible.

How can that be? A metaphysically possible world-state is a property the universe could have had. But surely, one is inclined to think, if the universe could have had w, then there can't be anything incoherent, or a priori inconsistent, in supposing that it does have w. And, if there is no such inconsistency, then w won't be knowable a priori not to be instantiated. In short, any metaphysically possible world-state should be epistemically possible. Since this contradicts our earlier result, one of the suppositions leading to the contradiction must be abandoned—either (i) that there are instances of the contingent a priori, (ii) that (5) is correct, or (iii) that it is never a priori inconsistent to suppose, of any metaphysically possible world-state, that it is instantiated.

That there are instances of the contingent a priori is shown by the fact that, when S is contingent, anyone who, at @, knows the a priori (6a) is in position to derive the contingent (6e) by steps that can be known a priori to be truth-preserving.[11]

> (6a) S iff S.
> (6b) So, it is true at this very world-state (said demonstrating @) that S *iff* S.

---

[11] A version of this argument is given in Soames (2005a, pp. 120–2).

(6c) So, it is true at this very world-state (said demonstrating @) that S *iff it is true at this very world-state* (said demonstrating @) *that S*.

(6d) So, S iff it is true at this very world-state (said demonstrating @) that S.

(6e) So, S iff actually S.

The step from (6a) to (6b) is based on the principle that for any proposition p, if at world-state w, an agent A knows p, then A needs no further justifying evidence to come to know, of w, that it is a world-state at which p is true. Thus, our a priori knowledge of proposition (6a) is sufficient to allow us to come to know (6b)—i.e. to know, a priori of @, that it is a world-state at which proposition (6a) is true. But if we know, of *this very state* @, that it makes the proposition expressed by ⌜S iff S⌝ true, then we need no further information to come to know the same thing about the proposition expressed by ⌜S iff it is true at *this very state* that S⌝. Thus, proposition (6c) is knowable a priori. The next step, to (6d), is based on the principle that if a use, at w, of ⌜It is true at this very world-state that R⌝ (said demonstrating w) expresses knowledge based on evidence E (where E may be null), then a corresponding use of R does too. Given the apriority of (6c), we conclude that the proposition expressed by (6d) and (6e) is also knowable a priori—despite being contingent. Hence, there is an instance of the contingent a priori for each contingent truth.

Niceties aside, we may, therefore, take it that for every metaphysically possible world-state $w \neq$ @, there is a proposition (expressed in @ by (6e)) which is false at w, despite being knowable a priori. So, if (5) is true, all metaphysically possible world-states other than @ are epistemically impossible. However, (5) isn't true. The temptation to think otherwise is linked to the temptation to accept (7)—which (in the presence of EP1) is interderivable with (5).

(7) If p is true at w, and it can be known a priori that p is false, then w can be known a priori not to be instantiated (in which case w is epistemically impossible).

The initial plausibility of (7), as well as its ultimate falsity, is illustrated by (8).

(8a) Saul philosophizes iff actually (i.e. it is true at @ that) Saul philosophizes.

(8b) ¬Saul philosophizes ∧ actually (i.e. it is true at @ that) Saul philosophizes.

Since it is contingently true that Saul philosophizes, there is a metaphysically possible world-state w at which (the proposition expressed at @ by) (8a) is false, and (8b) is true—despite the fact that (8b) is knowable a priori to be false. Thus, the antecedent of (7) is true for <w, (8b)>. If (7) were true, it would follow that w was knowable a priori not to be instantiated. But (7) isn't true.

World-states, it will be remembered, are properties defined by sets of basic, world-describing propositions—where the propositions true at w exceed, not only those that define w, but also those the truth of which is calculable from the ones that do. Crucially, the truth-values, at w, of propositions that ascribe truth-values to propositions at other world-states are determined, not by the complete story about the universe told by w, but by the space of world-states of which w is a part. The following table applies this idea to example (8).

A SIMPLIFIED SPACE OF WORLD-STATES

$P1$ = the proposition that Saul Kripke philosophizes.
$P2$ = the proposition that Scott Soames philosophizes.

@	w	w^*	$w\#$
$P1$	$\neg P1$	$P1$	$\neg P1$
$P2$	$P2$	$\neg P2$	$\neg P2$

Here we pretend that complete world-stories can be told in terms of $P1$ and $P2$. Of course, in any realistic example, the number of basic propositions would be greater, and the world-state-defining sets larger, and more numerous. However, this doesn't affect our result, as long we retain the assumption that world-states are not defined in terms of the truth-values of propositions at other world-states. Given this, we can reduce the question 'Can the world-state w in which (8b) is true be known a priori not to be instantiated?' to the question 'Can it be known a priori that the propositions defining w, $\neg P1$ and $P2$, aren't jointly true?' Since this can't be known a priori, it can't be known a priori that w isn't instantiated. Thus, the consequent of (7), (7) itself, and (5) are all false—as is (7_{AP}).

> (7_{AP}) If it can be known a priori both (i) that p is false, and (ii) that p is true at w (i.e. that if w were instantiated, then p would be true), then it can be known a priori (iii) that w is not instantiated (in which case w is epistemically impossible in the sense of EP1).

When p is (8b), and w is a world-state in which p is true, we have already shown that (i) is knowable a priori, and that the consequent of (7_{AP}) is false. Thus, (7_{AP}) is false iff (ii)—which amounts to (9)—is knowable a priori.

> (9) If it were true that ($\neg P1 \land P2$), then it would be true that ($\neg P1 \land$ it is true at @ that $P1$).

This is knowable a priori iff it is knowable a priori *that it is true at* @ *that P1*. But, as I argued using the world-state Tiny, when the truth of q is calculable from the propositions defining w, it is always knowable a priori that q is true at w. Since $P1$ is a defining proposition for @, (9) is knowable a priori, and (7_{AP}) is false.

The falsity of (7_{AP}) is another example of an earlier result: a priori consequences of propositions that are knowable a priori are sometimes themselves not knowable a priori. In this case, one proposition—(i) of (7_{AP})—can be known a priori only when @ is presented indexically—as in 'It is false that ($\neg$ Saul philosophizes $\land$ actually Saul philosophizes)'—while another proposition—(ii) of (7_{AP})—can be known a priori only when it is known a priori that Saul philosophizes at @—which requires @ to be presented non-indexically, in terms of its propositional content. Since there is no way of merging the a priori routes to (i) and (ii) into a single route to (iii), an agent can't derive (iii) from a priori knowledge of (i) and (ii).

To recap, propositions like those expressed by ⌜S iff actually S⌝ are genuine examples of the contingent a priori. Initial appearances to the contrary, the metaphysically possible world-states at which they are false are also epistemically possible in the sense of EP1. Why, then, doesn't knowledge of these propositions require empirical evidence to rule out the epistemically possible world-states in which

they are false? The answer is illustrated by (6), which shows how
certain contingent propositions expressed using the actuality operator (or an analogous indexical) can be derived, by uniformly a priori
steps, from corresponding truths the necessity and apriority of
which are uncontentious. Because of this, these contingent propositions can be known a priori at the world-state, @, they are about.
What rules out world-states at which they are false is not empirical
evidence, but the transparent, indexical reference to the very world-
state at which the knower evaluates them. This contrasts with
standard instances of the Kripkean necessary a posteriori, which
don't involve reference to the actual world-state.

VII

A Unified Treatment of the Two Uses of 'Actually'. I now return to
the two uses of 'actually' with which I began. The first, rhetorical,
use is one in which an utterance of ⌜Actually S⌝ signals that the information expressed by S, which one is asserting, may be unexpected, or may contrast with possibilities one's hearers find salient. In
such cases, assertive utterances of S and ⌜Actually S⌝ say the same
things, while differing in what they implicate or convey. The second,
rigidifying, use is one in which the addition of 'actually' affects the
(modal) truth conditions of what is asserted. Despite their differences, these uses can be seen as two sides of the same coin, sharing a
single indexical semantics, in which 'actually' directly refers to the
world-state of the context.

This reference is responsible for its rigidifying effect on definite
descriptions, and for the fact that ⌜Actually S⌝ is necessary when S is
contingent. It follows from the nature of world-states that the
former is a priori when the latter expresses an a posteriori truth, calculable from the propositions defining the referent of 'actually'. As
we have seen, the apriority of the proposition expressed by ⌜Actually
S⌝ is consistent with the fact that, in practice, our knowledge of it is
often a posteriori. The indexicality of 'actually' allows speakers rou-
tinely to pass back and forth between S and ⌜Actually S⌝, even
though the propositions they semantically express differ dramatical-
ly. Because of this effortless inferential interchange, an assertive utterance of either sentence standardly results in the assertion of the

propositions semantically expressed by both.

This assertive equivalence is responsible for the rhetorical effect of uttering ⌜Actually S⌝. Since adding 'actually' doesn't change what is asserted, one who adds it is presumed to have some non-assertive reason for referring to @, and explicitly saying that the proposition *p* (expressed by *S*) is true *in it*, rather than simply asserting *p* by using *S* on its own. Standardly the reason is to contrast @ with other states that one's hearers find salient, or expect to be instantiated. For example, when I said 'Actually I live in California', I did so in recognition that some people may have thought that I still lived in Princeton. By calling attention to the actual world-state, and explicitly saying that *in it,* I live in California, I implicitly contrasted it with possible states in which I live elsewhere. Thus, the indexical semantics that gives 'actually' its logical and philosophical punch also explains its rhetorical use in ordinary conversation.[12] The same rhetorical effect could, of course, also be achieved by referring to @ non-indexically—as 'the world-state that is actual' (in the philosopher's sense of being instantiated). However, since the indexical 'actually' is needed independently, the rhetorical effect provides no reason to posit a second, non-rigidifying sense. If there is such a sense in ordinary language, it must to be motivated in some other way.

VIII

Broader Issues. Having illustrated a framework for thinking about actuality and possibility, I will briefly consider some challenges to it. The first concerns indexical reference to the actual world-state— which, I have argued, is the property of making a certain set of basic propositions true. Although the property that plays this role varies from inquiry to inquiry, in many cases the one that does will be very complex, often outstripping our cognitive capacities. In these cases, any knowledge *that p is true at* @ which we possess will be knowledge in which @ is presented to us by the actuality operator, or some indexical variant. It is, therefore, crucial that our acquaintance with,

---

[12] This argument parallels Grice's argument (1989, pp. 56–7) that the performative effects of uttering ⌜it is true that S⌝, rather than *S*, noted by Strawson, are conversational implicatures arising from the semantics of 'true', rather than additions to that semantics.

and ability to directly refer to, complex properties should enable us to know singular propositions about them in roughly the way in which our acquaintance with, and ability to directly refer to, complex physical objects enables us to know singular propositions about them, despite being ignorant of many of their features.

That it does is suggested by an example involving a box on my shelf. Three sides of it, which you can see, are square. Two others are square, and the back is a pyramid—though you can't see them. We agree that a certain property, which we name '*S*', is the shape of the box. By looking at the box, you know, of *S*, that its instantiation involves sides 1, 2, and 3, being square—knowledge you express you by saying: '*S* (this three-dimensional shape) is one that involves sides 1, 2, and 3 being square'. In so doing, you succeed in directly referring to, and expressing your knowledge of, a complex property, despite the fact that you are only partially familiar with it's content. Adding complexity—more sides, or shapes—doesn't seem to change the situation. Knowledge expressed using the actuality operator is a more complex version of the same thing.

It is, of course, true that direct reference plus propositional attitudes sometimes produces strange results. You may, after hearing me referred to by name, learn something that you express to me by saying 'You are Scott Soames'. However, what you learned is (arguably) not the proposition semantically expressed by your sentence—which is also expressed by the uninformative 'You are you'. Similar remarks apply to my box. When, after examining all sides, you say 'This shape, *S*, is one that involves 5 square sides plus a pyramid', you may express new (empirical) knowledge, despite the fact that the proposition semantically expressed by your sentence may (arguably) be one you have known (a priori) all along. Similarly peculiar cases can be constructed with 'actually'. Though potentially puzzling, these peculiarities arise for all directly referential expressions, and so do not count specially against the analysis given here. At most, they locate questions about it within a larger debate.[13]

Once indexically-based knowledge of properties like @ is accepted, the next question is whether the complexity of these properties prevents us from having the non-indexical knowledge-by-content of them needed to know a priori that certain propositions are true at

---

[13] Solutions to the puzzles of direct reference are proposed in Soames (2002; 2005b).

them. For many highly complex world-states, there is certainly a sense—analogous to the sense in which I can't dunk the basketball, because I can't jump high enough—in which I can't derive the truth-values of propositions from sets of propositions defining them—and so cannot know a priori which propositions are true at them—because I am psychologically incapable of entertaining those sets. In what sense, then, is it knowable a priori *that p is true at @* (or at *w* generally), for many propositions *p*? It is knowable a priori in the sense that it is *possible* to know such propositions a priori—where a use of ⌜It is possible to know a priori that *S*⌝ in a context *C* expresses a proposition that is true (at w_1) iff there is a world-state w_2 that is metaphysically possible (from w_1) in which we, or beings relevantly like us, know the proposition expressed by *S* (in *C*) a priori. For example, it is knowable a priori *that, at @, hundreds of thousands died in the Civil War* because there is a metaphysically possible world-state in which we—or similar agents without our limitations on intelligence, memory, and attention span—can, and do, derive *the proposition that hundreds of thousands died in the Civil War* from the basic propositions defining @. In this way, the possibility of knowing propositions to be true at @ a priori is explained in terms of cognitively enhanced versions of ourselves whose a priori knowledge of these propositions parallels our own unproblematic a priori knowledge of propositions true at the world-state, Tiny.[14]

If this is right, then, in many cases, when *S* expresses a true proposition *p*, it is possible to know *that p is true at @* either indexically, corresponding to (10a), or by content, corresponding to (10b).

(10a) It is true that *S* at *this very world-state*.

(10b) It is true that *S* at *the world-state at which it is true that Saul is a philosopher ∧ Alfred is a logician ∧ …* (one conjunct for each of the basic propositions defining @).

Does this conception falsely assume that these sentences semantical-

---

[14] This modal perspective also sheds light on certain puzzling examples. Suppose that the proposition expressed by ⌜*S* ∧ it is never known that *S*⌝ is calculable from the propositions defining @. Then this proposition is true, even though it is never known—at @, or any other metaphysically possible state. However, this is no barrier to the apriority of the proposition expressed by ⌜Actually (*S* ∧ it is never known that *S*)⌝.

ly express the same proposition (in their respective contexts)? I don't think so. First, it is not evident that such an assumption would be false. If world-states are the complex properties I take them to be, then it is natural to regard the semantic contents of the italicized phrases in (10a) and (10b) as bearing the same relation to one another as those in (11a) and (11b) do.

(11a) *This very proposition* (said demonstrating the proposition that Saul is a philosopher $\wedge$ Alfred is a logician $\wedge$ ...) is true.

(11b) *The proposition that Saul is a philosopher $\wedge$ Alfred is a logician $\wedge$* ... is true.

Since the semantic contents of these phrases is, arguably, the same, the idea that (10a) and (10b) semantically express different propositions may be another of the familiar illusions connected with direct reference. Second, and more importantly, my argument doesn't assume that (10a) and (10b) express the same proposition. What it assumes is that understanding and justifiably accepting (10b), and thereby knowing the proposition it semantically expresses, is sufficient for knowing, or coming to know, *de re*, of @, that p is true at it, and hence for knowing the singular proposition *that p is true at @*—whether or not this proposition is semantically expressed. Since knowing the proposition in this way doesn't require empirical evidence, while knowing it when @ is presented indexically does, we get the result that it is possible to know *that p is true at @* in two different ways, without having to decide what (10b) semantically expresses. For what it is worth, I do take (10a) to semantically express the proposition *that p is true at @*, and I find it plausible to think that (10b) does too. But the latter is an optional part of the package.

The conclusion that some possible agents know a priori *that p is true at @* raises another worry. In identifying world-states with properties incorporating complete stories of what the universe would be like if they were instantiated, I argued that it is no part of the story told by any world-state to specify what the universe would be like if a different world-state were instantiated. This was one reason for excluding world-state-indexed ascriptions of truth-value from the basic propositions defining world-states. This exclusion may seem to be threatened by our recognition that agents at some world-states know certain of these ascriptions about other states. Let's see whether it is.

We may assume that when agents at a world-state w have beliefs, the set S_w of propositions defining w will include propositions ascribing beliefs to them. Since the truth, at w, of (12) requires only the truth of p at w^*, the truth, at w, of (13) doesn't require (12) to be an a priori consequence of S_w.

(12) p is true at w^*.

(13) A believes truly that p is true at w^*.

What about (14)—which may take to be true at w?

(14) A knows that p is true at w^*.

If (14) is a priori calculable from (13), plus members of S_w specifying the causal sources of A's belief, the reliability of A's cognitive processes, etc., then S_w needn't include any propositions from which (12) can be derived. Thus, the truth of (14) at w requires no modification of the story I have told, provided that (15) is an a priori consequence of the basic propositions about belief, reliability, etc. used in defining w.

(15) If S, then A knows that S.

However, if (15) isn't an a priori consequence of those propositions, then S_w will have to include (14), thereby having (12) as an a priori consequence.

This presents a problem. For if the propositions defining certain world-states have world-state-indexed truth-value ascriptions about other states as a priori consequences, then instances of the contingent a priori will create trouble for the definition of epistemic possibility given by EP1. For example, let @ be the actual world-state, and w be a metaphysically possible world-state at which the contingent a priori proposition (expressed at @ by) (8a) is false, because the proposition (expressed at @ by) (8b)) is true.

(8a) Saul philosophizes iff actually (i.e. it is true at @ that) Saul philosophizes.

(8b) ¬Saul philosophizes ∧ actually (i.e. it is true at @ that) Saul philosophizes.

Suppose further that proposition (8b) is known, at w, by some agent A, and that the proposition, (8c), ascribing this knowledge to A, is one of the propositions defining w.

(8c) A knows that: ¬Saul philosophizes ∧ it is true at @ that Saul philosophizes.

Under these assumptions, it is knowable a priori that w isn't instantiated.

First, it is knowable a priori that w is instantiated only if (8c) is true. So, it is knowable a priori that w is instantiated only if (8b) is true. Hence, (8d) is knowable a priori.

(8d) If (8b) isn't true, then w isn't instantiated.

Second, since (8a) is knowable a priori, it is knowable a priori that (8b) isn't true. Thus, the claim that w isn't instantiated is an a priori consequence of (8a) and (8d), both of which are knowable a priori. Moreover, it is possible for us (here and now) to know both of these propositions a priori when @ is presented indexically. (It doesn't matter that A's knowledge, in w, of @ is non-indexical.) Thus, it is knowable a priori that w isn't instantiated. If one assumes, as I do, that metaphysically possible world-states, like w, are always epistemically possible, this result contradicts EP1, which defines an epistemically possible world-state as one that is not knowable a priori not to be instantiated.

In sum, if knowledge ascriptions aren't a priori consequences of more basic claims about truth, belief, and other factors, then the fact that agents at some world-states know the truth-values of certain propositions at other states requires rejecting EP1, in favour of EP2. Since EP2 stipulates that w is epistemically possible iff it can't be known a priori that w couldn't be (or have been) instantiated, examples of the contingent a priori can't pose problems for it. Given that the metaphysically possible world-states in which such examples are false are, by hypothesis, states that could have been instantiated, knowing that they couldn't have been instantiated is impossible. Nor, as far as I can tell, would the replacement of EP1 by EP2 undermine other aspects of the overall picture. However, since it hasn't been shown that knowledge claims aren't a priori consequences of more basic claims, such replacement isn't mandated. I am sceptical that it can be, since doing so requires much more than showing simply that knowledge isn't definable in more basic terms. Therefore, I continue to favour EP1, while recognizing that the issue remains open.

What about other ways of liberalizing the simple Carnapian framework? In setting up the structure of world-states, I used a simple, first-order language. The basic propositions used to define world-states were expressed by atomic formulas, and their negations, relative to assignments of values to variables. The truth-values of the remaining non-modal propositions at a world-state w were determined by the basic propositions of w, plus recursive rules for quantifiers and truth-functional operators. Truth-values of modal propositions at w followed from the truth-values of propositions at other world-states, related to w, in the total space of states. On this conception, both the richness of individual world-states and the scope of the total space of states varies with the richness of the underlying language, the properties expressed by its predicates, the domain of objects talked about, and the uses to which the language is put. It is not important that there be one absolute space of world-states with respect to which all inquiries are conducted. What is important is that every space of states we need can be understood within the broad outlines of this framework.

What might an extension of this simple system look like? No matter how syntactically and semantically complex the underlying language, nothing essential to the framework is threatened by allowing many propositions expressed by non-atomic, non-modal formulas (relative to assignments) to count as basic. How, in this setting, should we distinguish those sets of basic propositions that define world-states from those that don't? Putting aside syntactic criteria for completeness and consistency, we might stipulate that to be complete a world-state-defining set must determine (a priori) the truth-value of every non-modal proposition, and to be consistent it must be epistemically possible in the sense of EP1 (or of EP2, if EP1 turns out to be unsustainable).

What about propositions which, though not overtly modal, have consequences that are? Are they world-state-defining? They can be, and often are. Suppose, for example, that truths about what causes what are constitutive of w, without being a priori consequences of other, more basic, truths of w. On this supposition, causal propositions will play a role in defining w, even if they constrain which world-states are metaphysically possible from w. This is not unusual. It is routine for the constitutive truths of a world-state w—e.g. that Saul Kripke is a human being and that I am the father of Greg and Brian Soames—to have modal consequences by partially determining which world-states are metaphysically possible from w. The sensitivity of metaphysical possibility to the contents of world-states is no threat to the framework. There is, however, a related question that could be raised. In excluding modal propositions from those that define world-states, the framework presupposes that world-states that agree on all non-modal facts are identical. Thus, those that support different modal truths must also differ non-modally. Although I find this plausible, those who don't may avoid this result by allowing definitions of world-states to sometimes to include modal propositions.

A deeper question involves the ontology of the framework. Do world-states other than @—i.e. properties that the universe doesn't have, but which it can coherently be conceived to have—(actually) exist? Of course they do, just as other complex, but uninstantiated properties do. However, it is also true there could have been world-states different from those that actually exist. Since world-states are properties the constituents of which are objects and properties, (actually) existing world-states are those the constituents of which (actually) exist. Since there could have been many objects that don't actually exist, and since they could have been constituents of world-states, there could have been world-states that don't actually exist. Accordingly, what the truth of ⌜It could have been that case (i.e. is metaphysically possible) that S⌝ really requires is not that there exists a metaphysically possible world-state at which S is true, but that there could have been such a state. This, of course, precludes giving a reductive analysis of modal notions in terms of possible world-states. However, that should have been obvious anyway—since, on my account, the notion of a possible world-state is itself defined with the help of modal notions.[15]

REFERENCES

Almog, J., J. Perry and H. Wettstein (eds.) 1989: *Themes from Kaplan* (New York: Oxford University Press).

Carnap, R. 1947: *Meaning and Necessity* (Chicago: University of Chicago Press).

Grice, P. 1989: 'Logic and Conversation', in *Studies in the Way of Words* (Cambridge, MA: Harvard University Press).

Kaplan, D. 1989: 'Demonstratives', in Almog, Perry and Wettstein (1989).

Kripke, S. 1980: *Naming and Necessity* (Cambridge, MA: Harvard University Press).

Salmon, N. 1989a: 'Tense and Singular Propositions', in Almog, Perry and Wettstein (1989).

——1989b: 'On the Logic of What Might Have Been', *Philosophical Review*, 98, pp. 3–34.

Soames, S. 2002: *Beyond Rigidity* (New York: Oxford University Press).

——2005a: *Reference and Description* (Princeton, NJ: Princeton University Press).

——2005b: 'Naming and Asserting', in Z. Szabo (ed.), *Semantics vs Pragmatics* (Oxford: Oxford University Press).

——2006a: 'Saul Kripke, the Necessary Aposteriori, and the Two Dimensionalist Heresy', in M. Garcia-Carpintero and J. Macia (eds.), *The Two-Dimensional Framework: Foundations and Applications* (Oxford: Oxford University Press), pp. 272–92.

——2006b: 'The Philosophical Significance of the Kripkean Necessary Aposteriori', *Philosophical Topics*, 16.

——2006c: 'Understanding Assertion', in J. J. Thomson and A. Byrne (eds.), *Content and Modality: Themes from the Philosophy of Robert Stalnaker* (Oxford: Oxford University Press).

——forthcoming: 'Kripke on Epistemic and Metaphysical Possibility: Two Routes to the Necessary Aposteriori', in A. Berger (ed.), *Saul Kripke* (Cambridge: Cambridge University Press).

Stalnaker, R. 1976: 'Possible Worlds', *Noûs*, 10, pp. 65–75.

——1999: 'Indexical Belief', in *Context and Content* (Oxford: Oxford University Press); originally published in *Synthese*, 49, 1981.

---

[15] Thanks to Nathan Gadd, Ali Kazmi and David Manley for useful comments on an earlier draft.

INFORMATION FOR SUBSCRIBERS

The Aristotelian Society *Supplementary Volume* is published annually in one volume. Institutional Print and Premium Online subscription prices for 2007 are: £83 (Europe), US$146 (The Americas), £97 (Rest of World) (VAT and GST to be added if appropriate). For more information on pricing and other options, and more detail about online access to Blackwell Publishing journals, including access information and terms and conditions, please visit www.blackwellpublishing.com/supa.

Single issues from the current and previous volumes are available from Blackwell Publishing. For ordering information, claims and any enquiry concerning your journal subscription please contact your nearest office:
UK: Email: customerservices@blackwellpublishing.com; Tel: +44 (0) 1865 778315; Fax: +44 (0) 1865 471775.
USA: Email: customerservices@blackwellpublishing.com; Tel: +1 781 388 8206 or 1 800 835 6770 (Toll free in the USA); Fax: +1 781 388 8232 or Fax: +44 (0) 1865 471775.
Asia: Email: customerservices@blackwellpublishing.com; Tel: +65 6511 8000; Fax: +44 (0) 1865 471775.
Earlier issues may be obtained from Periodicals Services Company, 11 Main Street, Germantown, NY 12526, USA (e-mail: psc@periodicals.com).

Proceedings of the Aristotelian Society, ISSN 0309-7013, is published in print in one volume per year. US mailing agent: Mercury Airfreight International Inc., 365 Blair Road, Avenel, NJ 07001, USA. Periodical postage paid at Rahway, NJ and additional offices. Postmaster: Send all institutional subscription address changes to Proceedings of the Aristotelian Society, Blackwell Publishing Inc., Journals Subscription Department, 350 Main St., Malden, MA 02148-5020.

The *Supplementary Volume* is published by the Aristotelian Society and distributed by Blackwell Publishing Ltd, 9600 Garsington Road, Oxford OX4 2DQ, UK (Tel: +44 (0) 1865 776868; Fax: +44 (0) 1865 714591).